Campaign Craftsmanship

Campaign Craftsmanship

A Professional's Guide to Campaigning for Elective Office

Edward Schwartzman

UNIVERSE BOOKS
New York

To my wife Robin
who makes so many good things possible

Published in the United States of America in 1973
by Universe Books
381 Park Avenue South, New York, N.Y. 10016

© 1973 by Universe Books

Library of Congress Catalog Card Number: 72-91198
Cloth edition: ISBN 0-87663-173-1
Paperback edition: ISBN 0-87663-906-6

Printed in the United States of America

Contents

Preface

I have been involved professionally in more than thirty political campaigns, from district leader to presidential primary. I have never advised presidential candidates or written campaign strategies for president or determined the expenditures of millions of dollars in any one campaign. I have, however, been a professional political "mechanic" for more than a decade, having first become involved as an activist in reform Democratic politics in Bronx County in 1961. I have participated in campaigns at virtually every level of political life—for president, governor, senator, congressman, mayor, judge, city councilman, borough president, assemblyman, and district leader —as a technical consultant specializing in research and telephone work. I have worked on the East Coast, mainly in New York City and New York State, but the experience of colleagues in other parts of the country indicates that the problems and techniques of political campaigning are basically similar throughout the United States and Canada.

Political mechanics receive no press attention, nor do they require it for ego gratification. They are detail men; they do jobs the public is not aware of but that must be done for successful campaigns. Even experienced politicians sometimes are not too knowledgeable about these details—petition collecting, petition binding, which typeface to use in a brochure, how a sample survey is selected, to name only a few. This book is about these details, all of which I have done myself, except for the preparation of a television campaign.

Many books are available by advisers to presidents and senators, some of which are brilliantly written and some of which are inaccurate and even offer dangerous advice. But there is hardly anything on the day-to-day substance of campaigning, and as far as I know, there is no other book by a professional political detail man that covers all aspects of campaigning.

The book is intended for a number of audiences but primarily for the local candidate who faces a campaign for the first time in the 1970s, when many people are realizing that political campaigning is not a mystique accessible only to lawyers and public relations men, and when more and more citizens—notably women and minority group leaders—are bringing their talents, ambitions, and sense of community priorities to the political arena. At the same time, urban problems are becoming so massive that new types of governmental responses are clearly necessary, and new types of candidates are seeking and are needed to provide them.

Some books regard political campaigning as a sport or game and suggest ways to win. I don't see it that way. There is no magic way to win an election, and no honest technician or political mechanic in his right mind would say that there is or could be. I do not guarantee that using the ideas and approaches contained in this book will *win* elections. That would be extraordinarily presumptuous. But a candidate who uses the book will not waste his or her money and energy on the imbeciles and imbecilities that are common in many campaigns. Instead, the candidate should be able to provide and sustain an early sense of direction and get the greatest possible benefit from the effort and money he invests in the pursuit of elective office.

New or potential candidates will get a realistic appraisal of what a political campaign involves in time, money, and work. Candidates concerned about the many press reports on the expense and mechanization of campaigning will perhaps realize that professionalism and rationalization can produce more economical campaigns as well as more expensive ones. Experienced politicians whose backgrounds do not include systematic concern with political research may find the book particularly useful.

Another group of people who may be helped is that sizable body of citizens who, campaigning every year for local organizational offices, receive little public attention but contribute significantly to the responsible functioning of their communities. Many of the techniques described here can be adapted effectively for such campaigns.

Particularly in view of their growing role in local and national campaigns, I would be especially gratified if high school and college students gained insights into an important component of the American political process.

I hope that concerned citizens will gain additional understanding of why the much-heralded "New Politics" depends in considerable part on a new professionalism and on their own substantial contribution.

Finally, the tens of thousands of amateur campaign workers who do poll watching, carry petitions, and listen to speeches and pep talks may get an idea of total campaign strategy and of how critical their efforts are.

The basic thesis of this book is that the use of professional techniques can provide a real chance for winning public office for candidates who otherwise could not hope to compete successfully. The key to professional-style campaigning is sensitivity to *detailing*—the main subject of this book. The proverb associated with the architect Mies van der Rohe, "God is in the detail," describes the necessary emphasis for campaign work. Many campaigns—even those organized by experienced politicians—are conducted as if no precedent existed, as if one could not learn from the experiences of other campaigners. The staggering escalation of campaign costs makes "learning by doing" a luxury that few candidates can afford and makes emphasis on proper detailing absolutely essential. Saving money is important for even the wealthiest campaigners. It is critical for the first-time campaigner, whose resources are usually limited and, in most cases, no match for those of the incumbent. Well-planned detailing also spares the candidate considerable irritation—a surplus commodity in most campaigns, even in the best of circumstances.

Although there will never be an exact science of political campaigning, each good campaign, like any good work of art, is based on a sound technical structure and is characterized by a sensitivity to real and potential turning points. Sensitivity to such pivotal opportunities is a political instinct that probably cannot be acquired through reading or instruction. Building a good technical structure, however, can be learned, and it is accomplished by the most carefully planned and executed detailing. Proper detailing involves professional standards in research, petitioning, brochure design, and other campaign procedures and products, with constant concern for proper follow-through and implementation, whether what is at issue is something as exciting and dramatic as a public policy reversal or as prosaic as looking up telephone numbers for an opinion survey and copying them correctly.

Campaigns have been lost because campaign workers concerned themselves exclusively or primarily with presumably more important policy questions but forgot to check something so "simple" as whether the signatures on the candidate's nominating petitions were properly signed and witnessed. This book examines such not-so-prosaic and not-so-unimportant details and makes recommendations that my experience suggests are appropriate for every good political campaign.

Examples of research questionnaires, advertising messages, issue papers, survey cross-tabulations, and other campaign materials are included in the book, and a selected bibliography gives students and other interested readers an opportunity to pursue their special interests further.

If you're a candidate-to-be, I wish you luck and joy in a tough job. If you're a student, I envy you—there is no more fascinating field than political science, and good young politicians are as desperately needed now as they always have been. John F. Kennedy is said to have remarked, "Every American mother seems to want her son to be President, but none wants him to be a politician." However, there is no more responsible or exciting profession than politics; corruption and selfishness are only a small, if pervasive, part of the business. The positive side receives less public attention: You, as a candidate, can respond to community ideas, provide influence and a sense of direction, and use power and discretion with compassion, intelligence, and a sense of equity. You can try to do what needs to be done. No other profession provides so great an opportunity to benefit society.

This is my first book, and I've learned that even an unpretentious effort like this is quite complicated. I would particularly like to indicate my gratitude to Melvyn Spain and Dr. Susan Tolchin, who went over early drafts very carefully and provided many constructive suggestions. In addition, Arthur B. Levine and Morris Sweet read parts of the book and offered many valuable ideas. Beatrice Reinfeld first challenged me to write the book, which I had only talked about for the previous three years, and provided encouragement as the task went on. Lou Barron taught me a great deal about the English language; I hope I've taught him something about politics.

I appreciate the graciousness of Jeff Barrett, Walter Diamond, Ronnie Eldridge, Zane Klein, and Nat Sorkin, who allowed me to interview them. Doris Gelberg, Elizabeth Diamond, Ethel Bunin, and my sister Martha Schwartzman cheerfully gave their time and skills to translating my terrible handwriting and typing the manuscript. My wife helped immeasurably both in editing the manuscript and in recalling experiences from the campaigns on which we have worked together.

Finally, I wish to acknowledge the cumulative contributions of politicians and political mechanics I have worked with over the years. Some were brilliant and deeply involved, some were men of integrity with little political instinct for the jugular, and some were of such incompetence that it amounted to a positive flair. The book in part originates from them, for, one way or another, I learned from all of them—and some of them tell me that they have learned from me.

Men are of necessity so mad that not to be mad were madness in another form. [Pascal] thought it quite in order that Plato and Aristotle should have written on politics as though they were laying down rules for a madhouse.

—ERIC HOFFER

Until the moment of truth, a candidate does not know whether he is the bullfighter or the bull.

—STIMSON BULLITT

1 Setting Up Your Campaign

I wouldn't think of making a move nationally if I didn't have my state in good hands. The first lesson is don't sleep too long, don't trust too much, don't take anything for granted.

—HUBERT H. HUMPHREY

When you start to campaign, you will have to confront many troublesome details of housekeeping, from budget allocation to who gets a new desk and who gets the pretty secretary (sometimes literally as well as figuratively). Many candidates find these things boring, burdensome, and of little consequence, but cumulatively they can significantly influence the efficiency and success of campaign operations. To administer a campaign properly, you should personally work out all these details in advance of the active campaigning, in consultation with your key staff, your close advisers, and perhaps your principal contributors.

Although most campaign offices are managed inefficiently and a considerable waste of time and money is not only frequent but taken for granted as normal, that need not be the case. It is both possible and essential for a candidate whose funds are limited to set up a campaign office in a businesslike way.

Space

The first problem is usually how much space to rent and where to look for it. Hotel suites are commonly used, but although their central locations have an obvious advantage, their convenience rarely justifies their high prices. Some politicians choose storefronts to give visibility to the campaign. In my experience, however, the value of such visibility (as well as that of large signs on the fronts of headquarters offices) is greatly overrated. You can get a short-term lease on an empty store for perhaps three or four dollars a square foot per year (prorated), but since empty stores are not always available in all sizes, you may have to take a much bigger one than you need, so that you not only spend too much but are also burdened with a large, half-empty headquarters, which gives the impression of a lackluster campaign. Often campaigners or their representatives rent thousands of square feet of prestige office space, realizing later that only a fraction of it was really necessary. Such a mistake has a cumulative impact: larger stores mean higher maintenance expenses, more staff, larger signs. Often the signs stay in place for years after the campaign is over as shabby testimonials to the nagging economics of American campaigning.

Neatly kept space, moderate in expense and expanse, is perfectly adequate. The candidate is seldom there, in any case, and the public-relations impact of a modest but well-kept headquarters can be very positive. Six dollars a foot per year (prorated) is the most that should be spent for rent; in many circumstances, it is perfectly all right to campaign from your home or from the offices of a local club.

Few real estate men handle short-term space, and in many cities and towns, well-located and reasonably priced space is hard to come by for a short period. However, there is always some space available. In every city, there are offices that are empty between leases or scheduled for alteration in the near future. The only sure way to find appropriate accommodations is to start several months before campaign time. You may have to pay rent for an additional month or so when the space won't be fully used, but the certainty that you have the right space makes that a good investment, and the extra time allows you to plan the proper use of the space and to hire carpenters and install telephone wiring, air conditioners, and other necessities.

In a 1970 campaign, New York Congressman James H. Scheuer had difficulty finding appropriate short-term leases in a new district, so he rented trailers and moved them throughout his area. This relatively inexpensive tactic undoubtedly helped him beat a strongly entrenched incumbent, and, indeed, this device is increasingly utilized by campaigners for reasons of both mobility and economy.

In another major campaign, a senatorial candidate in a close race had three separate offices in midtown New York that cost him between $50,000 and $100,000 for the campaign and deprived him of thousands of dollars he might have spent for other more important campaign needs. Presidential campaigns get similarly bogged down by high-rent space that often serves little useful purpose. Senator

Edmund S. Muskie's presidential campaign, for example, was reported several times in 1971 and 1972 to be cutting back staff for lack of funds; yet more than a year before his first state primary, Muskie had already rented an entire floor in an expensive downtown Washington building. Unwise allocations of funds such as this undoubtedly contributed to Muskie's decision to drop out of active primary campaigning in April 1972.

Estimating space requirements with precision is difficult, but sensible planning can help. You should start by deciding exactly which people, performing which functions, you want at headquarters. Basically, you will want to include space for a receptionist-secretary, your personal secretary (to handle your schedule and appointments), the campaign manager, and two assistants to supervise petitioning, research, press relations, follow-through on special problems, and club liaison. In a professionally directed campaign, most of the technical work will be done by outside consultants and specialists, such as photographers, speech writers, and people for research, polling, brochure preparation, and TV setups, none of whom will occupy your headquarters space. Your headquarters should have some reserve space for small-scale conferences, storage of brochures, and other miscellaneous purposes. A reception area will be needed for visitors, as well as for press and possibly TV interviewers.

It may be necessary to reserve some space for volunteers, who will be involved in checking telephone numbers, running mimeograph machines, and getting out mailings. However, this aspect of the campaign should perhaps be housed separately. It is distracting to the regular headquarters staff to see volunteers come and sit around waiting for someone to assign them work.

Some thought and care should be given to how the office looks to visitors and the press. Many campaign headquarters are completely disorganized and look it; certainly this does not contribute beneficially to the candidate's appeal. Disarray is seldom attractive in any office.

It is usually advisable to rent headquarters furniture, typewriters, calculators, and other office equipment. The rental of refrigerators, air conditioners, and fans would also be a prudent investment. Cold drinks, beer, liquor, and some food should be available. There seems to be an unwritten law that much campaigning work is done late at night. I personally have found the availability of a folding army cot in a campaign office very useful. Three or four telephones will be necessary, and it may be worthwhile to engage an answering service for night calls.

Adding up all the items mentioned thus far indicates an expenditure of about $10,000 for office overhead to mount an urban congressional campaign. When you include cleaning, insurance, maintenance, and miscellaneous expenses, this estimate is probably conservative, and salaries for secretaries and full-time staff members may increase the operating costs for a twelve-week campaign by about another $12,000. Perhaps $25,000 would cover the basic needs and emergencies in a medium- to large-scale campaign.

Staffing

The smaller the staff, the better, in almost every instance. An ideal full-time staff for most campaigns up to and including congressionals is five to eight workers; for most mayoral, senatorial, and gubernatorial campaigns, twenty key staff people should, in my judgment, be the absolute maximum. (Governor Nelson Rockefeller reportedly used more than 300 in his 1969 campaign; Senator George McGovern was reported to have 250 full-time paid staff members throughout the country when he made his presidential race in 1972.) The more people, the more infighting for position with the candidate.

A full-time staff chart, such as the one on the following page, should provide for all the critical functions.

It is not always necessary to have one person handle only one function. Circumstances will dictate the size of the total staff among whom duties can be divided.

Campaigning involves relationships with contributors, legal advisers, and technical consultants. The campaign manager and the candidate should handle these personally in setting policy and priorities. The manager should be completely in charge, naming a deputy in his absence. Other members of the headquarters staff should not be personally involved in the controversies that characterize most campaigns. Nor should the candidate intervene, except in unusual circumstances, in the daily operations of his staff. Violating the basic administrative rule—each worker should have only one boss—contributes significantly to waste and poor morale and is an error made in many campaigns.

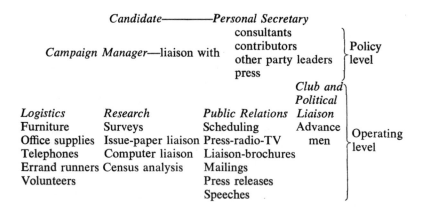

Amateurs or professionals?

Jesse Unruh of California has observed that in politics, as in everything else, you tend to get what you pay for. Most candidates like to have young volunteers at their headquarters, because they add to the appeal of a candidate and many amateurs are energetic, devoted campaigners. In the view of seasoned campaign managers, however, the use of experienced professionals is clearly advisable when judgment and efficiency are called for.

Amateurs can do many important things in a campign, but they tend to require much supervision, and because they are unpaid, it is difficult to control them. They like to discuss their assignments in great detail, sometimes taking as much time with that as in actually doing the job. Many volunteer in the hope of being elevated to policy-making positions after two days' work on details and become disappointed when that doesn't happen. On balance, volunteers are useful, but you have to pick their spots carefully, delineate their roles sharply, and keep them out of procedures in which timing and the exact following of instructions are primary considerations. One regular staff member should be charged with supervising them and keeping them happy.

In some circumstances, notably the presidential primary campaigns of Eugene J. McCarthy in 1968 and George McGovern in 1972, the role of volunteer canvassers was absolutely critical. They gathered petition signatures in large numbers (proselytizing very effectively in the process), distributed literature, manned sidewalk stands in areas of heavy pedestrian counts, hand addressed envelopes, made telephone calls, "pulled" (got out the vote) on election day, and in general provided an enthusiasm that caught on. Since it meant so much to these nice young dedicated people, many voters began to feel that maybe the candidate was worth thinking about after all.

Throughout this book I emphasize the necessity for professionalism, for rationalization of campaign procedures. However, many more laymen and women are participating in public affairs than ever before—perhaps 10 to 20 percent of the populace is now involved in public decision making in some manner, compared to 1 or 2 percent only a decade ago—and any candidate should encourage volunteers to join his campaign. They can be recruited by you and your family, by your campaign area chairmen, and by your other campaign workers during the course of their petitioning and canvassing (see pages 61–72) or at kaffeeklatches or other small gatherings (see page 42). Lists of prospective workers can be borrowed from your political party headquarters, from local political clubs with which you are associated, from the previous campaign files of elected officials with whom you are friendly, from women's and men's clubs, and from civic and religious organizations. Many women, in particular, have considerable time to devote to political campaigning. Your canvassers and other possible recruiters should carry with them 3×5 cards on which they can enter the names, addresses, and telephone numbers of people who are interested in working for you. The cards should look something like this:

Name:
Address: Telephone:

I have done		I'd like to do	I'll have time to work on these days from _____ to _____
___	Bookkeeping	___	Sunday _____ to _____
___	Filing	___	Monday _____ to _____
___	Publicity	___	Tuesday _____ to _____
___	Reception work	___	Wednesday _____ to _____
___	Research	___	Thursday _____ to _____
___	Shorthand	___	Friday _____ to _____
___	Typing	___	Saturday _____ to _____
___	Canvassing	___	
___	Petitioning	___	
___	Telephoning	___	Primary Day _____ to _____
___	Other	___	Election Day _____ to _____

In smaller campaigns, volunteers can be crucial, and even in major campaigns they can play a critical role. But you should know exactly how to use them—both for your sake and for theirs. I have seen volunteers used in demeaning ways—doing "make-work," for example, so that campaign headquarters looks busy, or sitting around waiting for someone to tell them what to do. Such activities cannot possibly benefit your campaign and may actually harm it, either by taking the attention of your regular staff away from more important work or by alienating the volunteers.

Volunteers can usefully serve many campaign functions, including:

- distributing literature
- organizing kaffeeklatches or small money-raising events
- accompanying you on walking tours
- gathering petition signatures
- canvassing (proselytizing voters door to door)
- checking and binding petitions
- challenging opponents' petitions (a time-consuming job that entails checking individual voters' registrations and signatures at the local board of elections)
- telephoning voters to discuss you and your views
- researching census and related data covering the district
- researching past voting patterns in the district
- preparing voter cards and lists
- conducting personal or telephone research interviews
- setting up street stands for literature distribution
- in primary elections, identifying persons who actually voted in previous primaries by checking the records of past elections at the board of elections
- "pulling" on election day by telephone and household canvass
- poll watching on election day
- providing transportation to the polls for the elderly and infirm
- manning loudspeaker trucks and bullhorns
- putting up posters
- typing correspondence
- filing
- bookkeeping
- manning the office to take calls and answer questions
- recruiting other volunteers

Most of these functions are discussed in detail in the following chapters. It should be emphasized that for many of these functions the presence of experienced professionals is advisable, especially for the more sensitive and difficult tasks, which include conducting research interviews and answering inquiries. But many candidates can't afford to retain paid consultants for every function. If you are in this situation and you have no option but to use volunteers, be sure to give them specific directions and careful supervision.

The campaign manager

Your campaign manager will probably have to work full time—and more—and, unless you've promised him a job once you are elected, he will expect to be paid professionally. Fees as high as $1,500 a week plus expenses have been reported. (When I startd in politics in 1960, campaign managers in congressional campaigns were happy to get $100 a week plus expenses.) For smaller campaigns, managerial fees will often consist of expenses and the promise of a future job.

Some experienced politicians believe that a good manager can account for 10 percent of the total vote depending, of course, on the competence of the opponent's campaign manager. When Assemblyman Manuel Ramos challenged Congressman Herman Badillo in a 1972 Democratic congressional primary in the Bronx, some politicians offered 20-to-1, and even 50-to-1, against Ramos, but when it became public knowledge that Walter Diamond, a seasoned politician, would manage the Ramos campaign, the odds dropped to 5-to-1. Obviously, you should get the best manager you can.

But you can't go into the job market looking for a full-time campaign manager. Some successful ones are business or professional colleagues of their candidates. John N. Mitchell, for example, who managed Richard M. Nixon's presidential campaign in 1968 (and who subsequently was appointed U.S. Attorney General, a position he held until he resigned to manage Nixon's 1972 campaign for reelection), had been Nixon's law partner. Few candidates, however, are so fortunate as to find a good and willing manager among their close professional associates.

Ideally, you want someone who is politically experienced, loyal, and equipped to raise funds and to represent you in important and critical negotiations; who can work sixteen hours a day six or seven days a week and will charge you only expenses; who is brilliantly sensitive to the opportunities that present themselves in campaigns; who can analyze 10,000 pieces of election data and find exactly what you have to know; who can draw other good people to work for you; who is completely honest and beyond party or press criticism; who will make no demands on you after you win; who can handle probblems rapidly and well without troubling you; who can write speeches, keep financial records, read all the papers, and see and hear all the TV and radio reports about the campaign; and whom your wife, family, and contributors will love. That is what you want and need, but you're not likely to find it.

As soon as you decide to run, start inquiring about prospective campaign managers in journalistic, academic, and political circles. City hall reporters may suggest people who could help you; professors of political science, law, or sociology may have competent colleagues or students. Other sources of leads are political leaders in your own party or even friends in the opposing party. (There is a surprising amount of camaraderie among political mechanics, regardless of their registration, and they do cross party lines from time to time to work for candidates of another party.)*

The choice of a campaign manager is critical. He spends your money and allocates your time. There are many smooth, confident, and persuasive talkers around who know the ball game but are without imagination, courage, or intellectual honesty, let alone modesty. You won't get a good man for nothing. Politics is no different from any other profession, and competent altruism is a special taste— a minority predilection.

If you intend to provide the creative direction of the campaign yourself, you may want a campaign manager who is strong in administrative talents. If you expect to go heavily into television, you probably want someone who has a reputation and experience in that area. If you're planning a campaign geared to issues, you may want a professor or academically oriented man, although you'll find few politicians who will recommend this course, since the concepts of

---

* Many professionals work for members of one party only. Some professionals specialize in representing one segment of a party. Others, like myself, prefer to work for candidates of ability representing the progressive segments of both major parties.

political theory have little in common with the specifics a campaign manager must contend with. Don't worry too much about what other politicians may think—you have to pick a manager whom you can trust to spend your money and represent your best interests. It has to be someone you're comfortable with both intellectually and emotionally. The "vibrations" had better be good, because you and your manager are going to be married to each other for several months, living through the genial and ugly terrors and the constant turmoil of campaigning, and your eccentricities had better be mutually compatible.

Most first-time candidates are best off with an intelligent personal friend as manager, if he has sufficient time for all that the job entails. There is a natural temptation in campaigns involving substantial investments of time and money to assume that only the most seasoned managers can do the job. This is not always the case. Some very good men are emotionally unstable, some are too demanding in the event of a victory, some take kickbacks, some feel they have to go the "safe" way—to do only what is expected and what has been done in the past. A politically sensitive friend or colleague, devoted to your interests, someone with whom you can discuss things honestly and openly, can often do the job better and may well be your best campaign manager.

In a recent statewide campaign, one candidate, an experienced politician with a brilliant and loyal personal staff, felt obliged to go outside for his top people because he felt that his own staff members weren't up to the job in such a major race. In retrospect, it is clear that his experienced assistants understood his needs better than the campaign manager he chose, although the manager was a practiced and highly regarded campaigner. Some mistakes were made during the campaign that probably cost him the election. (In fairness, there is no way of knowing whether the outcome would have been different had he used his own people.)

According to some politicians, campaign managers and candidates are natural enemies. On the one hand, candidates often feel that their managers presume too much and take prerogatives no one ever gave them. When they see money flow out for expenses no one bothered to mention in advance, many candidates think the manager is padding the bill or arranging kickbacks; and, as a matter of fact, both practices are probably as common in political campaigns as in business affairs generally. On the other hand, many managers consider their candidates unappreciative of the energy, initiative, and dedication they pour into the campaign. At times, each may be right in his condemnation of the other. This natural enmity may be based on considerations of ego. For example, it was reported that Robert Price, Mayor John V. Lindsay's 1965 campaign manager, who practically ran New York City as deputy mayor after Lindsay was elected, was annoyed when his complete control was questioned. Price left the Lindsay administration early in its first term. (Richard Aurelio, who became Lindsay's 1969 campaign manager and deputy mayor, was also reported to have really run the city before he resigned to manage Lindsay's abortive presidential campaign in 1972.)

Many candidates feel an overwhelming need to be their own managers. That is seldom wise. Usually the candidate is too busy literally running to involve himself in the minutiae of the campaign. (In England, politicians "stand" for election. In the United States, politicians "run" for election—and that is exactly what they do.)

There is another important reason why the candidate should completely discount the idea of being his own campaign manager. Each campaign is of critical importance to a candidate, and he cannot expect to see a race clearly. Mario Procaccino, running against Lindsay for mayor of New York in 1969, couldn't conceive the possibility of losing, since he received such a warm reception on the streets wherever he campaigned. The principals in a political campaign can't be expected to have an objective overview of how the campaign is going and what still needs to be done. Basic policy direction should come from the candidate, perhaps in consultation with his family, contributors, and close friends and personal advisers, but implementation should be completely in the hands of the manager. If a candidate really wants to manage a campaign, his best course may well be to resign his own candidacy and find another candidate to manage.

In many campaigns, managers make basic policy decisions for candidates and initiate major public pronouncements. This should be avoided except in emergencies. The manager is not running for office (although some managers do use their candidates as surrogates for their private ambitions), and only the candidate himself must ultimately live with the policies enunciated in the course of the campaign.

Many managers can dazzle an inexperienced candidate with the arcane details of a campaign, so that the normal response is, "OK, you take care of it—but don't spend too much." It is much better for a candidate, before he enters the race, to make a quiet, reasoned inquiry into what is involved, what he can expect to get for his money, which expenditures are mandatory, and which discretionary. *Before the campaign,* he should familiarize himself with the costs of such things as advertisements in local newspapers, 30-second TV commercials, giveaways, mailing 25,000 pieces, preparing 10,000 brochures, so that he can plan at least an outline of campaign strategy and required disbursements.

Some candidates feel they must be involved in every aspect of the campaign. That is exhausting and largely unnecessary. Once you appoint your campaign manager and define his responsibilities and their limits (indicating which decisions must be reserved for your approval), let him get on with the job. Make your appraisal of his capacity within three to four weeks; if by that time you have no confidence in him or don't like the way he does things, or what he has done, get a new manager. Many campaigns have been lost by the failure to do this. Frequently, when candidates lose confidence in a manager, instead of replacing him, they appoint a coordinator or executive assistant who gradually preempts the manager's prerogatives. This is bad for staff morale and leads to conflicts and subversion of decisions, none of which benefits the campaign. The basic rule is that only one man can be in charge.

Other paid staff members

One of your first staff appointments will be a secretary to cover the office in the early stages of the campaign, take calls, keep files, and handle appointments. Many candidates take secretaries from their professional or business practice or ask their wives to do the job. In a smaller campaign, either one of these courses is acceptable, if your business or family life won't suffer. In a tough campaign, when fourteen hours a day, seven days a week of work may not be uncommon, someone conditioned to political campaigning may be a better choice—someone from a political club, perhaps, or a volunteer who seems competent and strong, or the friend of a friend in politics.

Recruiting other staff members involves personal recommendations of people whose abilities you value; referrals from political allies; and your own observation of club workers whose honesty and ability are known to you. Putting together a group that can work well with you is the first requirement, but almost as important is their ability to work well together. This takes some doing; if each of your personal staff is busy trying to make points with you, the overall interests of the campaign may be sacrificed in the process.

Outside consultants
According to an experienced New York politician, every candidate in a major campaign ultimately panics in one way or another:

> If they have money, they try to buy security by hiring all the expert advice they can. They're faddish, like mutual fund managers: they buy whoever was hot last year. Very few candidates know exactly what they want and who the best consultant is to do it. The consultants are in business, you know, and politics is very seasonal—they have to make their money, and some are really thieves. But the good ones are more than worth their money—you just have to make sure you pick the good ones, and for the services *you* really need, not those *they* think you need.

Both the amount of money involved and their potential impact on the outcome of the election render the selection of outside consultants in larger campaigns very important. The basic rule in choosing outside consultants is to determine right at the start precisely which services you need, and to do your shopping early. The candidate should make the time to interview possible consultants personally.

The Political Market-Place (edited by David L. Rosenbloom and published by Quadrangle Books in 1972) provides fairly comprehensive lists of firms that specialize in campaign services, but it is not a Michelin Guide to relative quality. Anyway, ratings change even faster in politics than in the restaurant business. One list, published in 1971, mentioned William J. Ronan as an available campaign manager, although at the time the list was published, Ronan was director of the New York State Metropolitan Transportation Agency and, as one of Governor Nelson Rockefeller's closest advisers, he had limited his campaign activities to Rockefeller's campaigns. It was unlikely that he would have provided his services to any other candidate. Published lists such as these are helpful but must be used with caution.

My advice is to select *one* good consultant whom you have checked out thoroughly. Talk to his technicians about exactly what has to be done and how they intend to do it, and do not hesitate to ask for detailed explanations of technical terms even if you think you may sound naive. (Such questions are far from foolish and should be asked.) Professionals of quality are happy to discuss their work with potential clients, and, as in other fields, the good ones are usually enthusiastic about what they do. Questions about price should be discussed equally openly.

Once you've invested your time in searching for and hiring one specialist, ask him to recommend specialists in other aspects of campaigning.

Consultants may include the following:

An *advertising agency* to write copy, develop themes, work up radio and television commercials, buy space and time, etc. To choose an advertising agency, check those in your community first. Which have had political experience and are well regarded by other politicians? Which agencies specialize in the media you wish to emphasize—television, newspapers, or radio? The agency that is best for you will not necessarily be one that has won a political campaign. An innovative agency that is willing to assign a creative team to your campaign may be better for you than a more conventional agency that may invest only a minimum of creative energy on your behalf. The agency must have an advertising style with which you can feel at home. For example, a current television advertisement for an oral antiseptic hits the product's weakest point, its bad taste, and makes that its selling focus. You may like this approach, but you may not.

The approach of the agency should be consonant with the rest of your campaign. If you are running for a judicial post, you will not want an advertising agency that specializes in psychedelic graphics. If an appropriate agency is not available in your locality, you may hear of someone in the area who does this sort of work on a free-lance basis. If not, you may have to shop for an agency in a larger city. Agencies throughout the United States are listed (with their personnel and clients) in the *Standard Directory of Advertising Agencies*, available at many public libraries or by mail (priced at $22.00) from the publisher, National Register Publishing Company, 5201 Orchard Road, Skokie, Illinois 60076. Another useful publication is a twenty-page booklet, "Political Campaign Advertising and Advertising Agencies," available without charge from the American Association of Advertising Agencies, 200 Park Avenue, New York, N.Y. 10017.

In all but the smallest neighborhood campaigns, you will surely need a *printer*, who should be selected with the assistance of your staff. There are differences among printers, not only in prices but also in quality of work and—most important in tightly timed elections—in reliability. Missing a deadline by a week or ten days can destroy a brochure's effectiveness and negate the energies and monies invested in preparing and distributing it. In order to avoid arousing the antagonism of organized labor, political campaigners generally use only union printers and include the printer's union "bug," or stamp, somewhere on each piece of literature.

Your advertising agency, if you have one, may have an established relationship with a printer. Whether or not this is the case, you should interview a number of printers, inspecting samples of their work and asking for the names of local clients. Check with their clients to learn whether they were satisfied with both the quality of the work and the printer's ability to meet deadlines. Political clients of prospective printers may be particularly helpful to you in this regard.

If you decide to use the printer recommended by your advertising agency—and sometimes you may feel you have no choice but to do so—the agency will probably receive a percentage of your printing bill from the printer, a common business practice called the "finder's fee." If you are able to deal directly with the printer, you may be able to convince him to reduce his price by the amount—probably 5 to 10 percent of your total bill—which he would otherwise give to the agency that referred you.

For a *radio-television consultant* you may want one of the well-publicized hotshots, or you may get a local person. If you have a personal contact with an advertising agency, you may not need a separate radio-TV specialist. If not, and you see something on television that you especially like, call the station, find out which agency did the ad, try to trace the man who did it, and get in touch with him. He may be willing to take a three-week leave of absence to do a job for you. (Some agencies stay out of campaign work and prefer to have any political work in which their staff members are involved done on a free-lance basis.)

Novelty specialists are agencies or companies that handle giveaway items such as balloons, matchbooks, rulers, and ballpoint pens. You might try premium houses that work with advertisers; but I feel that you really shouldn't spend much time or money on such items. Except for shopping bags, which serve as walking posters, giveaways are generally nonproductive unless you can come up with something genuinely new and useful that will attract favorable public attention. Buttons are expensive and largely ineffective in producing new votes. In local campaigns, I would recommend your buying perhaps 200 or 300 buttons for your children, friends, and workers. Anything more would be wasteful. On election day, special buttons are sometimes given to staff to gain access to campaign headquarters and to identify those who are newcomers to the regular staff.

Other politicians will usually tell you who supplied their buttons and shopping bags; these suppliers will be able to lead you to other novelty merchants if they themselves cannot provide the products you desire. As in the case of printers, it is best to deal with novelty specialists directly rather than through your advertising agency, since the agency may expect to receive, as an additional fee, a percentage of the price you pay, and that may result in your paying a higher price for the novelties. The over-all problem of giveaways is treated more fully on pages 197–98.

In a smaller campaign, you probably won't need a professional *speech writer* at all. In that case, write a basic speech and try it out on your friends and colleagues. Then use it in kaffeeklatches and smaller gatherings before attempting it in front of a larger audience. Try not to sound pompous, and use a style you're comfortable with —don't mouth phrases you don't believe or care about, or that aren't natural to you. Keep your speeches short—ten minutes or so.

Senator Hubert H. Humphrey, in his presidential campaigns, was constantly criticized for speaking twice as long as the audience's attention span lasted. The joy of having a captive audience is great, but don't talk longer than you need to. Any time you speak in public, extemporize as much as possible, or at least appear to do so.

In larger campaigns, however, you may need a professional speech writer. Ask local political reporters whose political speeches they think highly of, and who wrote them. Interview the speech writers and consider whether your political sympathies and concerns are close enough so that they can understand your views and help communicate them effectively to the electorate. You might meet potential speech writers in the academic community by asking a supporter with connections at a local university to arrange to introduce you to politically oriented faculty members and graduate students whose ideas are compatible with yours. When you talk with them, you can judge which people may be interested in working for you and which have a style and philosophy consistent with your own. Unless you have previously heard or read speeches written by someone whom you are interested in hiring, start out by commissioning one relatively minor speech from him or her. If you are comfortable delivering that speech and it is well received by the audience, you will feel confident entrusting more important speeches to that writer.

Survey specialists, whose services are discussed in detail in the advertising and research sections of this book, may suprise you with the magnitude of their price per interview, but keep in mind that good samplings can be done with no more than a few hundred interviews for a large area. Among the nationally famous firms are George Gallup, Louis Harris, National Opinion Research Center, Oliver Quayle, Burns Roper, and Daniel Yankelovich (who does political work exclusively for *The New York Times* and *Time* magazine). Small firms that are somewhat less prestigious and probably less expensive may be as good or better for local candidates than more widely known ones, since your account is more likely to be personally handled by a principal in a smaller firm.

Many survey firms are reliable, but some are not, some are incompetent, and some are simply thieves. In considering any survey firm, you should interview both the principals and the technicians who would actually do the job, examine their work, and talk to a number of their earlier clients—not so much because of the amount of money involved as because their performance will contribute significantly to campaign strategy and will influence every critical decision you'll make.

In medium- to large-scale campaigns, your choice of a *computer firm* can be extremely important because a good computer service company can greatly increase your campaign's effectiveness or can significantly waste your money and time. Most of these firms—conventionally referred to as "houses"—are small service bureaus. Your computer house's integrity and sensitivity to your research requirements will provide the context for much of your thinking in relation to the electorate and for many of your specific decisions on allocating your resources. Good houses will allow the political logic of your campaign to guide them in what they do for you, while lesser quality firms may simply manipulate data, often in ways that achieve only minimal results. Sending out thousands of computer letters generates a lot of activity and income for them. Many houses will simply be happy to send out letters to whomever you want. Good computer technicians will question you closely on which groups should get letters. There are advantages to dealing with a computer firm that has a political mechanic on its staff—only a few do. Even the best computer men know very little about campaigning, although they can talk knowingly. The best bet is a political technician who knows computer capabilities.

Many computer firms handling political advertising accounts are merely "list brokers"—they buy or develop lists and send out mailings for candidates as a purely mechanical process. The mailings are usually of limited utility, possibly because they are sent to the wrong people and run the danger of creating neutral or even negative impacts. (In 1972, for example, it was rumored that hundreds of thousands of computer letters intended for voters in Oregon were sent instead to Illinois residents because the firm used the wrong tape and no one bothered to check.) On the other hand, a creative house can contribute very substantially to campaigns.

In retaining computer service consultants, you should look for these characteristics:

1. *Reliability.* Do they deliver exactly what is required on time? Mistakes require reruns, whose cost is passed on to the candidate, since most firms charge their clients per hour of computer use. Since timing is so critical in campaigns, a computer mistake or delays that cause a mailing to go out late can seriously limit its impact.

2. *Political experience.* The firm's principals should have been involved in campaigns conceptually as well as mechanically. They should know how strategy is formed, the limits of mailing effectiveness, how to determine which client groups are crucial, how to develop ethnic-select lists, how to find the raw data and make it useful for you.* Unless they've been through a campaign from beginning to end, they won't be able to contribute creatively to yours.

3. *Innovational capacity.* There should be some evidence that the firm can handle each situation on an individual basis, and not simply repeat what they or someone else did in a previous campaign. You must make this judgment on your impression of the principals of the firm and the professional assigned to your campaign, as well as on past performance. Much of their value will depend on the rapport you establish with them. If you have doubts, the probabilities are that the doubts will be a self-fulfilling prophecy.

4. *Technical capacity.* In a fair-sized campaign, the firm should have an IBM 360-30 or similar equipment. For major city and state-wide races, there should be access to two computers of this type.

5. *Competitive pricing.* Prices should be established with precision —whether costs for computer mailings will include envelope stuffing and labeling and bagging for delivery to the post office, whether a printout will be provided in addition to cards, labels, and/or letters, and so on.

In many smaller areas, only one competent, reliable firm is usually available to perform a given service, and that firm may already have agreed to handle your opponent by the time you approach it. That happened in a major congressional race in New York City in early 1972, when a highly specialized computer firm informed each candidate that it was handling both accounts. One executive handled one

---

* The concept of client groups is discussed on p. 49. Ethnic-select lists— voter lists broken down by ethnic or other basic characteristics—are discussed on p. 204.

candidate, while another handled his opponent. You should agree to such an arrangement only if you have full confidence in the firm's professional integrity.*

A *telephone specialist* is almost a necessity if you intend to make over 10,000 calls. Check the charges and list of past clients, as well as the principals' operating philosophy and technical background, for each firm you consider. There are local telephone advertising firms in most parts of the country, but there may or may not be one in your area that is experienced in political work, a factor to be considered. If no politician you know can recommend a good firm, look for telephone research and marketing specialists under "Market Research" in your classified telephone book. Or, since major advertising agencies hire these firms, you can get recommendations by talking with friends in the advertising business. You are likely to get the best results, however, by asking other candidates and politicians about the consultants and processes they have used: Did they make much difference in the campaigns in which they were involved? Was there a higher turnout than expected? Was the vote in the areas called significantly higher than that anticipated by the polls or than that in areas not called? The answers to these questions should enable you to pick a consultant who justifies his costs.

As in any professional relationship, once you decide to hire a consultant, you should be certain that the contract stipulates exactly what is to be provided and when. Have an experienced political attorney review proposed contract specifications carefully. Most telephone consultants will charge you a flat fee per call, which includes an unspecified profit for them. Some may also be willing to accept an arrangement whereby you pay all costs directly, paying them either a percentage of the costs or a consulting fee. Few consultants will be willing to advance you credit. That is not unreasonable, since political finance committees disband instantly at the end of the campaign, and often no one is available to take fiscal responsibility after election day. Because of the poor payment record of many politicians, most consultants require 50 percent of the contract total on

* Situations like this are practicable for data processing, but usually impossible for research survey and advertising firms, since their functions require a more partisan involvement by the firm's principals. In such cases, you may have to go outside your own locality to shop for a consultant.

signing, 25 percent during the campaign, and the final 25 percent shortly before the election.

Campaign voyeurs

Try to minimize the time you spend with the campaign buffs who hang around headquarters. If you win, they may think that they helped and expect you to feel a sense of obligation to them. If you lose, they can always say, "Well, he didn't want to listen to me when I warned him that . . ."

Many of these "sometime *mavens*" have participated in so many political discussions that at times they sound quite profound.* Use any of their ideas that seem to you to be sensible, but bear in mind that most of them have never invested anything in a campaign except talk. These campaign voyeurs are harmless, except that they will take as much of your and your campaign workers' time as you will allow them. One tactic is simply to make a policy of allowing only those with business to transact into campaign headquarters.

Unfortunately, your friends and relatives may be among those who enjoy this role. If you make an exception for your intimates at campaign headquarters, you will find it hard to deny the others.

Budgeting

That additional money is often regarded as the only solution to problems in government programs may in considerable part originate from campaign practices, where "more" is the usual operative strategy. Many candidates and their managers regard more money and more workers as the only solution for campaign problems. Although sufficent monies are indeed critical for basic expenses—overhead, salaries, mailings, and promotion—large additional expenditures that fall outside the overall campaign strategy may simply deceive the candidate into believing that everything that can be done is being done, while, in truth, the results of this additional spending may be all but negligible.

You must remember throughout every campaign that most voters make up their minds quite early and that their voting decisions are

* *"Maven,"* a Yiddish word meaning an informed or expert person, is often applied sarcastically, as in this case.

controlled largely by their predispositions rather than by anything said or done in the campaign. Perhaps only 10 percent of this large group will ever change their minds—and as many as change *to* you will probably change *from* you. The best you can really expect is a split. It is to the *undecided* vote of 20 to 30 percent, then, that you must direct a major portion of your energies and your funds. For this reason, expenditures for saturation mailings, billboards, and posters are not sensible investments, since they are directed at everyone, including the 70 or 80 percent who have already made up their minds. Marginal increment analysis—the practice of evaluating the probable practical effects of any proposed additional expenditure— is as important in campaigning as in business. This technique cannot always be practiced with precision, but even roughly applied, it may save you significant sums of money that might better be used elsewhere. For example, mailing only to areas where the outlook is promising is a much more efficient use of funds than a saturation mailing to every voter in a district. Thus, you might rank the election precincts in your district according to the number of voters in each who are undecided about the election. After determining the cost of sending the mailing to every voter in each district, you can easily calculate the cost per undecided voter reached in each of the districts. You might then cut off your mailing at the point at which mailing expenses average 22 cents per undecided voter reached.

For another illustration, take the question of deciding among various types of visual material. The choices may be:

- five painted outdoor signs for clubhouses: $1,500
- ten billboards throughout the district: $5,000 (including preparation, space rental, etc.)
- one thousand posters: $500 (design, putting up)
- ten thousand car stickers: $1,000 (design, printing, distribution)
- ten thousand general purpose stickers: $600 (design, printing, putting up)

Separately, none of these may seem particularly expensive, but combined, they add up to $8,600, a significant amount.

In most campaigns, what happens is that the policy group and/or the manager decides at first that the billboards at key locations are important, since they've heard via the grapevine that these locations are already being considered by the opponents. (Information on strategy and tactics—much of it erroneous—generally flows from one candidate's group to another and is a main topic of conversation over drinks during most campaigns.) No one is likely to ask how effective the billboards are, how many people will be reached, and how many votes will be changed. If these questions do come up, the response usually is that billboards have been put up in every campaign for as long as anyone in the district can remember and that therefore they must be effective. That may have been true in the past, but the expenses of campaigning are much higher today and the technological alternatives are altogether different. Because there is no scientific evidence for evaluating the impact of each of the campaign media, it is natural to rely on mechanisms that apparently have worked in the past. You must learn to avoid this habit. If you think the choices through, you will probably change your emphasis and save money, since the impact per $1,000 invested clearly will be greater from one or two thoughtfully planned visual promotions than from indiscriminate saturation. The following table illustrates this point.

ITEM	COST	NUMBER REACHED	COST PER VOTER REACHED
Clubhouse signs (5)	$1,500	5,000	$3.00
Billboards (10)	$5,000	10,000	$0.50
Posters (1,000)	$ 500	10,000	$0.05
Car stickers (10,000)	$1,000	15,000	$0.07
General stickers (10,000)	$ 600	15,000	$0.04

(These figures are estimates, and costs will vary from place to place. Traffic and pedestrian counts for various street corners, often available from city traffic departments, will assist you in judging the number of people who may be reached by signs, billboards, or posters. There is no scientific way to judge the number of people reached by stickers, but you or your manager should be able to come up with a reasoned estimate based on your knowledge of the community.)

In an area containing 50,000 registered voters, the distribution may approximate that shown in the table above. All of the types of visual media listed in the table are probably effective with the same segment of the voting public, so to buy all of them, as is common in many campaigns, does not make good fiscal sense. If you feel you must buy any, keep in mind that car stickers advertise the campaign quite cheaply and are not offensive. They will not change many votes, but they will give the people who like your candidacy a chance to feel they are contributing to it, thereby reinforcing their vote at little cost. With conspicuous billboards or multitudinous posters, however, as with loudspeaker trucks, mass mailings, and stickers posted indiscriminately on mail boxes and telephone poles, you run the risk of irritating citizens and losing votes, including those of the important undecided bloc.

This approach to decisions on expenditures for visual media has wider application; for every significant expenditure you should consider alternatives and try to evaluate the impact of the various options. In many campaigns the temptation is very strong, after investing in billboards, for example, to respond to a campaign worker's plea for stickers for his district and then accede to a club's demand for a sign so that its candidates may be advertised at your expense. You cannot altogether dismiss the goodwill that these expenditures probably buy, but the object is to win, and the goodwill of club officials alone will not produce all the votes necessary. Generally, you are better off focusing your expenditures on potentially receptive voters.

I am often struck by the fact that many major budget decisions are made without the benefit of any objective research. Polls are common in campaigning, but few candidates and managers seem to base their advertising commitments on research showing the impact of different media. If you are having a sample poll conducted by professionals, it may repay you to try to establish which investments in media seem to be most effective. (For sample polls, see Chapter 3.) Advertising agencies do this kind of research for commercial clients, but it is rarely done in political campaigns, partly because everything in most campaigns is conducted in a frenzy and partly because managers, intent on protecting their ignorance of how to weigh the options sensibly, tell their candidates it is unnecessary. The time for the careful analysis of options is at least six months before the campaign starts in earnest. Opportunities for quiet reflection are nonexistent once the campaign is under way. Good decisions and policies cannot be made in the confusion, panic, anger, or resentment that often prevail during the heat of the campaign. Chapter 5 offers practical suggestions.

Control of expenditures

Who authorizes expenditures is always the key question. In well-funded campaigns, my experience is that the candidate prefers to disburse everything through his personal accountant. This procedure makes for control of the money but often involves costly delays. If the budget is mapped out carefully in advance, it is preferable for the candidate to tell the manager exactly how much can be spent on a certain item and how much is available for emergencies, and then to instruct his accountant to release funds in each category as requested by the manager. To have to clear with an accountant, however, who in turn may have to clear with the candidate and contributors, does not make for a smooth operation. But since most campaign managers are not intimates of their candidates, and since substantial sums of money do change hands and kickbacks are not unheard of, a candidate should protect himself by requiring the manager to account for expenditures. A detailed weekly accounting is frequently required of those campaign managers with a large degree of control over expenditures.

Major items such as advertising, mailings, computer printouts, polls, and television and radio spots should be contracted for *in writing* early in the campaign, and the candidate's attorney and accountant should carefully check *all* contract stipulations in advance. In some campaigns, for example, media consultants receive a fee from the candidate plus a 15 percent rebate from the newspapers or radio and television stations. This can add up to a great deal of money, some of which may be saved if the consultants' contracts are written carefully.

How to raise money

A basic premise of this book is that the candidate who uses accurate research and devotes some time and thought to his campaign while it is still in its early stages can conduct an effective, sophisticated campaign relatively economically. Money counts, of course, but spending money is, by itself, no guarantee of victory. From my own experience, I know that a well-financed campaign can lose to a well-directed, less-well-financed one. This occurs often enough to make it worthwhile for those who are so minded to consider campaigning even if they know in advance that they cannot match their opponents' financial resources. There is ample evidence to argue that almost anyone can win and that almost any candidate, no matter how well entrenched, can be beaten.

Incumbents have a considerable advantage over new candidates, if for no other reason than that they may have done favors for individuals and business firms. In the natural course of events, they may also have extended themselves for certain individuals, arranging introductions, helping to obtain zoning variances, getting a job for this or that one, or recommending new business loans. (The topic of patronage—of which this is one aspect—is the subject of Martin and Susan Tolchin's book *To the Victor* [New York: Random House, 1971].) Often these favors are arranged "contracts," with the proviso that the recipient of the favor will buy a seat or a table at the annual testimonial dinner at $50 a plate, provide campaign workers or campaign services, pay for printing costs, or make an appropriate campaign contribution when requested.

Basically, a new candidate is selling "futures" when he raises funds—he can't do anything else until he obtains office and some discretion. The incumbent, however, is selling "nows"—he can do things right away for his constituents. As long as campaigns cost what they do, these problems will exist. Not every such political contract is necessarily a personal favor against the public interest. A firm may have been waiting six months to be paid for goods the city purchased from it. If an official in the city government can see that the bill is is paid relatively promptly, the public interest is not substantially harmed, yet the firm is likely to be grateful.

Since raising money for new candidates is difficult, a candidate should name an experienced finance (or fund-raising) chairman who has extensive contacts in the business community and among civic groups.* In larger campaigns, friends and colleagues may volunteer

* The critical importance of a finance chairman is exemplified in Fred L. Zimmerman's description of the activities of Eugene Wyman, who was associated with Hubert Humphrey's presidential bid in 1972. ("The Money Man," *Wall Street Journal* [New York edition], March 8, 1972, pp. 1, 13. [The *Journal* consistently provides some of the best political reporting in the nation.])

their services, since, if you win, you may be able to recommend them for appointments to judicial posts or to prestigious jobs (such as chairman of a commission). Many wealthy people do not desire public office but want to be involved in public affairs to satisfy their need to express themselves on public matters that they are concerned about. In smaller campaigns, you're best off asking political colleagues for the names of effective finance chairmen in past campaigns. Bankers, builders, and attorneys with contacts in the business community and with civic groups are probably your best bet. Unless they are close friends or family, you'll probably have to offer some concrete incentive—for example, your support for a judgeship or for mayor or your support for a public issue of concern to them. In an ideal situation, this chairman should organize all fund-raising events.

If a contributor wants specific assurances of "favors," the candidate, not the finance chairman, should judge the propriety of the request. Many people contribute without asking a specific favor, expecting simply to be able to speak to the candidate, if he wins the election, on matters affecting them. They expect a sympathetic ear without specific assurances.

Senator Birch Bayh (Democrat, Indiana) spoke frankly about this matter in an interview on CBS's "Face the Nation," April 30, 1972:

> Every contribution we take, I think we ask ourselves, all right, now what does this obligate you to? And in my judgment, the most it should obligate us to is to provide a forum to listen to the problems of anyone who makes a contribution. In the final analysis, I as a senator have a responsibility to listen to the problems and listen to the case of those who don't make contributions, even those who support my opponent.

Many candidates prefer not to beg, which fund-raising often seems to involve, and many will not trade elements of their official discretion in order to raise funds. One New York politician I know refuses contributions in excess of $100 from any individual, on the theory that although he owes a contributor a hearing on any given problem, he does not want to incur any specific obligation beyond that. Unfortunately, this view is usually possible only in relatively small districts.

Campaign budgeting can't be done with precision. The unexpected expense can easily play havoc with your estimates. Even so, you can certainly anticipate the major expenditures: office overhead, paid staff, research, printing, mailing, radio and television time, newspaper advertisements, novelty giveaways, etc. Prepare your budget for the basic necessities and worry about the refinements later. If you find that you need $20,000 to make the race and that you can afford only $5,000, while the finance chairman thinks he can raise only another $5,000, you may decide not to run. But if making the race means a great deal to you, you may decide to go into debt, a course many campaigners are forced to follow.

If you are a new candidate, your best sources of funds or services will include the following:

1. *Your own money*. Ask yourself some fundamental questions. How much of your family's savings are you willing to commit? Most financial advisers believe a prudent family should have one year's income in the bank for emergencies. Do you want to mortgage your home or borrow funds?

2. *Relatives*. It may be unpleasant for you to ask them for money, but close relatives will often find the idea of your running for office exciting and will want to contribute money as well as to volunteer to work in your campaign. They also can interest their friends and colleagues in helping you.

3. *Friends*. The people you work with and old family friends can be surprisingly generous with their time and money. Young attorneys, with an eye perhaps on a judgeship, will often contribute, hoping for a friend in the party. People you know in civic groups may sympathize with your stands on the issues and be willing to help.

4. *Cocktail parties, teas, and kaffeeklatches*. Your friends and neighbors may be willing to sponsor small gatherings (20 to 25 people) for you, with each guest contributing perhaps $10 to your campaign. You will not make a great deal of money, since you should pay for the food and liquor, but each such party can raise a hundred dollars or more, and, in addition, you will be able to discuss your views in a relaxed setting. You may gain additional workers and contributions from those voters whom you impress as a good candidate. These parties should be arranged with careful attention to such detail as how much, if anything, should be charged, how

many and which people should be invited, the form of the invitation, and the type of food and entertainment.*

5. *Newspaper and radio advertisements soliciting contributions* are sometimes effective if your stands on controversial issues attract certain groups. In addition to bringing in small donations, such appeals may attract rich people you might not otherwise know how to approach. (In New York City, for example, the press has reported that two millionaires, Carter Burden and Stewart Mott, have contributed hundreds of thousands of dollars to various candidates whom they did not know personally.)† Advertisements of this sort tend to be costly and usually do not produce a great outpouring of money. They may, however, have beneficial side effects: Volunteers may offer their services, your campaign will be dramatized and publicized, and the idea that you have to appeal to the public for funds may be effective in developing the fact of your honesty and independence. George McGovern used this device to great advantage during his primary campaigns in 1972.

6. *Testimonial dinners* are a most important source of funds for both incumbents and new candidates. Your political club or a civic group in which you are an active member can sponsor such events. Dinner tickets can be $25, $50, or even more, depending on the precedent in the area. Usually a prominent politician appears as a speaker. It is advisable to supplement the speeches with entertainment (preferably entertainment that is donated)—music for dancing, a comedian, a singer, or whatever else is customary or might be well received in your locality. In a large city, if you use a good hotel banquet room with quality food, liquor, and service, the cost may be from $15 to $20 per person, but you may raise several thousand dollars if you sell enough tickets. In a smaller community, costs, as well as proceeds, will of course be smaller. You may be able to gain additional money from a testimonial dinner by publishing a program (sometimes called a journal) in which contributors buy ads wishing

---

* For a detailed account of how to organize kaffeeklatches on a local level and how to maximize the results, see Dick Simpson, *Winning Elections: A Handbook in Participatory Politics* (Chicago: Swallow, 1972), pp. 41-47.

† Regarding Burden, see Thomas Meehan, "The Carter Burden Question," *The New York Times Magazine*, November 7, 1971, pp. 33 ff; regarding Mott, see the Profile by E. J. Kahn, Jr., in *The New Yorker*, November 27, 1971, pp. 56ff.

you well. These devices are the chief moneymaking techniques of most experienced politicians.

In organizing a testimonial dinner or any other fund-raising affair, attention to detail is important. Many political functions literally leave a bad taste in people's mouths—the food is served cold and the wine may be bitter. The prices normally charged for tickets to these affairs should justify a choice of quality entrées, and, since some people don't eat meat, fish should be available. The temperature of the room should be comfortable and the seating uncrowded. The microphones should be tested for the speakers and the band. The seating list should be sensitive to who is not speaking to whom, and care should be given in general to a sensible placement of guests at the tables. You may or may not want to have a published seating list, since such lists have been used by reporters to ask why a certain contributor was there and what favor was requested in return for the contribution. (The seating lists of most political dinners are filled with the names of architects, planners, attorneys, builders, union officials, and others whose work and income involve dealing with the government. Recently, such lists have been harder come by, since they make some political relationships clearer than ticket buyers and officeholders may wish.)

7. *Political club and/or party.* The political organization you belong to may provide some campaign funds, but generally it is still paying off debts from previous campaigns. Increasingly, the individual candidate must rely on his own financial resources, while the local political club may even ask him funds. The club and the county or city organization can often "contribute" experienced campaign workers, which is a considerable help and sometimes even more important than cash. (In New York City, a political club with only ten reliable, experienced workers is generally regarded as a strong club.) The organization can also be helpful in providing expertise on when and how to file petitions, the best and most reliable printer, and other practical, important campaign matters.

8. *"Piggybacking"* is an often-used technique that involves sharing mailing and printing costs with another candidate—perhaps a better-financed one—on the party ticket. If you're running for the state legislature, for example, the party's congressional candidate can include your brochure in his mailing, and your only cost will be the

printing of the brochure. Generally, you will be asked to provide workers or other campaign serivces in return for your colleague's help.*

9. *Direct-mail solicitation.* Letters soliciting contributions from voters registered in your political party are a common fund-raising device that I regard as most promising for candidates in medium- to large-scale races. Preparation, paper, copywriting, design, and postage (at the bulk rate of 4.5 cents a letter) bring the average cost of such appeals to about 10 cents a letter—and to that must be added about $25 per thousand for the commercial mailing lists that are used in most cases. To be economical and worthwhile, thousands of these letters must be sent out at once. In small campaigns, this method is not economical; but the principle of establishing lists of possible contributors who are likely to be receptive to your candidacy and then appealing to them for funds is a good one. Businesses and individuals who are potential contributors might be identified by going through local newspapers to see which local groups have taken positions on which issues, or by having a member of your staff check through the city commercial directory and chamber of commerce and professional association membership lists.

The financial returns from large-scale direct-mail solicitations may not be great enough to justify the investments of time and money that they require, but since the process has the added virtue of advertising your candidacy, you may wish to make use of it anyway. The technique was used by Senator George McGovern in the winter of 1971 to raise funds for his presidential bid, and there were reports that the effort was notably successful, raising some $1.25 million.

Most commerical concerns that specialize in direct-mail fund raising charge a percentage of the total amount collected, but others charge a flat fee of 12 to 14 cents a letter, or a few cents more per letter than the cost of doing the mailing directly from the candidate's own headquarters. The additional expense may or may not be justi-

---

* The term "piggybacking" is also used to describe an unethical practice in campaigning or in business generally. Some consultants, for example, set up a computer program or a telephone or other research study for one client, who pays the full rate, and then sell the same operation to other clients at reduced rates without the permission of the first client, who is not informed of the questions that are added to his research.

fied by increased rates of contributions. This is how *The New York Times* described the situation:

> The direct-mail professionals are devoting increasing attention to writing more skillful letters for their clients and to the application of numerous technical advances that make the over-all package more attractive.
>
> Computers can scatter the individual prospect's name throughout a typed letter, and now there is even a way to produce an appeal that is faintly smudged so as to look even more like the work of a secretary.
>
> But all these elaborate touches depend entirely on the quality of the mailing list, according to the direct-mail experts. . . .
>
> The direct-mail experts borrow the names of contributors from some friendly politicians, or they rent the subscription lists of liberal or conservative publications at rates that average three or four cents a name. . . .
>
> But the professional carefully records the names of those who respond to his own appeal because these he can legitimately add to his own stock and, after a suitable interval, approach again. . . .
>
> By working in campaigns around the country and renting lists of one kind or another, he slowly begins to identify the people who are most forthcoming and, equally important, those who are least generous.*

10. *Professional fund raisers.* There are people who make their living as professional fund raisers, but their charges are generally too high—30 percent or more of the total contributions received—to be of practical value to a new campaigner.

11. *Do-gooders.* There are people in most urban communities who are truly devoted to the public interest. Very effective national campaigns on ecological problems have recently been led by private groups of such concerned citizens. They and others like them may be willing to support your candidacy, providing funds and campaign workers, if you have taken a favorable stand on their positions. Reviewing local newspapers and discussions with city hall reporters can

* Walter Rugaber, "Politicians Turn to Direct Mail to Bring in Campaign Funds," *The New York Times,* September 8, 1970, p. 29.

usually provide you with a list of organizations and people with whom you should get in touch.

12. *Anti-incumbent groups.* Any incumbent is bound to incur the disapproval of some voters and some special-interest groups. Reviewing the incumbent's record should give you a good idea of which people he is likely to have alienated. Many of these people or groups may wish to contribute to your campaign simply to get even with him.

13. *Local religious organizations.* In cities and in suburban areas, churches and other religious organizations that own large properties are interested in assuring that proper public services remain or become available, and they are often willing to purchase blocks of tickets for political functions or provide other support to candidates in their area.

14. *Local business organizations.* There are groups, usually business oriented, who contribute to both sides in order to have a sure winner and, therefore, they hope, a sure friend in government. It takes some research and questioning of newspapermen and other politicians to find out which groups make a practice of contributing to all candidates in your area, but the financial return may well make it worth the effort.

15. *Contributions in services.* Finally, you should be able to think of numerous sources for contributions in services rather than cash. The printers' union, for example, may not be willing or able to give you a cash contribution, but it may agree to provide free printing of your brochures if you provide the paper. Other unions might be willing to provide workers to distribute your material or even to mail some campaign material for you. If you live in a university town, you may be able to get capable graduate students to write position papers for you without charge. Your specific needs and your ingenuity will dictate other possible sources of contributions of necessary services.

As soon as possible after receiving a campaign contribution, make certain to acknowledge its receipt and your gratitude to the contributor in the form of a personally signed letter. This is not only common courtesy but also an inducement for the contributor to help you again later in the campaign or in a future campaign.

No one owes you a contribution just because you have decided you want to run. Many potential contributors will be discouraged if they see evidence of waste and misuse of funds. Don't commit funds you don't have, and don't spend money on discretionary items before the basic expenses of the campaign are met. Careful spending of money is also a habit worthwhile in your term of office, should you win. Taxpayers around the country have voted down many bond issues because they have seen evidence of government waste around them. Additional money is not the solution to every problem, in political campaigns or in government.

It must be emphasized that campaign fund-raising activities and commitments made to obtain contributions may "contract" or obligate you to such an extent that your discretion in office may be severely limited. A candidate who has too many "contracts" outstanding may not be able to serve his own political needs or the needs of his constituency effectively. Sometimes it may be wise to turn money down, hard as that course always is, so that you retain some maneuverability as an official and as a human being.

2 Detailing

Nova's law is simple: Do it yourself, and believe no one. If you have a commercial to send from Washington to Minneapolis, carry it to the airport, hand it to Bill and tell him what flight to take. Run back to the office, call Harry in Minneapolis, tell him to meet the flight, then take a cab to the TV station, ask for Charley, and stand over Charley while he puts the commercial on the film chain. It's the only way.

—BARRY NOVA

This chapter discusses specific campaigning details, as distinguished from the structuring elements described in the previous chapter. Usually there is nothing glamorous about these specifics—although advance men, for example, may encounter hectic, tense conditions—but in many campaigns the quality of the detailing described here makes the difference between winning and losing.

Client-group analysis
The most important detail is the identification and analysis of voter client groups, for this determination will key the campaign in numerous ways by providing the focus through which you see all options in a campaign.

Client-group analysis identifies groups of voters who are united by feeling, attitudes on given issues, racial or religious identity, or other relationships or opinions. The members of one client group are likely to react to events and issues in roughly the same manner and intensity. An ethnic minority, the elderly, welfare recipients, and parents of schoolchildren are examples of client groups. Nothing can save more money and more campaigns than competently applied specific client-group analysis. Nonetheless, it receives cursory attention in most campaigns, and only the most brilliant, experienced, intuitive campaigners seem to use it properly. This problem is part of a considerably more general issue, the role of research in a campaign, which is examined in detail in Chapter 3. Here, one principle must be emphasized: *No campaigner should try to make everyone a convert.* Although only a completely inept candidate would ever think it possible, too many primary and general election campaigns have proceeded on the singularly absurd assumption that everyone is a potential convert. Shutouts take place in baseball, not in political contests.

Once this fact is acknowledged, the critical question becomes "Whom can you reach?" or, to put it another way, "Who is potentially sympathetic to your programs, priorities, and personality?" These are your particular client groups. Identifying these people should provide the cornerstone for your campaign, for once they are established, your allocations of time and money investments can be more effectively focused.

Client-group analysis is used in market research, in urban planning, and in other professional fields. In political campaigns, it can determine where your potential strength is and help maximize the potential there. The data can come from two sources: past voting records (usually by geographic district) and sample surveys (showing voter attitudes by age, sex, ethnic background, party, income, and other demographic characteristics). The required research procedures and their potentials are described in Chapter 3.

At this point, a simple example may demonstrate the utility of client-group analysis. In a primary campaign involving 50,000 registered voters, perhaps 15,000 people will vote. Analysis of past primaries would suggest the likely geographic and demographic distribution of these 15,000, enabling you to tell your local workers or election district captains where they can most profitably invest their time. Instead of touring the streets of the entire area indiscriminately, you can spend most of your time in locations where the actual voters are—canvassing buildings, meeting voters at subways, bus stops, and train stations, and anticipating the issues that interest the client groups in these areas. Rather than saturating every registered voter, mailings can be selective, and telephone campaigns, focusing on areas containing most of the probable voters, can include appeals to which these groups can relate.

If your research polls are carefully designed, they will establish the characteristics and attitudes of voters in the prime areas (those with particularly heavy votes in previous elections), as differentiated from the voters in secondary areas. In some cases, your major appeals may be to women (who generally make up the majority of voters), or to certain ethnic groups, or to the young or the old.

It is prudent to set up the client-group analysis considerably in advance of the actual campaigning, since the necessary coordination of surveys with information from experienced local workers is extremely difficult during the tense period of day-to-day campaigning.

As a practical matter, all candidates must concern themselves particularly with one client group: the undecided. Although there can be no assurance that one or two characteristics unite the members of this group, any information from surveys regarding the undecided is extremely worthwhile, for this group is worth at least one-third of your campaign funds and time.

Decision-making

Important policy decisions should be made rapidly and sensibly, with provisions for good implementation and follow-through. In too many campaigns, there is never a clear definition of who makes the decisions, and the process is thereby delayed. Sometimes the decision-making group may consist of the candidate, the manager, and technical consultants. Too frequently, however, the group making the decisions may vary from day to day, based on who is around campaign headquarters, or which contributor or party representative has an interest in the matter, or who last met the candidate in the men's room. In a well-managed campaign, a policy guidance group, established early and held constant, provides continuity in overall direction as well as proper coordination of each sector of the campaign.*

The composition of the policy guidance group varies from candidate to candidate and from situation to situation. Normally, however,

* Murray B. Levin describes this aspect of Edward M. Kennedy's senatorial campaign in Massachusetts in 1962 in *Kennedy Campaigning* (Boston: Beacon, 1966).

it includes representatives of major contributors and the party in addition to the campaign manager, close friends of the candidate, and sometimes the candidate's spouse. The policy guidance group should meet once a week for a general review of the campaign. In addition, it should be summoned whenever a major problem occurs. When you bring the group together to deal with a specific problem, you may wish also to include whichever consultant is involved in the problem.

In dealing with your policy guidance group, remember that only one person can be in charge, and that person must be the candidate. Listen to everyone, but if there is disagreement, you are the one who must make the decision. The policy guidance group has an advisory function only; you must have the final say.

Robert F. Kennedy, an experienced and effective campaigner, used to say that all the big campaign decisions are made quickly, synthesizing experience and insight in a way that is not fully explainable. In politics as in personal life, the most profoundly important decisions may be made from essentially unconscious sources. An inexperienced campaigner tends to defer to his advisers who have been through this before. In part, there is absolutely no way to avoid this. But you must develop your own instincts as soon as possible; you will not always have time to think about the proper action, phrase, or strategy. Sometimes, a misguided phrase to a reporter can destroy six months of work. It is, after all, *your* career, *your* money and energies that are at stake. If you can't develop your political instincts, you will have to go the most careful route in every situation, and your campaign staff will have to learn to guard you in a structured way, to screen you from dangerous questions and issues until a thoughtful strategy has been developed. They will have to anticipate such things as the questions that are likely to come up in a press conference, so that answers can be prepared and you won't have to extemporize. Similarly, you will always have to screen speeches with your staff and avoid speaking off the cuff unless it is absolutely necessary.

Scheduling

Scheduling is a problem in every political campaign. In many campaign offices, as the campaign gets under way, speaking engagements, meetings, and other events are entered on a giant calendar. As time passes, however, advance scheduling, while obviously sensible, becomes difficult to guarantee. Conflicts about time and place become complex; fund-raising and party problems sometimes arise that must take precedence; late-breaking issues demand an immediate response. For these reasons, flexibility is necessary in scheduling.

Underlying most campaign strategies is the assumption that the more often the candidate speaks, the better, since TV news spots and the press may feature the candidate if he is making news or being interviewed. Also, many candidates believe that unless they're actually doing something or in constant motion, they're losing ground. The focus should be exposure but in a strategic way—making news and reinforcing campaign themes. The object of making campaign appearances is to get votes. In every campaign I have seen, at least 10 to 20 percent of the candidate's time has been wasted with protocol appearances at political functions, wedding receptions, or honorary dinners. These activities keep the candidate moving but can hardly be expected to produce new votes in significant numbers. There is such a thing as running too hard and in the wrong direction.

In some situations, candidates seem to think that speaking engagement with specific client groups assure the support of those groups. In a recent campaign in a predominantly Jewish area of the Bronx, one of the candidates, who later became a New York Supreme Court judge, felt that he could not lose, since his calendar showed he had an appointment to speak before each important synagogue group. He lost, and to this day he probably doesn't understand how or why.

Mario Procaccino, in his 1969 New York mayoralty campaign, provided another example of mistaken scheduling commitments. Since at the beginning of the campaign he was far ahead of John V. Lindsay, some of his advisers told Procaccino to hold his public appearances to a minimum, so that he would avoid losing votes. One commentator, perhaps facetiously, went so far as to suggest that Procaccino get sick and leave the country during the campaign. Procaccino disregarded this advice, campaigned actively, and lost the election to Lindsay. You can't always assume that more street campaigning and more speeches are more effective than selective campaigning.

Whenever possible, coordinate your scheduling with your research on probable voting patterns, the distribution of the undecided vote, and other aspects of the campaign. Similarly, if you have scheduled a speaking engagement at a community center weeks in advance, your walking tours should include that neighborhood the day before the speech. If you have a telephone campaign going, the "message" should go into the area in which you're speaking, with the information, if interest develops, that you'll be there at a certain time and place.

The scheduling function should rank priorities in a specific way. For example, the following list might apply to some candidates: (1) presentation of major positions in speeches and at press conferences; (2) interviews with press, radio, and television; (3) addresses to local political clubs; (4) addresses to local religious and ethnic organizations; and (5) street campaigning.

The proper coordination of your schedule requires both administrative talent and thorough knowledge of your research. It can come only from the campaign manager and should never be a function of the loudest screamers or most active arm twisters on the staff or in a related political club. Your manager should see to it that your time and energies are invested as efficiently as possible in making voters conscious of your candidacy and in motivating them to vote for you.

Advance men

When a circus or carnival comes to town, it is preceded by ballyhoo men who drum up interest and encourage ticket sales. In campaigning, the ballyhoo men are called advance men. Their responsibilities are many and important, but the basic purpose of their work is to stimulate public interest as well as press and television attention for the candidate. They arrange interviews with journalists, make hotel reservations, rent halls for speeches, get police permits for street rallies, try to insure large turnouts for public appearances, coordinate with local party officials on such matters as who is to be invited to a function and who is not and which important contributors and potential contributors should be contacted when the candidate is in the area, and attend to myriad other details.

Advance men must see to it that all aspects of the candidate's public appearances go smoothly. Are there major events scheduled at the same time that may take away from the candidate's press and television coverage? Are public functions scheduled at hours when people are on the streets?* Are hecklers expected? If so, what type of police security is needed, and with whom must arrangements be made? What size audience can reasonably be expected? A good advance man knows that it is far better to book a small hall and fill it than to fill a large hall only half way. Will the guest list of a rally offend anyone who is important to the campaign effort? Local workers should be given the opportunity to check such lists in advance so that no such unintentional offense is committed.

Being an advance man is a full-time job in state and national races.† In local campaigns, the functions of advance men are often performed by the staff member who is responsible for the candidate's schedule or by another experienced person working under his direction. Whoever functions as your advance man must be familiar with your overall campaign strategy, so that he has a good idea of where and with whom the candidate should be spending his time. In large-scale campaigns an advance man has to concentrate on getting television and newspaper coverage, since that is now generally regarded as having more impact than paid ads.‡ In smaller campaigns, the scheduler-advance man must work closely with the campaign manager (who sometimes performs this function himself) to keep the candidate in areas where he can meet different voters, since there is little to be gained by his repeatedly meeting the same voters. In New York, for example, shopping centers, parks, and subway entrances are prized locations, because their constant streams of passersby maximize the candidate's investment of time and energy. Since there are limited numbers of such locations in most districts, advance

* Observers noted that during Senator Edmund S. Muskie's presidential bid in 1971, his staff sometimes scheduled parades for the dinner hour, when no one was on the street.

† *The Advance Man,* by Jerry Bruno and Jeff Greenfield (New York: Morrow, 1971), describes the experiences of an advance man in a major campaign. Bruno was an advance man in Robert F. Kennedy's senatorial campaign and Arthur Goldberg's gubernatorial campaign. Allen L. Otten wrote an excellent article describing the work of advance men (whom he referred to as "schedulers") in the Democratic presidential primaries in the *Wall Street Journal* (New York edition), March 1, 1972, p. 1. In presidential campaigns, schedulers and advance men may do separate jobs.

‡ More and more politicians are becoming convinced that making news— breaking into television news shots—is more important than television advertising (*TV Guide,* June 1, 1972). In smaller campaigns, the focus is on developing controversies and sustaining the interest of local newspapers.

men who recommend appearances there must consider strategies to be followed should the opponent choose the same location at the same time.

In these details of campaigning, as in all others, coordination with research findings is very important. Which areas and groups have doubts about the candidate and the issues that concern them should be uppermost in the minds of staff members involved in scheduling and advance work.

The tasks of advance men sometimes seem trivial, petty, or insignificant, but they make the difference between a successful campaign trip, walking tour, or speech, and an unsuccessful one. Don't assign these tasks to anyone unless he is an experienced administrative detailer and has some political instincts. Advance men represent you, and they can cause real harm to your campaign if they are incompetent. It can be a major error to yield to the temptation, common to many candidates, to assign a volunteer or a young staff person to handle advance details. Inexperienced people should not be allowed to serve as advance men until they have spent time accompanying someone who is competent and experienced in advance work.

Street rallies

Street rallies are used to drum up interest and excitement. The important decisions are when and where the rallies should take place and which speakers should appear with the candidate. The campaign should be off the ground before street rallies are scheduled; a street rally that falls flat is far worse than no street rally at all. Saturdays, Sundays, and early evenings when good weather is anticipated are the best times. Pick a corner with high pedestrian counts: a location in or near a shopping center or near a theater where a popular movie is playing is likely to be a good one. Be sure to obtain the proper permit from the local police.

Leaflets announcing the rally should be distributed to pedestrians and residents of the neighborhood a few days before the rally, and an ad should be taken in the local paper. If you have a telephone campaign, coordinate it with your street rally and have your callers remind people in the neighborhood that they can see the candidate at the rally and form their own impressions. Sound trucks can also be used to advertise the meeting. Some candidates like to use live or taped music to create a stir. An outside speaker—a leader of the party, some other gifted orator, or another person well known in the neighborhood—adds appeal to the program.

Use your research to anticipate the questions that people in the neighborhood are likely to throw at you, and be ready with specific answers or proposals. Pronounce people's names perfectly, and make sure you recognize every local leader in the audience. Above all, don't forget what neighborhood you're in, as many politicians have, including Edmund S. Muskie in the 1972 presidential campaign, who repeatedly mentioned the wrong city in a major speech. Be sure to have appropriate literature and campaign workers to distribute it. Finally, see to it that the litter is cleared up. Don't antagonize residents of the neighborhood by abandoning the massive amounts of paper that pile up after a rally. (Assemblyman Antonio G. Olivieri of New York, in his subway campaigning, uses a large barrel where voters can throw his literature away.)

Speakers' bureaus and speakers' guides
In some larger (city-, state-, or nation-wide) campaigns, a formal speakers' bureau is established, and when a candidate cannot meet all demands for his presence as a speaker, substitute speakers cover the appearances of lesser importance. The speakers may be friends, staff members, members of the candidate's family, or teachers from a local university. A senior staff member should be present when an untested speaker makes his first presentation, and obviously, ungifted speakers should not be permitted to represent the candidate.

It is prudent to prepare a speakers' guide—a collection of statements on important issues—which makes it possible for the speeches of substitutes to be authoritative as well as lively, informative, and to the point. It also enables the candidate's surrogate to respond to audience questions accurately, without running the risk of misrepresenting the candidate.

Some compilers of speaker's guides try to avoid sensitive issues. That, in my judgment, is a serious mistake, since most voters come to public meetings precisely to hear a candidate's stand on controversial matters. You will lose votes if your representatives are unable to state positions on these issues lucidly. Some issues are

NEIGHBORHOOD CITY HALLS

1. Set up in councilmanic districts
2. "Open door" policy to all Departments and Mayor's office.
3. Greater personal involvement of citizens.

JOBS

1. Strong City action for immediate increased job opportunities for all.
2. Press for trade union membership for minorities.
3. Hold back payments and cancel contracts for city work where job discrimination is practiced.

ANTI-POVERTY

1. More federal aid on a continuing basis.
2. Separate city agency with full-time head responsible to Mayor.
3. Active role for the poor in local areas.

REAPPORTIONMENT

1. Immediate special session of Legislature to set up non-partisan group to devise fair plan and take subject out of partisan politics. In keeping with Supreme Court one-man-one-vote principle.

CIVIL SERVICE

1. Review and update Career & Salary Plan.
2. Make pay and fringe benefits comparable to federal-state jobs and private industry.
3. Cross-promotions by competitive exam,s on a service-wide basis.

AIR POLLUTION

Summary

1. Equip buses and other city vehicles with after burner
   devices.
2. T ke the lead in regional and interstate control projects.
3. Enlarge Department of Air Pollution Control.
4. Strict enforcement and stiffer penalties.
5. Mandate up-grading of sub-standard incinerators.
6. Launch public education program.

1. Seven point air pollution program.
   a. Title "To Clear the Sewer in the Sky."

2. The City must take the initiative.
   a. Seek out and correct defective city owned installa-
      tions and equipment.

3. Telegram sent to Mayor Wagner, by Mr. Beame.
   a. Require all "future" city owned buses and vehicles
      to be equipped with after burner devices.

   b. Require all city vehicles, owned by city to be
      equipped immediately, if possible.

4. Seven point program is as follows:
   1. City leadership in regional and interstate Air
      Pollution projects.
   2. Enlarge the City Department of Air Pollution Control.
   3. Strict enforcement of rules with stiffer penalties
      for violations.
   4. Up-grading of sub-standard incinerators.
   5. Correction of defective city equipment.
   6. Creation of advisory citizens committee.
   7. Intensive public education program.

Factual Information

1. 60 tons of soot per square mile fall, every day, on New
   York City.

2. Pollution is from:
   1. Burning of fuel oils for power and heating.
   2. Burning of waste from cars, buses and trucks.
   3. Demolition and construction.
   4. Littered and dirty streets.
   5. Dry cleaning operations.
   6. Surface coating operations.

(Continued on Page 2)

dynamite in their potential to damage your campaign: if they come up when you are not present, your spokesmen must be prepared to meet them as you wish them met.

On pages 58–59 are two pages from a typical speakers' guide—this one compiled for the spokesmen for the Democratic candidates for mayor (Abraham Beame), city council president (Frank O'Connor), and comptroller (Mario Procaccino) of New York City in 1965. The first deals extremely briefly with five of the twenty-four subjects that are treated more extensively (as is the second, on air pollution) in one-, two-, or three-page summary form.

Election law

Knowledge of the technicalities of local election law is absolutely crucial to any campaign. Some candidates have been literally knocked off the ballot because their petitions were invalid; no one had bothered to read the laws governing elections. Most states have a political calendar advising candidates of filing dates and other important legal deadlines. In some states, a board of elections publishes the calendar; in others, it is the secretary of state. Part of a sample political calendar appears on pages 62–63.

State law generally regulates not only when but how election petitions are filed—for example, on what form, how many signatures are required, and who can witness signatures. The form usually calls for a committee on vacancies—that is, a group of people you name who are on the ballot, so that, in the event of your illness or death, they can name a replacement. Ironically, although campaign headquarters tend to attract many young lawyers, few seem to enjoy examining the election law or checking petitions. It is extremely important to have a lawyer on your staff who has been through petitioning and knows the laws regarding elections, including how to challenge opponents' petitions, how to file petitions, and the results of previous court challenges. (Petitioning requirements are discussed more fully on pages 64–65.) Your lawyer should also be on call on election day for advice about action to be taken if your poll watchers report voting irregularities.

An example of how crucial legal technicalities can be was provided by Richard L. Ottinger's campaign for the U.S. Senate from New York in 1970. Ottinger's staff believed it important to have two lines on the ballot, the Democratic Party and one other, since each of his two opponents was running on two separate lines. Since Ottinger was well known for his strong stand on issues involving the conservation of natural resources, someone decided to use the name Conservation Party. A great deal of effort and expense was exended to get the required thousands of signatures throughout the state in each county for the Conservation Party.

Political journalists and experienced political attorneys warned Ottinger's campaign staff that Conservation was too close to the already-existing Conservative Party name (probably one of the reasons the name was chosen) and that a court case might deprive them of the second line. In fact, Ottinger's Conservative Party opponent, James L. Buckley, did take the matter to court, and the Conservation Party line—which was thought to be worth 25,000 to 50,000 votes—was voided.

Canvassing

The basic strategy in conducting a campaign is to get on the ballot, develop reasons for voters to vote for you, construct a list of favorable voters, and, finally, to get them to the polls—or "pull" them—on election day.

Canvassing—visiting households in a district in person ("hand canvassing") or by telephone ("telephone canvassing")—has traditionally played an important role in two of these jobs. It is done in the early stages of a campaign to gather signatures for nominating petitions and to proselytize on a candidate's behalf, and in the final stages of the campaign to pull favorable voters to the polls. Although hand canvassing used to be regarded as the key to successful campaigning, the rising importance of the mass media and the concomitant destruction of many city political machines have recently diminished the reliance on local captains that hand canvassing entails. (Radio and television bring the candidate himself into the voters' living rooms, so canvassers, while serving other necessary functions, no longer need to introduce the candidate to the voters.) In smaller assembly or council races or in suburban or rural districts, however, hand canvassing is important. In some cities, the regular organization has access to election district captains, some

POLITICAL CALENDAR
1971

214 CENTRAL PARK AVENUE

White Plains, N. Y. 10606

WH 9-7418 or WH 9-1300

This Calendar contains only the information most generally sought and is presented in concise form.

For complete details, refer to the Election Law.

NOTE: Dates and offices to be filled are listed as known at time of printing.

WILLIAM J. VAN WART	JOSEPH A. McNAMARA
ALBERT T. HAYDUK	WILLIAM D. BRUNS
Commissioners	Deputy Commissioners

CHRONOLOGICAL DATES (Continued)

	SECTIONS
August 31—First day for qualified voter or spouse, parent or child accompanying such voter, outside of County because of duty, occupation or business may apply for absentee registration.	153-a, Sub. 8
September 4—THE DAY for filing first statement of Receipts and Expenses (Primary).	323
September 14—PRIMARY DAY (Hours of voting 12:00 Noon to 9:00 P.M.)	149-a, Sub. 13
September 17-18—Period to hold Judicial District Convention.	149-a, Sub. 16
September 20—First day to file Independent Petitions.	149-a, Sub. 17
September 20—First day to file Certificate of Party Nomination. (Village of Ossining ONLY).	149-a, Sub. 17
September 22—Last day to file Independent Petitions.	149-a, Sub. 17
September 22—Last day to file Certificate of Party Nomination. (Village of Ossining ONLY).	149-a, Sub. 17
September 24—Last day to file Acceptance or Declination of Independent Nominations.	149-a, Sub. 21
September 24—Last day to file Certificate of Acceptance or Declination of Party Nomination. (Village of Ossining ONLY).	149-a, Sub. 21
September 27—Last day to file Certificate to Fill Vacancy caused by Declination of Independent Nomination.	149-a, Sub. 24
September 27—Last day to file Certificate to Fill Vacancy caused by Declination of Party Nomination. (Village of Ossining ONLY).	149-a, Sub. 24
September 30—First day of Local Registration—4:00 P.M. to 9:00 P.M.	354, Sub. 2
October 1—Second day of Local Registration—4:00 P.M. to 9:00 P.M.	354, Sub. 2
October 2—Last day of Local Registration—9:00 A.M. to 9:00 P.M.	354, Sub. 2
October 2—Last day for all qualified voters (except military voters) to file application for absentee registration.	153-a
October 4—Last day to file final statement of Receipts and Expenses (Primary).	323
October 21—Last day for Division for Servicemen's Voting to receive applications for military ballots.	305, Sub. 5
October 22—Last day for any qualified person who has changed his residence within County since October 1 to be registered at Central Registration Board.	149-a, Sub. 30
October 23—THE DAY for filing first statement of Receipts and Expenses. (General Election).	323

CHRONOLOGICAL DATES (Continued)

	SECTIONS
October 26—Last day to apply for absentee ballot.	117, Sub. 2
October 30—Last day (12:00 Noon) for military voter to personally file an application with County Board of Elections.	205, Sub. 8 and 10
November 1—Last day (12:00 Noon) voted absentee military ballots can be received by the Division for Servicemen's Voting.	305, Sub. 1
November 2—GENERAL ELECTION (Hours of Voting —6:00 A.M. to 9:00 P.M.)	191
November 22—Last day to file final statement of Receipts and Expenses. (General Election).	323
December 3, 1971—First day of Central Registration for General Election of 1972.	335

1971 ENROLLMENT

	Rep	Dem	Con	Lib	Blk	Vac	Miss	Total
Bedford	5003	1839	116	72	1086	17	79	8038
Cortlandt	7898	4880	384	134	2286	57	160	14549
Eastchester	11880	8885	246	129	2021	77	108	17846
Greenburgh	20543	12034	476	424	6127	159	206	40029
Harrison	5756	2196	86	67	1563	22	44	9784
Lewisboro	1800	613	42	26	305	14	8	2812
Mamaroneck	8335	4708	163	127	1452	41	70	14885
Mount Pleasant	9687	8467	216	92	3333	70	222	18856
New Castle	5152	2115	103	69	1261	34	46	8780
North Castle	3762	766	39	28	594	15	35	4369
North Salem	988	440	43	18	286	3	3	1779
Ossining	9877	6198	113	147	2805	66	182	19364
Pelham	4119	1500	79	38	550	15	43	6348
Pound Ridge	1174	418	10	18	190	5	10	1835
Rye (Town)	8222	3964	142	138	6259	58	113	18864
Scarsdale	4908	2889	60	91	1233	38	68	9407
Somers	2244	961	113	40	545	16	15	3934
Yorktown	5878	3165	267	83	1784	39	108	11337
Total of All Towns	110451	66951	2681	1787	28016	787	1416	209749
Mount Vernon	12091	11089	280	323	8692	163	103	22790
New Rochelle	14225	11978	414	413	6163	147	214	33554
Peekskill	3136	3143	87	63	2256	35	87	6816
Rye (City)	4979	1658	52	65	1032	17	45	7738
White Plains	13740	5974	174	180	2725	82	150	23025
Yonkers	39064	42014	1784	925	8911	429	361	93459
Total of Cities	87235	76696	2591	1965	25749	853	860	194611
County Totals	196686	137687	5573	3706	66764	1590	2426	292180

Form 39—5M—1971

RESIDENCE
Sec. 150

August 2—Last day to become a resident of the County in order to vote at the General Election.

ENROLLMENT
(For 1971 Primary)

Sec. 187
Sec. 386
Sec. 387
Sec. 388

August 13—Last day to:

Enroll upon becoming of age.
Enroll after acquiring citizenship.
Enroll after acquiring residential qualification.
Enroll because of military service.
Transfer enrollment after moving within the County; and re-register.
Correct enrollment due to mistake made at time of original enrollment. [Limited, as it applies only to certain registrations made in 1970].

Above only by personal appearance at Board of Elections.

CENTRAL REGISTRATION
Sec. 355

The office of the Central Registration Board, located in the office of the Board of Elections, White Plains, N.Y., is open for the convenience of ALL VOTERS as follows: (Holidays excepted)

January 4, 1971 through August 30, 1971
Reopens December 3, 1971
Monday through Friday—8:45 A.M. to 4:30 P.M.
Thursdays to August—8:45 A.M. to 9:30 P.M.

October 22—LAST DAY FOR ANY QUALIFIED PERSON WHO HAS CHANGED HIS RESIDENCE WITHIN COUNTY SINCE OCTOBER 3 TO BE REGISTERED AT CENTRAL REGISTRATION BOARD.
Sec. 149-a, Sub. 30

COUNTY CHAIRMAN'S CERTIFICATE
Sec. 149-a, Sub. 2

June 8—Last day to file statement with the Board of Elections of party positions to be filled at Primary Election.

PRIMARY PETITIONS

Sec. 135
Sec. 136
Sec. 137

To designate candidate, a Designating Petition, must be signed in ink by not less than FIVE (5%) percentum, as determined by the preceding enrollment of the enrolled voters of the party residing within the political unit in which the office or position is to be voted for, but need not exceed the number of signatures required for the larger subdivision in which the political unit is situated, which required signatures need not exceed the following limits:

1000 signatures for any County Office.
500 signatures for any office to be filled by the voters of a city of the second class.
250 signatures for any office to be filled by the voters of a city of the third class.
250 signatures for Delegates and Alternate Delegates to a State or Judicial District Convention.

June 22—First day to sign Designating Petition. Sec. 149-a, Sub. 3
July 26—First day to file Designating Petitions. Sec. 149-a, Sub. 5
July 29—Last day to file Designating Petitions. Sec. 149-a, Sub. 5
August 2—Last day to object to petition filed on July 29. Sec. 145

August 3—Last day to Accept or Decline Designation. Sec. 149-a, Sub. 7
August 6—Last day to Fill Vacancy caused by Declination of Designation. Sec. 149-a, Sub. 9

PARTY NOMINATIONS
(VILLAGE OF OSSINING ONLY)

September 20—First day to file Certificate of Party Nomination. Sec. 149-a, Sub. 17
September 22—Last day to file Certificate of Party Nomination. Sec. 149-a, Sub. 17
September 24—Last day to file Certificate of Acceptance or Declination of Party Nomination. Sec. 149-a, Sub. 21
September 27—Last day to file Certificate to Fill Vacancy caused by Declination of Party Nomination. Sec. 149-a, Sub. 24

RECEIPT AND EXPENSE STATEMENTS
Sec. 323

September 4—THE DAY for filing first statement. (PRIMARY)
October 4—Last day to file final statement. (PRIMARY)
October 23—THE DAY for filing first statement. (GENERAL ELECTION)
November 22—Last day to file final statement. (GENERAL ELECTION)

PRIMARY
Sec. 149-a, Sub. 13

September 14—Hours of Voting: 12:00 NOON TO 9:00 P.M.

PARTY POSITIONS
Party Rules

ALL PARTIES—Delegates and Alternate Delegates to Judicial District Convention.
Republican and Democratic Parties—Members of the County Committee. [2 from each E.D.]

PUBLIC OFFICES — PRIMARY

A Judge of the Family Court
A County Judge
A District Attorney
17 County Legislators
Local Offices which may be required to be filled at the General Election.
Sec. 146

PUBLIC OFFICES — GENERAL ELECTION

2 Justices of the Supreme Court
Plus all public offices listed under PRIMARY

WRITE-IN NOMINATIONS
Sec. 149-a, Sub. 14

Persons who are nominated by write-in may Decline or must Accept within 5 days after notification of his nomination, otherwise such nomination shall be null and void.

If a Declination is filed, the vacancy may be filled not later than 3 days after the Declination was filed.

REFERENDUM, PROPOSITION OR QUESTION

September 13—Last suggested day for the submission of a Referendum, Proposition or Question to be voted for at the General Election. [Preliminary work of printing pamphlets, etc., should have been completed].

of whom are paid $25 to $50 for a day's work.* This is no longer a great deal of money, but it provides some motivation for people to show up and do their jobs.† In a judicial delegate race in New York in 1970, a district leader whose funds were limited did not spend anything at all on loudspeakers, mailings, or other such traditional campaign devices. Instead, he relied entirely on canvassers, asking his 115 captains to bring in 15 votes apiece. The resulting 1,725 votes were decisive in electing his ticket.

In the New Hampshire presidential primary in March 1972, for example, Senator George McGovern received 37 percent of the vote after public opinon polls had predicted only 25 percent as his likely share of the vote. It seemed clear to me as a professional involved in the early stages of McGovern's campaign in New Hampshire that the efforts of an estimated 2,000 volunteer canvassers during the campaign and on primary election day were a significant, and possibly decisive, factor in his excellent showing. (An effective professional telephone campaign and McGovern's public disclosure of the names of all his contributors also played major roles in the outcome.) Although it is impossible to say exactly how much any one thing contributed to his extra 12 percent, it would be difficult to dispute that the saturation canvassing by enthusiastic volunteers was an important factor.

Petitioning

State election laws specify the form in which petitions are to appear and the number of signatures required to place a candidate's name on the ballot. (Part of a sample petition is reproduced on pages 66–67.) Before your workers begin canvassing for petition signatures, someone on your staff—preferably an attorney, but otherwise someone who is experienced in petitioning and who knows something about local election law—must read your state's election law very carefully. This staff member should also examine the review procedures used by the local board of elections, whose members may

---

* Some candidates pay petition canvassers as much as 50 cents a signature. I would advise against this course except, where it is legal, in emergencies; in many places it is illegal, and where it is legal, it is likely to result in forgeries.

† Similarly, running a slate of county committeemen (party posts) provides motivation for people to work for the candidate, since their names are on the ballot as well.

be political appointees who can express their political biases in their rulings. After the signatures have been collected, he should take personal charge of "binding" the petitions—checking to make sure that they are legally signed and witnessed and then literally putting them into binders and presenting them to the board of elections. Among the things that should be carefully checked under his supervision are the following: Signatures should be collected in homes and not on the street or in parks. Signatures collected in public places— so-called boardwalk petitions—are invalid in many localities. The petitions must be properly witnessed, usually by an adult who resides in the election district in which the signatures are being collected. Petitions have been set aside and candidates knocked off the ballot because of seemingly minor irregularities in witnessing.* It is imperative that each voter sign the petition exactly as he is listed on the voting rolls, that the address be noted properly, and that the signatures be in black or blue ink. In many localities, if a voter's middle initial is listed in the election books, the voter's signature on the petition must have his middle initial or it will be disqualified. Married women should be particularly careful to sign their names exactly as they appear in the registration book.

Another common cause for petition signatures to be thrown out is that the signer signed more than one petition for the same office. A surprisingly large number of people are apparently willing to sign almost anything that is thrust at them, including the petitions of several different candidates for the same office. Your workers should impress potential petition signers with the fact that they may legally sign only one candidate's petition per office. This problem becomes even more acute when candidates running for several different offices share petitions, a practice that is common in some localities. Generally, the first petition a person signs for any given office is determined to be his only legal signature for that office.

Usually, each canvasser is given ten petitions with spaces for ten signatures per sheet. This should be the canvasser's quota. If he can do more, fine; but in my experience, after twice the number of valid signatures required by law has been obtained, the canvasser can

---

* Many courts will review petition challenges only if a substantial number of irregularities can be demonstrated. However, I have seen candidates removed from the ballot because one or two canvassers, providing many signatures, had made only minor errors.

DEMOCRATIC PARTY – BRONX COUNTY
Designating Petition

To the Board of Elections in the City of New York:

I, the undersigned, do hereby state that I am a duly enrolled voter of the Democratic Party and entitled to vote at the next primary election of such party, that my place of residence is truly stated opposite my signature hereto, and that I intend to support at the ensuing primary and I do hereby designate the following named persons as candidates for nomination of such party for election to party positions of such party to be voted for at the primary election to be held on the 14th day of September, 1971, as hereinafter specified.

PARTY POSITIONS

Delegates to Democratic Judicial Convention from the
1st Judicial District from the 84th Assembly District, Bronx County, New York

Names of Candidates   **Places of Residence**

Names of Candidates	Places of Residence
ALGERNON M. MILLER	5232 Arlington Avenue, Bronx, N.Y. 10471
ANN A. KAPLAN	4455 Douglas Avenue, Bronx, N.Y. 10471
ISADORE LEVIN	3 Hudson River Road, Bronx, N.Y. 10471
MARILYN R. MILLER	3020 Johnson Avenue, Bronx, N.Y. 10463
ROSE JACOBSON	500 West 235th Street, Bronx, N.Y. 10463
ALFRED SATIN	3516 De Kalb Avenue, Bronx, N.Y. 10467
MOLLIE BLOOMENFELD	555 Kappock Street, Bronx, N.Y. 10463
FREDERICK FORMAN	3400 Ft. Independence Street, Bronx, N.Y. 10463
DAVID S. POPPER	3411 Irwin Avenue, Bronx, N.Y. 10463
CATHERINE V. HEAVEY	5714 Faraday Avenue, Bronx, N.Y. 10471

PARTY POSITIONS

Alternate Delegates to Democratic Judicial Convention from the
1st Judicial District from the 84th Assembly District, Bronx County, New York

Names of Candidates	Places of Residence
BARRY FEDERMAN	5420 Mosholu Avenue, Bronx, N.Y. 10471
GLORIA KLEINBERG	645 West 239th Street, Bronx, N.Y. 10463
DOROTHY MISHKIN	5700 Arlington Avenue, Bronx, N.Y. 10471
PAUL P. HECHT	5440 Netherland Avenue, Bronx, N.Y. 10471
ALEX E. SHIER	225 West 232nd Street, Bronx, N.Y. 10463
BETTY R. EDELSTEIN	4525 Henry Hudson Parkway, Bronx, N.Y. 10471
ELEANOR NEWMAN	25 Knolls Crescent, Bronx, N.Y. 10463
DANIEL GROSS	5400 Fieldston Road, Bronx, N.Y. 10471
CLAUDIA H. HECHT	5565 Netherland Avenue, Bronx, N.Y. 10471

I do hereby appoint:

BENJAMIN WICHNER, residing at 3935 Blackstone Avenue, Bronx, N.Y. 10471
JOHN SORENSON, residing at 142 Van Cortlandt Park South, Bronx, N.Y. 10463
CONSTANCE MILLER, residing at 5232 Arlington Avenue, Bronx, N.Y. 10471
DOROTHY EFFRON, residing at 620 West 232nd Street, Bronx, N.Y. 10463
DAVID AVRACH, residing at 2711 Henry Hudson Parkway, Bronx, N.Y. 10463

all of whom are enrolled voters of the Democratic Party, as a committee to fill vacancies for the above party positions in accordance with the provisions of the election law.

IN WITNESS WHEREOF, I have hereunto set my hand the day and year placed opposite my signature.

DATE	NAME OF SIGNER	RESIDENCE	Bronx County State of New York	
			Election District	Assembly District
1	, 1971	Borough of Bronx, New York City		84th
2	, 1971	Borough of Bronx, New York City		84th
3	, 1971	Borough of Bronx, New York City		84th
4	, 1971	Borough of Bronx, New York City		84th
5	, 1971	Borough of Bronx, New York City		84th
6	, 1971	Borough of Bronx, New York City		84th

STATEMENT OF WITNESS

I, _____ , state: I am a duly qualified voter of the State of New York;
(Name of Witness)

an enrolled voter of the Democratic Party and now reside in the _____ election district of the _____ Assembly District
(Fill in Number)   (Fill in Number)

in the City of New York, in the County of Bronx, in such state, at _____
(Fill in Street and House Number and Post Office)

therein. I was last registered for the general election in the year 1970 from _____
(Fill in Street and House Number and Post Office)

_____ in the City of New York, in the County of Bronx, in such state. The said residence was

then in the _____ election district of the _____ Assembly District. I know each of the voters whose names are
(Fill in Number)   (Fill in Number)

subscribed to this petition sheet containing _____ signatures and each of them subscribed the same in my presence and
(Fill in Number)

upon so subscribing declared to me that the foregoing statement, made and subscribed by him, was true.

Date_____ , 1971

_____
(Signature of Witness)

SHEET No._____

440 Ira Rosenberg, Inc., 15 E. 125th St., N.Y.

probably be more useful in other functions. Some local political leaders seek large numbers of petition signatures which they use to gain a trading advantage in their dealings with candidates for such higher offices as congressman, mayor, senator, or governor. In these cases, the petitions are used as evidence of potential support, which is presumably influential in gaining endorsements (or at least preventing endorsements of opponents) and/or financial assistance. Unless you have a reason of this sort, however, I believe that you should simply come in with enough "good" signatures to prevent a challenge, and certainly twice as many signatures as are required is usually a safe number. Some technicians believe a candidate should get as many signatures as he can, to impress the voting public; but in my judgment, not too many voters know or care how many signatures any candidate obtains.

Politicians who are interested in testing a candidate's strength on the basis of his petitions sometimes look more closely at the number of petition witnesses than at the number of signatures. Since the person who carries a petition normally witnesses it, the number of witnesses a candidate has provides a fair indication of how many workers he has. People who carry petitions presumably also are willing to lend their efforts to other campaign activities which one can hope will result in additional votes for the candidate on election day.

The petitioning procedure should start as early as you can manage. As a first step, the current registration lists for your party should be purchased from the appropriate source—board of elections, department of commerce, or other body, depending on the locality. Any citizen may purchase or have access to these records, and you will probably be correct in suspecting a political motive if anyone tells you that they are not available, even if you are given some excuse such as that the election rolls are stored on computer tape or that mechanical problems make it impossible to make them available to you. However the rolls are stored, you are entitled to access to them, even if in a rare case you have to go to court to get them.

Using the roll books, the campaign manager selects the areas where canvassing can best be done—that is, the areas with the largest concentrations of voters (in a primary campaign, voters in your party) who can reasonably be hoped to be sympathetic to your candidacy.

It is usually unwise and practically impossible to cover each election district fully, and much time can be wasted in even attempting to do so. Some areas simply have to be written off as "no contest," or at best made the target of a minimal mail campaign emphasizing whatever issue or ethnic identification might salvage 10 or 20 percent of the vote in the area. Your research should determine the selection of the potentially favorable areas and groups the canvassers must reach.

Each voter in your target area should be listed on a 3×5 card containing items similar to the following:

SMITH, JOHN (Dem.)	29 A.D.
	32 E.D.
0000 Main Street, ZIP	
Canvass: Date _____	Worker _____
Signed petition _____	
Thank-you sent _____	Other family voters:
Literature _____	Jane (Rep.)
Kaffeeklatch sponsor ____ _____	
Volunteer for _____. _____	
Comments:	

The cards prepared for this purpose can also be used later as the basis of mailings. They are most useful for this purpose if members of a family are combined on a single card, to avoid duplication of mailings to a single household. The cards can be prepared by computer (somewhat expensive, but a massive saving of time) or by hand (less expensive, but very tedious work with a probable loss of quality).

If you can afford it and if there is a good, politically oriented computer house near you, it will probably be well worth your while in a medium- or large-scale campaign to have the cards prepared by computer. Creatively used, computers can aid your petitioning effort in other ways besides preparing the cards. For example, in 1972 a New York computer firm developed a "finder's book" that provided the election district and assembly district numbers for any street address. Since New York had just been extensively redistricted, there was no other quick way to identify the election and assembly districts of each petition signer—information that was required alongside each petition signature. Checking them by hand would have been a laborious—and probably error-ridden—project.

Once they are completed, the 3×5 cards should be arranged according to street addresses; in the case of large apartment buildings, the canvassers' working decks of cards should normally be grouped by floor and apartment number unless some special situation makes it preferable to divide them by ethnic group or other such criterion.

Areas (blocks or buildings in the city) are assigned to a team of your canvassers, preferably a man and woman. There are security problems at night in many large cities, so women should not canvass alone. The teams should be supervised by the campaign manager after an orientation that gives them a good understanding of your background as well as your stands on major issues and your criticisms of your opponent(s). (A typical set of instructions for primary petition carriers appears on page 71.) You should make yourself available to answer questions from the canvassers.

Since you cannot get around to seeing or being seen by all the potential voters in your district, your canvassers are, in effect, your personal representatives. Their primary purposes in visiting households are to get your petitions signed, if possible; to identify issues that may affect their vote; and, in any case, to find out if the voters plan to cast their ballots for you on primary and election day. Canvassers should be able to tell voters where and when to register and where to vote. Depending on the type or amount of interest shown, they can let voters know in a few sentences what you are thinking or planning to do about issues and problems of local and national concern. They should understand, however, that they cannot commit you to new positions on issues. Voters who have further questions about you or who express interest in volunteering should be given the address and telephone number of campaign headquarters. The names of potential campaign workers should be turned in that evening so that someone in your campaign office will follow up their expression of interest and try to enlist their active support. After thanking the voter, and after putting down pertinent information, the canvassers should go on to the next household or individual on their list.

Literature should be available to give out during the interviews. This is often neglected since petitioning is the first step in the campaign and literature is generally not prepared until later. Such an omission is an enormous waste of potential strength, since litera-

INSTRUCTIONS FOR PRIMARY PETITION CARRIERS

1. **Who May Circulate the Petition.** In order to circulate the petition and witness signatures, you must be a registered voter, enrolled in the party and living in the district where you carry petitions. All signatures witnessed by you will be invalid if these conditions are not met.

2. **Who May Sign.** Petition signers must also be registered voters, enrolled in the party and residing in the district.

3. Signatures must be in black or blue ink. Carriers should have pens.

4. The voter must sign his own name in the presence of the witness.

5. The witness must see the petition being signed by each signer.

6. No carrier may witness his own signature.

7. Do not fill in Election District and Assembly District numbers. These will be filled in later at headquarters from the enrollment lists. Leave the "Sheet No." blank also.

8. The date and address should be filled in carefully by the carrier before the signer signs his name. If an error is made, strike out the entire line and start over on the next line. Write dates out in full, without abbreviations. Dates should be consecutive on any one sheet.

9. Never use ditto marks--for dates, addresses, or anything else.

10. Each person's name should be signed in full or in the same manner as they appear in the voter registry. Women should sign their full first names (Elizabeth Scotto, not Mrs. Donald Scotto).

11. On a separate piece of paper list each signer's name, together with your name. This will be used for checking the voter list and defending challenges.

12. Return petitions and lists to headquarters as soon as possible. It is better to turn in a sheet with only a few signatures on it than to risk losing or damaging it.

13. **Statement of Witness.** Print your name carefully in the first blank and print the address at which you are registered in the second blank. Leave all other items blank. Sign your name at the bottom. Put your initials at the edge of any line containing erasures, strike-overs, or other changes (which, however, should be avoided if at all possible).

14. If your address at the time of the 1971 general election was the same as it is now, on the back of the petition write in pencil "1971-same." If your address has changed, write the old address lightly in pencil on the back of the petition with the notation "1971 address."

ture given out in a personal canvass is much more apt to be read than literature received in the mail.

Some voters will ask for favors: "Do something for me and I'll probably vote for you." Your canvassers should not promise anything! However, they should know the name and telephone number of the police precinct captain; where the local hospital is; whom to call for public housing; where to obtain services for the aged; and similar details about other public services. This type of helpful information can be listed on a small card that the canvasser can carry. Although canvassers must not make any commitments in response to requests for such things as public housing assistance, a new street light, or more police protection, they should note them on the 3×5 cards and/or report them to the campaign manager, for two reasons: (1) you may be able to do something about them; and (2) they may prove to be important campaign issues.

· As in every other aspect of campaigning, details are important. Canvassers should take care to use the correct spelling and pronunciation of voters' names. People get annoyed if these particulars are in error. Evenings are best for canvassing—after the dinner hour until perhaps 9:30 or 10:00 is ideal. Some of your canvassers may want to interview neighbors as they arrive home from work, but it is better to interview strangers in their homes after dinner.

Personalized thank-you notes should be sent to all the people who sign your petitions.

Petition challenges

In a three-way race, if your research determines that the presence of a third candidate will hurt you (see pages 101, 105), it is usually wise to examine the weakest candidate's petitions to determine whether to try to knock him off the ballot by legal procedures.

Challenging an opponent's petitions is a laborious, expensive, time-consuming task which involves court action and will take your workers' time away from other necessary work. To shortcut the procedure, start by checking the legal address of your opponent's witnesses. Usually, the campaign worker who carries a petition serves as the petition's witness, and legally, he is often called the petition's "subscribing witness." Generally, he must be a legal resident of the area in which he ostensibly carried the petitions. Since one man usually carries and witnesses ten to fifty petition sheets, each containing ten or more individual signatures, invalidating one witness can invalidate hundreds of petition signatures.

Although they are illegal in most places, "boardwalk petitions" (defined on page 65) are quite commonly used and, if that is so, they are sometimes "witnessed" *ex post facto*. If it can be proven that this has been done, the witnessing procedure can be declared invalid and the petitions can be set aside.

An example, which almost cost a man his professional reputation, concerned a lawyer who, although he was known to live in Westchester County, used someone else's address to witness petitions in New York City. As an attorney, he should have been aware that his act was a breach of election law. The witness was known personally to the opponent's staff, who, having discovered what he had done, confronted him with the evidence and offered to let him withdraw the petitions, or they would sue to invalidate them. Naturally, he withdrew all his petitions.

Unless you can challenge a witness privately, as in the foregoing case, a legal petition challenge will require that someone photocopy all your opponent's petitions—which may run to hundreds of pages—and check each signature against the registration cards at the local board of elections for validity of signature, accuracy of address, and any other features that are required by local law. Checking whether anyone signed more than one petition is particularly bothersome, since the signatures do not appear in any particular order on the petitions. If anyone did sign more than one, a check must be made to see whose petition he signed first, since the first signature will probably be declared the valid one.

Before doing a full-scale petition challenge, make a spot check to determine whether the opponent's petitions are so weak as to make the effort worthwhile. If you are sure you can eliminate your opponent on the basis of his invalid petitions, the challenge is certainly worth any effort it requires, but if you doubt that you can knock out enough signatures to do that, you will have to decide whether the advantage to be gained by finding even a large number of invalid signatures merits the diversion of your workers' time and energies from other campaign activities.

The need to count

The district leader referred to on page 64 was an experienced politician; he understood the need for counting. He estimated fairly closely how many voters would come out in a primary and how many of those he needed to win. Anyone who has ever had to pull for a close club election when one vote can be decisive knows how important counting can be. This leader reviewed previous campaigns for judicial delegates in an off-year and realized that asking for a saturation campaign was impossible—he didn't have the money or the workers such a campaign would require. Asking for fifteen votes per worker was realizable, and past voting records in his district indicated that would be enough to win.

Counting is also a vital and too-frequently-forgotten factor in allocating basic resources. You know the voter registration in your district. However, you must count how many households are represented, so that you can make appropriate contractual commitments for direct mail and telephone campaigns, allowing a single piece of mail or telephone call for each household. Similarly, you must count the number of available telephone numbers for these households, subtracting an estimated percentage for those with unlisted telephone numbers (up to 20 percent in some areas) and for those who have moved or died recently, to know how many telephone calls to contract for. The importance of counting in petitioning is discussed elsewhere in this chapter. Before ordering thousands of flyers or extra shopping bags, count the number of voters in the district. One candidate I know ordered 50,000 flyers to be printed for distribution the day before the election. Had he counted first, he could have saved part of his printing expenses, for his twenty volunteers could reasonably deliver only 500 flyers each, or a total of 10,000. Clearly, some of his money was spent unproductively. A basic rule of politics is "when in doubt, count."

First position

In horse racing, the horse in the first position—the one next to the rail—usually is regarded as having a slight edge. In political campaigning, where the first position is the top line of the ballot or the first column on the left, the design of the ballot and your position on it can be important.

In many states, each party's candidates used to be listed on the ballot in a single column or slate, and people tended to vote the whole party slate. In such a situation, the location of your name wouldn't mean much. But the design of the ballot has changed in many localities, and today many more people vote independently, crossing party lines and voting for the individual rather than the party. (Walter De Vries and Lance Tarrance examine the importance of such selective voters in *The Ticket Splitter: A New Force in American Politics* [Grand Rapids, Mich.: Eerdmans, 1972].) Experienced political mechanics are convinced that in a primary fight the first slot on the ballot is worth 5 to 8 percent of the entire vote, and in a three-way race such an edge can be decisive. In some states, first position in a primary election is drawn by lot, and in the general election the party that received the largest vote in the last statewide election gets the first spot. Different states have different formulas for determining the order of candidates on the ballot. New York City has solved the problem by changing the order in which candidates are listed from district to district. If you don't live in an area where the first position advantage is neutralized by some such method and if you are not assigned the first slot, you'll have to work harder in your campaign to make the voter want to seek your name out on the ballot.

Election day procedures

The first thing to do is to vote yourself and make sure your family and staff take the time to vote. If you're having a final canvassers' meeting, you should be there with the campaign manager. You should also make appearances at the telephone canvassing operation both to motivate the workers and out of courtesy to them. Campaigns are hard for everyone involved, but you'll be amazed at how effective such simple acts of courtesy and thoughtfulness can be.

Election day procedures should be set up so that your campaign manager knows where everyone will be working. On the previous day, meetings will have been held with your field supervisors, canvassers, telephoners, poll watchers, messengers, literature distributors, troubleshooters, and other campaign workers to make certain that they know what they will be doing at all times during the course of election day, how they are to solve whatever problems they encounter, and when they are to call campaign headquarters.

To coordinate the election day pull, a copy of the master list of favorables, organized alphabetically within election districts, should be made available to each area's team captain. (A list of favorables for each voting district within the larger area should be provided for each of your poll watchers.) The campaign manager should indicate which districts are to be covered by a hand pull, and which by a telephone pull. Arrangements should also be made for the distribution of palm cards (small replicas of the ballot with your slot clearly marked, designed to be carried into the voting booth) and campaign literature near voting places. In complicated elections, a sample ballot should be used instead of a palm card. (Examples of the two appear on pages 171 and 173.)

If your pull is being done mainly by telephone, your telephone consultant or research person should have identified the order in which districts should be called, but this may have to be altered during the day, since even with the best planning, the pressures of election day usually break down the organizational plan for canvassing. Therefore, it is particularly important to have a coordination committee that can communicate rapidly with people in the field to make changes when required. For example, if poll watchers report a light turnout in districts that are known to be favorable to you, the coordinator may wish to transfer some canvassers from other areas to these, where the numbers and probabilities are more advantageous. At the same time, the telephone operation can also easily be diverted into problem areas. The logistical problem is that many individual canvassers or area captains will have to call in to headquarters every hour to report results and to receive instructions. Walkie-talkies, if they can be rented, are useful on election days in large districts in which perhaps fifty teams of canvassers may be out at the same time.

Most of the principles of petition canvassing described earlier in this chapter apply equally to the election day pull, with one important difference: On election day, your canvassers call or visit only those voters who are known to be sympathetic to your candidacy. The election day pull in fact is frequently done by telephone rather than in person or "by hand," but if more than one technique is used, there should be some reasonable measure of coordination and communication so that duplication is avoided and the objective—to pull the favorables—is accomplished. The focus, of course, is on areas that you think are mostly favorable to you but that are identified by your poll watchers as having light turnouts.

It is not unusual for a hand canvass and a telephone canvass to take place in the same election district, or for one election district to be telephoned twice by different teams working for the same candidate. Voters who are saturated in this manner may become so irritated they won't vote for the candidate. Similar negative results are likely to occur when candidates for several different offices all seek to pull the same voters.

The election day pull uses the same basic method whether done by telephone or in person—and, if possible, is done by the same canvasser who made the original contact. A telephone canvass should be short, since it need only remind people to go to the polls. The canvasser identifies herself as calling on your behalf and asks whether the voter has voted. If he has voted, she thanks him and moves on. If he has not voted, she seeks to impress him with the importance of his vote for you and reminds him of where the polling place is and the hours when it is open. In every campaign, a surprisingly large number of voters indicate that they don't know if they are registered or where they can vote. Canvassers should be familiar with the rules of the board of elections and should have a list of voting places. They should be able to provide baby-sitters for mothers with small children as well as transportation to the polls for elderly or infirm persons. Weeks earlier, someone on your staff will have compiled a list of volunteers, some of whom have cars at their disposal, and organized them to be available for these services. There should also be a crew of troubleshooters with cars at their disposal to put out fires—for example, emergencies requiring poll watchers to go home, arguments between poll watchers of different parties, and opponents' people electioneering at the polls. Staff members or volunteers should also see to it that poll watchers and other workers are relieved from time to time and that they are provided with food and drink.

Your poll watchers, who have probably been selected because of their previous experience in doing that kind of work or because of their demonstrated good judgment, represent your interests at all the polling places in your district. Since each of them should have attended orientation and training sessions at your headquarters, they should know the election law for your state and district and whom to call to report irregularities. Elections do get "stolen," even today when machines are widely used. In some areas, for example, machines have an oddly fortuitous habit of breaking down when the challenger is expected to have a heavy vote in a district. Poll watchers should have some basic understanding of how the machine works. They should arrive at the polling places fifteen minutes or half an hour before the polls open so that they can read the counters on the side and back of the voting machines to make certain that they register zero. Where paper ballots are used, your poll watchers must see to it that the ballots are complete, bound, and unopened. As each voter signs the affidavit and his name is called out, the poll watcher checks it in the precinct poll list to make certain that he has the right to vote at that voting place. Whenever possible, the poll watcher compares the poll list with a list of your "favorables" and, from time to time, sends back to your campaign headquarters a list of your favorables who have not yet voted, so that your canvassers will know who should still be called and reminded to vote. After the voting is completed and the voting machines are opened at the back, your poll watchers (1) check the side and back counters to make certain their totals match and (2) record the number of votes you and your opponents have received, for transmittal to your headquarters. (Later on, if the announced vote differs from that recorded by your poll watcher, you can take legal action, if necessary.) One of your poll watchers should go with the election judges and clerks to the board of elections to see to it that no changes are made before the votes are handed in to the board.

You yourself probably should take some of the day off until the voting is almost over. Your campaign committee and manager can do what is needed. One thing, your congratulatory speech—for yourself or your opponent—must be prepared, but in most cases, only a brief statement is called for.

Many campaigners hire a hotel ballroom for a victory celebration. This can be embarrassingly morbid and depressing, even if there is eventually a victory to celebrate (and all the more so if there isn't), since people mill about waiting while results trickle in, looking for famous and/or important people. In major elections, the press and television newsmen interview the same people over and over again at these "parties" trying to build suspense as long as the election remains undecided. A party given to thank your staff a week after the election may be a much better idea. Then, they will not be exhausted and dirty after working hard since early election morning, and you will not have to maintain the candidate's artifice that seems obligatory at election night parties.

Many candidates maintain their own spot-polling operation on election nights, using representative precincts to get early results and predict the probable outcome of the election. This seems a needless waste. You'll know the outcome soon enough.

At the end of the evening, send telegrams of congratulations to victorious friends and respected political enemies. There is no law that says you have to go much further than that, and hypocrisy is not seemly.

Post-election chores
Whether you win or lose, certain things you've paid for belong to you and may be helpful to you in future elections or to political friends if you don't intend to campaign again.

You should keep:

- the canvass cards, by election district
- names, addresses, and telephone numbers of canvassers
- lists of favorables, unfavorables, and undecideds
- telephone canvass records (3×5 cards)
- campaign scrapbook (newspaper clippings, etc.)
- samples of literature
- samples of giveaways used
- copies of transcripts of speeches
- lists of contributors
- lists of debts and liabilities you've incurred

The final chore—if you've won a primary—is to start to prepare for the general election. Take a real vacation—you may be in good shape physically, but from primary day to the first Tuesday in November is a long time, and even if you really love campaigning, it is exhausting and seldom exhilarating. If you've won a general election, your problems will include staff selection and analysis of the legislative and service needs of all your constituents—as a beginning. But that is another book.

3 Political Research: How to Do It and How to Use It

> *Nothing is more dangerous than to live in the temperamental atmosphere of a Gallup poll, always taking one's pulse and taking one's temperature. . . . There is only one duty, only one safe course, and that is to try to be right and not to fear to do or say what you believe to be right.*
> —WINSTON CHURCHILL

Recently I was asked by an experienced district leader for professional advice on a primary campaign for judicial office. The candidate had been involved in politics for twenty years and was prepared to spend whatever he had to on a fully professional campaign. Only after several long discussions, however, was I able to convince both the district leader and the candidate that an initial budget allocation for basic research was critical before active campaigning began. These were my specific research recommendations:

1. Record and analyze the results of the two previous primary elections by individual election district to delineate reform-regular party-faction votes for various offices, and to show the level of "drop-off" from the top line on the ballot to the judicial line—that is, to determine the proportion of voters who vote for the top (and normally most important) office on the ballot but do not bother to vote for the lesser offices (in this case, judgeships), which are listed lower on the ballot.
2. Obtain U.S. census data by tract for the area showing distribution by age, sex, income, race, ethnic group, and nationality (country of origin).

81

3. Obtain the names of the voters in the previous two primaries from the original buff-colored signature cards filed at the board of elections.

4. Obtain the election district maps for the area from the board of elections and mount them together onto a single map showing the entire judicial district.

5. Obtain the names and addresses of new registrants.

6. Do a probability sample survey of all recorded primary voters and new registrants to ascertain their characteristics generally and their attitudes about the candidates and their views.

This chapter discusses the reasons for such recommendations, the ways in which they are carried out by consultants, and the ways in which your staff can perform such services directly, if necessary.

Political research can be defined as the scientific search for those aspects of political reality that can help concretely in making both immediate decisions and long-range campaign policy, using objective data that are amenable to detailed, precise analysis and evaluation.* As in business and in government programs, the existence of good research cannot by itself guarantee intelligent decision-making. It is nothing more nor less than a tool; to be effective, it must be used skillfully.

Good research can be employed in making bad decisions, and good decisions are sometimes made based on poorly done research or on no research at all. Sometimes intuition, guts, and the synoptic capacity of a politically skilled candidate can be as important as all the research in the world. Nonetheless, political research of professional quality should be regarded as mandatory in any reasonably well-financed campaign and should be a factor in all major campaign decisions. Most professionals agree on the necessity for research, but considerable controversy exists on how best to do it.

Types of political research
There are four basic types of political research: polling or probability

---

* Abraham Kaplan, *The Conduct of Inquiry: Methodology for Behavioral Science* (Scranton, Pa.: Chandler, 1964), a college text, contains a brilliant general discussion of research.

sample surveys, voting behavior analysis, supporting demographic analysis, and issue or policy studies.

1. *Polls*—more properly referred to as *probability sample surveys* —are the best known basic type of research work required in political campaigns.* Published polls often show little more than where one candidate stands vis-à-vis his opponent at given intervals during a campaign. More important, however, is the fact that polls can also be designed to provide specific indications of why you stand where you do. Surveys provide information on which issues are of concern to which groups of voters and on the adequacy of your appeals to the groups you wish to focus on; and a major goal of surveys is to establish as objectively as possible which groups you should try to appeal to. They can also indicate how voters respond to you as a personality. Surveys are critical in laying out campaign strategy and testing and revising tactics during the course of a campaign.

Many candidates pay only lip service to political surveys. They prefer to make basic campaign decisions on "gut response" or on the advice of trusted political intimates, even though they may make an investment, sometimes a sizable one, in research, simply because it is expected or might keep a contributor happy. If, for any reason, you don't expect to use survey results, don't go to the trouble and expense of commissioning these studies. If, however, you want and know how to use survey data, get the very best work that you can afford or that your staff can provide.

Some politicians still cannot believe that a survey of a few hundred voters can provide a sensitive, accurate reflection of the total electorate. Yet many studies demonstrate the reliability and accuracy of professional surveys. Based on extrapolations from only a few election district returns, the major radio and television networks for many years have fairly accurately predicted the outcomes of elections early on election evenings.

2. *Voting behavior analysis* consists of recording the results of previous elections by the smallest geographic units available (usually election districts, which are also called wards or precincts in various

---

* The use of the word "polling" dates from the time when surveys consisted almost exclusively of polls asking whom the respondent expected to vote for. Surveys include much more than this now, but the world "poll" remains in wide use. A probability sample of voters is one in which each voter in the area or "universe" has an equal chance of being interviewed.

parts of the country). In primary campaigns, you would use data from previous primary elections, while in general elections you would naturally study previous general elections. These data should be used in conjunction with an election district map of the area in which you are campaigning, so that supplemented by the results of the attitudinal surveys, decisions on geographical emphasis in your campaign strategy can be made.

3. *Supporting demographic analysis* consists of recording decennial U.S. census data and then mapping the census tract data as an overlay on a map of your election district, making separate maps to show the distribution of older people, young people, families with young children, nationalities, races, and any other variables that are important in determining your allocations of time, energy, and money in the campaign.

4. *Issue or policy studies* are written to aid a candidate and his staff in developing explicit positions on matters of interest to the electorate. These studies are issued to the press and the public in many campaigns. Positions on foreign policy, police protection, budget priorities, tax measures, and other issues of concern to local voters are prepared to indicate the candidate's views of what has to be done and how to do it. I find it extraordinary that candidates almost never feel public pressure to make a similar announcement of the appointments they intend to make if elected; in many ways, this would indicate a great deal more about how they intend to govern than do general policy statements.

Informal research and its limits

In addition to the formal types of research described above, all candidates, whether consciously or not, do informal research—they reach conclusions based on what they see around them, and they act on those conclusions by saying or not saying something, by emphasizing one issue over another, or in various other ways. The difficulty with informal research of this sort is that it is impossible to estimate its accuracy in advance. A common problem of even some experienced candidates is that they trust conclusions based on their subjective impressions from street campaigning more than those based on their objective research. Because he had received enthusiastic responses in his street campaigning for the New York mayorality in 1969, Mario Procaccino, in his disastrous campaign against John V. Lindsay, was said to have ignored a number of polls that showed him losing voter support. Had he heeded the surveys, he might have been able to alter his campaigning style in time to regain the lost votes and win the election.

Some politicians greatly emphasize what they hear from cab drivers. Others read and are influenced by political columns in local newspapers, often despite their knowledge that the columnist is merely pulling together a series of guesses to make a deadline. Some like to talk with people in bars or candy stores or shopping centers. The supposition that these conversations may be significant assumes that the people being interviewed in this way constitute a probability sample in which all voters have an equal chance of being chosen— which of course they do not. Such conversations may give you an idea of what's on people's minds, but you should not treat them as representative or use them to make any far-reaching decisions.

Many candidates have friends or acquaintances who turn up at headquarters two or three times a week to provide moral support or to suggest new perceptions, criticisms, or matters to be concerned about. Some are sincerely concerned; others trade on the doubts and worries most campaigners face daily. The latter are people who take cheap shots. The advice of these "ego-support advisers" should almost always be completely disregarded. Usually, their opinions are about as useful and constructive as that of the sidewalk superintendent who reports to you that there is a crack in the foundation of your house—*after* the house has been built over the foundation. If they make you feel good, keep a few around, but don't take their information or advice seriously.

Other secondary information usually originates from campaign *mavens.* In most cases, the time you spend with them is apt to yield little reliable information while weakening the morale of the staff and volunteers who are really extending themselves for you. It would be better to allow an hour a week for your headquarters staff and fulltime volunteers to air their gripes and tell you how they think things are going. That way, you'll benefit not only from keeping lines of staff communication open and from background information they are bound to have gained through working full-time on the campaign, but also because their effectiveness would be weakened if they couldn't get to you at least in this way: There's no satisfaction in working hard for someone who doesn't seem to know you're there. If you do choose to have such regular staff "bull sessions," remember the classic administrative principle: Compliment publicly when you feel it is appropriate, but criticize quietly and in private.

Minority problems and the growing political importance of blacks, Mexicans, Puerto Ricans, and other minority groups in the big cities of the United States have led to the emergence of a relatively new phenomenon. Most large-scale campaigns now have a "professional Negro" (or Jew, Puerto Rican, Chicano, etc.) to advise the candidate on how best to reach his group. In my experience, however, many of these advisers are openly opportunistic and don't represent their ethnic group as much as their own personal ambition. Their advice and liaison with community organizations may be useful, but I would emphasize the necessity of using sample surveys as the controlling data for any of your decisions about ethnic-group politics, rather than the views of individual, self-proclaimed "spokesmen" for these groups.

Types of political surveys

Only three basic types of surveys should be considered in your political research: household surveys, telephone surveys, and mail surveys.

1. *Household interviews* of respondents in their own homes constitute the best research source, but they are also the most expensive. Prestigious firms charge from $15 to $25 per household interview, and larger campaigns (major congressionals and city- and state-wide races) require at least 500 interviews. In the 1972 presidential primary in New Hampshire, for example, three candidates used samples of about 600 respondents each. (It would make sense if candidates hard pressed for funds pooled their survey expenditures, since professional-quality research should not vary according to who commissions it. Each candidate would interpret the data for himself, in any case.) These surveys are usually conducted from three to five times during a campaign to provide a picture of the direction in which public opinion is moving. If subsamples of quality are required, making it possible to obtain reliable data for given subgroups as well as for the group as a whole, such research can cost from $250,000 to $500,000 in a presidential campaign. If a key decision has to be

made and the whole campaign depends on it, a household sample in a large-scale campaign is probably cheap even at a high price, for without question, household interviews of respondents selected by a probability sample provide the highest quality of information available to any candidate. (To repeat an important definition, a probability sample—also called a random sample—of voters is one in which each voter in a given locale or "universe" has the same chance of being interviewed as any other. Sampling specialists are able to estimate the reliability of such well-designed probability sample surveys with great accuracy.)

2. *Telephone surveys*. Although household interviews generally are best in providing detailed attitudinal information based on face-to-face discussions, telephone surveys are often used when funds are more limited or informational requirements are of a lesser order of sensitivity. (The universe and the sampling process are basically similar in both techniques.) Telephone surveying has two advantages over household interviewing: it is considerably cheaper, and it can be done relatively quickly. If you need and can afford detailed answers to open-ended questions, household surveys are almost mandatory. (Open-ended questions are those for which responses cannot be fully anticipated. Structured questions are essentially multiple-choice questions whose range of response is predictable to a large degree.) Otherwise, telephone surveys using centralized locations with professional supervision offer a reasonably priced alternative. Details on telephone survey techniques appear in Chapter 6.

3. *Mail surveys* sacrifice so much in quality and quantity of response that they only have limited utility as a last resort when nothing else is possible financially but any information is regarded as better than none. Despite this, even experienced politicians sometimes use postcard surveys, often for their public relations impact more than for their research value. In early 1972, for example, a county leader in New York sent out 20,000 postcards asking voters' preferences for presidential candidates. A professional survey could have been undertaken for the same expenditure of money but without the public relations benefit.

Bastardized or eclectic techniques include "scientific" postcard surveys in which a given number of cards is sent to each election district, and comparisons of total newspaper linage given to your campaign with that given to your opponent. The press often picks these up and gives them a credibility they do not deserve. Although the public is sometimes influenced by such surveys, the candidate shouldn't take them seriously.

A notable example of the dangers of such pseudo-surveys occurred in the U.S. senatorial campaign of 1970 in New York. It was rumored (such things are difficult to prove, as the people involved are rarely willing to discuss them on the record) that *The New York Times* was prepared to endorse the incumbent Republican Senator Charles E. Goodell in a three-way race, but was afraid that Goodell could not win and that to endorse him would take votes away from his Democratic opponent, Richard L. Ottinger, and thereby give the senate seat to the Conservative candidate, James L. Buckley. Goodell's manager was said to have assured the *Times* that his research demonstrated that Goodell could win, even though no other available research confirmed such a conclusion. The *Times* allegedly checked with Goodell's polling company, which swore that the results of the survey were reliable; meanwhile, some leading Republicans were said to have told the firm to give the *Times* any assurances that were sought. Staff men close to Ottinger believed that what probably happened was that the *Times* was considering not making any endorsement at all and that Goodell supporters put pressure on the paper to back up its previous praise of the candidate. It was later reported that the surveys cited in Goodell's behalf were hardly professional, apparently consisting merely of comparisons of the linage given to each candidate in New York City newspaper coverage of the campaigns. The *Times* endorsed Goodell, who did not come close to winning but did split the liberal vote with Ottinger. The *Times* endorsement probably was the *coup de grâce* for Ottinger, and Buckley won the election.

Retaining a survey consultant

All other things being equal, half of the quality of a probablity sample depends on the precision and care exercised in choosing the people to be interviewed. The concept of picking samples is simple; proper implementation of the process, however, is a laborious task that requires a considerable degree of experience and skill. (In a 1972 congressional campaign in New York, for example, it took me four days to pull a sample of 500 voters for a telephone survey. This included the preparation of two additional substitution lists or "decks" of 3×5 cards for voters who had moved, refused to answer, were ill, or did not respond for other reasons. A single substitution deck is usually sufficient is most cities.) Since most political research contracts involve relatively small amounts of money for the research firm, which must pay top sampling design men fees as high as $500 a day plus expenses, some firms are forced to compromise on sampling quality. Sometimes, for example, a prospective survey consultant may want to economize by using a sample for you that has already been selected for another use and that may not be perfectly appropriate to the new situation, or by permitting shortcuts in the sample selection process. Such a sample may or may not be adequate for your needs. If it is not, do not permit its use, for such a compromise can seriously decrease the reliability of the results. Professional advice on this point is absolutely critical—but *you* must make the decision. However, if you can't afford to hire a professional to check the sample design, there are a few simple rules that may help you judge for yourself the representativeness and randomness of a sample:

1. Check the sampling proportions of men and women against the universe (the entire voting group that interests you).

2. If the sample is for a large district, say a state senatorial or a congressional, check the sample by comparing its distribution by assembly districts against the distribution by assembly districts within the actual universe.

3. If the proportions of one or two ethnic groups in your district are known to you—for example, 35 percent of the population are Italian and 18 percent are black—the sampling proportions should approximate this (adjusting for differences in the age distribution and registration habits of each group).

4. The sampling process should use the universe you're interested in. If you're concerned only about one group of voters or one area in your district, the sample should not be drawn from the entire district.

5. Acceptable reliability limits, expressed as 95 percent probability (meaning that there are 95 chances in 100 that the sampling

results are within 2 or 3 percent of the actual universe), should be stated.

6. The substitution process, absolutely critical in controlled sampling, should be spelled out explicitly for you.

If these questions are answered satisfactorily, you will have to have faith that you're in good hands.

Because of the critical nature of the sampling process, your research specialist and campaign manager should make a detailed inquiry of prospective consultants, including the following questions:

- What will be the nature of the sample and the universe?
- Who will design the sample?
- How will the sample size be determined?
- Which statistical reliability limits will be used?
- Who will pick (or "pull") the sample?
- How will the interviewers be trained, and by whom?
- Which quality-control routines will be used during polling?
- How will substitutions for non-respondents be done?

The best time to ask these questions is when you are considering retaining a consultant, before a contract is signed. Many candidates and their managers base their hiring decisions exclusively on the amount of the bid (choosing the lowest) or the prestige of the firm (choosing the highest). Neither way is correct. A low bid may mean that quality procedures and quality supervisors and interviewers will not be provided; prestigious names and high prices do not always guarantee top quality. Any professional should be happy to discuss his procedures in detail with you or your staff before expecting you to sign a contract.

Like all contracts signed in the course of your campaign, your research contracts should always be checked by a lawyer before you sign them. In addition to any recommendations your lawyer may make, you should insist that all tabulations of the survey results be made available to you as well as the original questionnaires used by the interviewers, the computer tapes used in producing the tables, and the IBM cards. In city- or state-wide races, it is likely that you will have a substantial (and not inexpensive) computer listing job done. The contract should give you exclusive rights over this list—you may be able to sell parts of it to other candidates running in smaller districts within your area and thereby recover a good part of your initial investment—but the computer house may insist on collecting part of the proceeds under such an arrangement. If you do obtain the original questionnaires, you should take the time to read the comments of respondents as recorded on the questionnaires. Professional questionnaires usually include open-ended questions, which must be edited and coded before they can be fed into the computer. Reading respondents' actual answers to such questions may provide you with interesting insights that are lost when the answers are processed for computer use. Most will be of value only as parts of the whole sample, but a few may provide you with ideas that are of importance in planning the rest of your campaign.

An illustration of the technique that was used by the staff of Senator Edmund S. Muskie to choose a survey consultant in his 1972 presidential primary campaigns may be useful here. Twenty-five nationally known firms were invited to bid for a research contract expected to fall in the $250,000-to-$500,000 price range, involving both national and regional samples. Each bidder was sent a list of possible research alternatives including alternative sample sizes. Quotes were invited for household as well as telephone interviews, central or localized supervision of the telephone interviews, and various numbers and types of questions to be asked.

After receiving the bids, Muskie's research director narrowed the field to five consultants, each of whom was invited to Washington to discuss his proposal in even more detail with the campaign staff. Each bidder was interviewed in depth about his sampling technique (developing a national sample is a very expensive and painstaking job), who his samplers and interviewers were, how they were to be trained and supervised, how the coding and editing were to be done, and other similar details. The consultant who was originally selected as a result of this process was not the most prestigious of those who had been considered, and since he guanteed top quality he probably was not the lowest bidder. Unfortunately—but demonstrative of a not uncommon fact of political life—the completely professional and ambitious research that was contemplated was reportedly never carried out, because the campaign staff was unable to raise the money to pay for it. Instead, a lower-cost compromise was worked out and another consultant was retained.

Costs of political research

Budgeting for research studies is difficult. Spending money on radio advertisements and brochures seems to result in something tangible, visible, or measurable, but many campaigners don't see direct productive results from research. Examples throughout this book should clarify and concretize the value of political research and demonstrate its importance in the budget of any well-run campaign.

In any large-scale, professionally conducted campaign, 5 to 10 percent of the total amount available can reasonably be budgeted for research.* Costs of thorough professional ·research surveys are approximately $15 to $25 per household interview and $7 to $9 per telephone interview, with several hundred interviews usually required in a sample. These fees include the following: (1) overhead, (2) profit, (3) training, (4) supervision, (5) interviews, (6) questionnaire design, (7) sample design, (8) sample selection, (9) coding schedules, (10) key punching (with 100 percent verification of the process), (12) cross-tabulation design, (13) computer program development and testing, (14) computer running time, (15) preparation of final tables, (16) analysis and presentation of final results, and (17) consultation with candidate and campaign staff.

This is the full job without short cuts. You can pay less and get less, but you would also run the risk of defeating the purpose of performing the research in the first instance: getting the best information in order to make the most informed and perceptive campaign policies and decisions. Research is not inexpensive, but it more than pays its way if done correctly.

Which decisions should be subjected to research

In designing political surveys, you should know in advance the questions you need answered. Too often, the right questions are not asked, so the results of the survey contribute very little to guiding decisions rationally, although that is the main purpose of any useful research survey. Every other purpose, such as public relations im-

* A large-scale campaign would be defined for this purpose as one costing in excess of $50,000. In smaller campaigns, the decision on the amount to spend on research would have to depend on how tight the race is and on whether adequate information is available from a political ally; it is impossible to establish even general guidelines for research expenditures in these instances. I would strongly recommend that even in smaller campaigns the requirements of objective research not be overlooked.

pact, should be secondary. This section describes certain major questions that every campaign has to answer in some fashion and that are susceptible to research.

Many professional politicians still think that modern campaigning depends too much on outside consultants and computer printouts; they maintain that the big "gut" decisions still have to be made intuitively or by the seat of the pants.* They are probably partly right: Many candidates don't understand the import of the data and don't trust their advisors' interpretation of data; in addition, some of the larger decisions aren't susceptible to statistical analysis. In some instances, research only identifies the larger problems without necessarily providing the answers, but at least the research enables the candidate to isolate, and concentrate on, the issues to which he must respond. Often, campaigners and their managers simply don't know how to use the data that may be made available to them. Nonetheless, nowadays, more than ever before, many more decisions in campaigns are made objectively on the basis of survey data. The decisions that research should influence include the following:

Which groups to appeal to and which themes to use are perhaps the most basic questions that campaign research has to answer for the organization of a successful campaign. There are several ways of using research to help answer them, all of which require the identification of relevant client groups. (The term "client group" is defined on page 49.)

In congressional and city- and state-wide campaigns, specific appeals usually are developed for specific client groups. In one area of your district, for example, the unreliability of garbage collection may be a hot issue. People will want to hear your ideas on improving garbage collection, and not on open space planning. For another client group in your district, narcotics may be the priority issue. You can speak in general terms to all groups, but that is rarely the most effective thing to do. The voters want specific answers to their own

* Former Governor Edmund ("Pat") Brown of California is one of these. He believes in paying some attention to polls, but "I give at least equal weight to my own sensing of how things are going, developed primarily from conversations with people I meet during the day's campaigning." Quoted in James M. Cannon (ed.), *Politics U.S.A.: A Practical Guide to the Winning of Public Office* (Garden City, N.Y.: Doubleday, 1960), p. 45.

problems, not platitudes and polite commiseration. If you don't have an answer, say so and ask for their ideas. Political research, supplemented by information provided by your experienced election district workers, should provide you with the themes that would appeal to the various groups in your district.

In a small sample John Kraft did for Herman Badillo's campaign for Bronx borough president in 1965, the analysis of the questionnaires suggested that Democratic women voters preferred Badillo in larger proportions than did Democratic men. A significant number of men appeared not to like Badillo's Puerto Rican origin and perhaps his attractiveness to their wives. The poll suggested a very close race in the primary (Badillo finally won by less than 200 votes), so an additional mailing was sent to middle-income Jewish areas mentioning that the candidate had worked his way through college, was graduated *magna cum laude*, and was both a certified public accountant and an attorney. This information—chosen to maximize Badillo's credentials among the undecided male voters—probably contributed to his victory.

Client groups in many areas are concerned about crime. The Manhattan congressional district represented by Congressman Edward I. Koch includes Greenwich Village, a neighborhood inhabited by large numbers of people who live alone. In recent years, the increasing crime rate in Greenwich Village has alarmed many of its single-woman residents. In the winter of 1971, Congressman Koch made the news by proposing that everyone who lived in the area carry a whistle. In the past, when someone screamed in the street, people hid in their apartments; Koch suggested that if anyone was heard screaming, everyone should come out and blow whistles. Community groups picked up the idea and began giving whistles to local residents; people began to feel safer walking in the streets; and Koch, in addition to doing a genuine service for his district, undoubtedly gained new supporters among his sizable client group of fearful women.

Sometimes your appeal is a counter-appeal. For example, should your research indicate that many voters resent the incumbent's having voted for tax increases after he had promised no tax increases, you may want to focus deliberately on the groups who are most concerned. It is probably unwise to promise no tax increases—urban problems have shown voters that some increases are necessary to provide the services they want. You may therefore want to focus on the unfulfilled promise and on how, specifically, you will work to eliminate wastage and duplication in government spending and meet the real priority needs.

It is common in political attitudinal surveying to learn that many voters feel an incumbent has been in office too long. The theme, "It's Time for a Change," has considerable merit in these instances. A number of other possible "anti-themes" can become apparent from survey data. Each one must be evaluated. Whichever themes you choose must be tested by your research during the campaign. Sometimes such a theme is a natural, and your campaign may catch fire from it, but such positive results are rare from anti-themes. It is more likely that your positive positions will catch on; the one that does will undoubtedly be one that your client groups can relate to personally. Ideally, it will be a phrase or an idea—like Roosevelt's New Deal or Truman's Fair Deal—that focuses on what you are like as a man, as a politician, and as a leader. Attitudinal survey research can contribute greatly to the development of themes by showing you which subjects are most important to your voters and what type of leaders they most admire.

Whose endorsement is helpful. The importance of endorsements was well illustrated in a recent Democratic primary election in New York City. In a light voter turnout, reform surrogate candidate Millard Midonick defeated organization candidate Frederick Backer by using an economical campaign of newspaper and radio spots emphasizing two themes: that Congressmen Herman Badillo and Edward I. Koch endorsed him, and that he had been selected by an independent panel of respected attorneys. (The obvious question not always asked in such cases is how the "independent panel" was chosen.)

Midonick's well-chosen endorsements were enough to overcome his opponent's endorsements (which came from regular Democratic organization leaders) and more liberal expenditures of money. (It was reported that Backer was paying his campaign manager $1,500 a week.)

Endorsements work both ways. They will attract some voters,

but they will repel others. It is important to do research on whose endorsements are valuable before asking for or accepting endorsements. The research should ascertain something that is quite basic but that is nevertheless lost sight of in many campaigns: whether, on balance, a given endorsement will help your cause or whether it will be the kiss of death, particularly among the groups of voters you wish to attract.

The impact of endorsements can be absurd but effective, like a famous ballplayer endorsing breakfast cereals for children: The endorsement itself isn't really relevant, but sales of the endorsed cereal increase markedly. In my home district, a regular Democrat, Leonard Farbstein, a steady if unglamorous congressman of some years, lost the 1970 primary election to Bella Abzug, an active and vocal partisan of Women's Strike for Peace and other causes. Having been personally subjected to the campaigns of both candidates, I believe that Ms. Abzug won for several reasons: (1) Farbstein, who was in his early seventies, did not campaign hard and did not get a great deal of active support from the Democratic clubs; (2) Women's Liberation sympathizers and some non-Jewish groups in the primarily Jewish district found Ms. Abzug's opposition to the establishment attractive; and (3) most effective of all, in my judgment, and what actually made the difference in a tight race, was the booming endorsement of Barbra Streisand, who made appearances and rode on the sound trucks with Ms. Abzug. Ms. Streisand's appearances gave a touch of romantic show business and excitement to the campaign. She had as much (or as little) relevance in the campaign as Marlon Brando or Jane Fonda would have had, but that strictly logical judgment was beside the point. Had Jane Fonda endorsed Ms. Abzug, the results might have been negative, but Barbra Streisand was Jewish and originally from Brooklyn, and her strident voice and down-to-earth manner were effective with Jewish women particularly, and probably with Jewish men as well.

To research endorsement potentials, include a direct query in your questionnaire: "Whose endorsement among the following names would be most important to you in deciding your vote?" or "Whom among the following names do you most respect?" You may also wish to find out what newspaper's endorsement would be most advantageous to your candidacy. Another device is to ask with which segment of the party the respondent is aligned. The exact wording of the question should be decided only after intensive pre-testing, or interviewing respondents to test the relative effectiveness of the various versions of the question in obtaining meaningful responses.

Associative questioning—using adjectives to describe an ideal candidate or an ideal party spokesman—sometimes suggests the traits the voter values most highly. The descriptive words are then applied to individual politicians, and the respondent is asked which word or words best describe the candidate or the potential endorser.

Not all decisions about endorsements are based on research. Some, perhaps including the decision to use Barbra Streisand in the Abzug campaign, may be based entirely on intuition or on intuition fortified by research. Always keep in mind, however, that such critical decisions should be based on the best information you can obtain within the short time available, so that the degree of risk can be established—and perhaps minimized as well.

Primary fights present a special endorsement problem. There, your problem normally won't be in associating with famous show business people, but rather in dealing with bitter intra-party rivalries. It's hard to know without some research who in the party may actually help you by lending you his name at any given time. In some cases, nobody the public is familiar with may offer any assurance of help; in such a situation, you may have to build up your endorsers as part of your campaign.

Where to spend time. Research can help enormously in deciding this essential question by keeping you advised about where and with what voters you are doing well and where that is not the case. To emphasize a point that has been made earlier in this book, most campaigns are decided by margins of less than 10 percent of the total vote. As the campaign progresses, you should be able to ascertain fairly closely the characteristics of the undecided voters and the reasons why they remain undecided. You'll have to examine your own conscience to determine how much you want to emphasize an issue that interests the uncommitted; it makes sense, however, to stay in the character and political form you've developed during the campaign. Too much switching around may make some voters uneasy about you; too little response may bother others.*

* The 1972 McGovern presidential campaign is the best example of this in the last generation.

Using research should help you to decided how to spend your time by showing you where the undecided are, what concerns them most, and to what appeals they are most receptive. For example, although enthusiastic receptions may seduce you into wanting to spend a large proportion of your time campaigning in the streets, research may show you that radio and television interviews have a greater impact on the undecided voters in your district. In such a case, quietly preparing for interviews by studying the major issues very carefully may be a better investment of your time than street campaigning.

Modulating campaign themes. Research is helpful in determining how the voters feel about developing controversies. Some of this research may come from a clipping file, from talking to people in shopping centers and on walking trips, from watching local television and listening to local radio programs, from talking to taxi drivers, or from other informal sources. The most reliable information, however, will come from telephone or household interviews with people chosen in a scientifically planned sample. Such a survey has two principal advantages over the informal sources of information: Its reliability is known, and it is relatively inexpensive—possibly even cheaper than feeding and caring for the hangers-on who often haunt campaign headquarters and are always ready to provide opinions and advice on policy.

A sequential "panel" or "continuity" approach is important in objectively establishing how the voting public is reacting to developing issues as well as in providing data indicating what bothers voters about you and/or your opponent. This technique consists of interviewing the same group of respondents a number of times during a campaign to see how their attitudes change in response to changes in the campaign. The virtue of the panel approach is simple: By interviewing the same sample at intervals during the campaign, you're able to develop a sense of which groups are responding to each appeal and which groups are not.

The U.S. Census Bureau Current Population Survey uses a modified panel approach in which a given percentage of the panel is carried over into each succeeding survey and the remainder of the panel is replaced by new respondents. Theoretically, any series of perfectly chosen probability samples should provide accurate comparisons. The panel approach is useful, however, because in practice it is almost impossible to draw a series of samples that is absolutely without some bias.

Although it is unwise to change campaign strategies and tactics frequently, some modulation of campaign themes is generally necessary. Often these changes will reflect opportunities that may pop up: an opponent's friend is accused of taking a bribe; the opponent has people call voters on their religious holidays and represent themselves as your workers (this reportedly happened to Richard L. Ottinger in his New York senatorial campaign in 1970), and you learn of the ruse and take it to the press, etc. Research can help you modulate your campaign appeals in a more sophisticated manner by showing you which appeals are getting through and which aspects of your program are ambiguous. The panel approach discussed above is probably most helpful in this regard. The results are of great value in adapting campaign literature to current needs and deciding on content and emphasis for television and radio commercials.

Establishing an opponent's vulnerability. Survey data can indicate with some specificity the content of the most effective attacks on your opponent. For example, research analysis may sometimes indicate the advisability of attacking the opponent's leader or party rather than the opponent himself. Many Democratic politicians used this tactic with great success against local Republican opponents when Barry M. Goldwater was heading the Republican ticket in 1964. In 1972, local Democratic candidates were reported to be disassociating themselves from George McGovern out of fear that an overwhelming Nixon victory would lead to their defeat, just as many local Republican candidates had been defeated as a consequence of Goldwater's disastrous loss in 1964. In some instances, particularly in primaries, survey analysis may indicate that the public really likes your opponent but doesn't think he has a real chance of winning. Your move then may be simply to compliment him whenever possible but keep indicating that he can't win.

When, where, and to whom to mail political literature are important decisions that can be made rationally on the basis of sample surveys and demographic analysis. The content of brochures is also a proper subject for research. An average congressional district may require as many as 100,000 letters and perhaps three separate mailings to have impact. Mailing 300,000 letters at a cost of about 8.5 or 9 cents a letter—plus the cost of design, preparation, computerized addressing, sealing, and bulk rate postage—amounts to about $32,000.* That is a lot of money even for wealthy campaigners. It makes no sense not to use it as effectively as possible by researching to establish the subjects to which voters will respond.

Voting behavior analysis and supporting demographic analysis (discussed on pages 83–84) can also be used to great advantage in targeting mailings of political literature for maximum economy and effectiveness. One campaigner did an analysis of past voting patterns by election district. He then mapped the results of his analysis on translucent paper and made a postal zip code map of the same election districts on the same scale, also on translucent paper. When he put one map on top of the other on a light table (that is, a table with a frosted glass top and lights inside), he was able to see at a glance which zip code areas were likely to be sympathetic to his candidacy and which were highly unlikely to be receptive to his appeals. Since mailings into the latter zip code areas were clearly not a good investment, he directed that the computer addressing the mailings "suppress" or discard all addresses having those zip codes. As a result, mailings were sent only into districts where optimal impact was probable, and money was saved that would in effect have gone down the drain in mailings to hostile areas. Supporting demographic analysis might have been used in a similar way, to identify the zip code areas having a high concentration of certain client groups—for example, young voters or Spanish-speaking voters. Specially prepared brochures could then have been sent into those zip code areas.

Survey research in some areas may reveal that 90 percent of the people of a certain ethnic ancestry really hate you. In such a situation, you certainly don't want to remind them to come out and vote —in effect, you would be pulling for your opponent. It is possible

---

* Congressional incumbents have an advantage in this regard; they often manage to use their franking privilege—which may not be legally used for purely political literature—for semi-political mailings to their constituents.

to design computer programs to suppress surnames suggesting a certain ethnic background. Such programs cost money to write, but they produce substantial savings in large-scale operations. (This is a variation of what is known as "ethnication," which is treated more fully in the section on computer mailings, page 204.)

Position papers

Almost every campaign includes substantive research papers, which are usually called position papers, white papers, or issue statements. (The term "white paper" comes from the nomenclature and cover paper used by the British Government for its evaluations of policies and programs.) In some campaigns, I have seen much staff time and money go into preparation of these papers for no other reason than that the opponents were doing it. Don't do position papers merely to do what your opponent is doing. Use them to dramatize your priorities and your feelings about problems.

If you're running in a small area, you probably won't need or even wish to ask professional help for preparing position papers, but you will probably be generally familiar with local issues and will want to bring yourself up to date in great detail for participating in public debates or providing sensible answers to questions you may be asked about problems that confront the community. On highly critical issues, or in larger areas, you will need background papers by specialists to give you an overview of problems with which you may not be as familiar. Your political survey research will be supplying you with ideas of what's on people's minds. This information should indicate which topics require position papers. Before the papers are typed for distribution, go over them critically with your principal advisers and associates to make certain they reflect your views accurately. Have copies made for distribution to persons who will be speaking on your behalf as well as to interested voters, civic groups, editorial writers, and the press generally.

On pages 102–4 are excerpts from a twelve-page white paper from John V. Lindsay's first New York City mayoral campaign in 1965.

Reconciling research with your instincts

Although research is critical for a sensibly run race, sometimes the data are not totally conclusive. Ambiguities in survey data often

<u>FOR RELEASE:</u>

5:30 pm Thursday
October 22, 1965

A "White Paper" on Reorganization of

New York City's Government to Achieve

Effective Planning and Administration

and Responsiveness to Local Need

****

Issued by JOHN V. LINDSAY,

Republican, Liberal, Independent Citizen's
Candidate for Mayor

<u>INTRODUCTION</u>:

There can be no doubt that New York City has failed to
provide the conditions which we all take for granted we are entitled to have. Safe streets, clean air, water and streets,
decent education, good jobs to name only a few.

I have spent five months detailing the programs I
would institute to make these services readily available. But
I now want to discuss how the various programs can be achieved.
For we all are painfully aware that good ideas do not get trans-
lated into effective programs automatically. In fact, for the
last twenty years expert opinion, new ideas, creative programs
have all failed to help the city because no one acts. No one
acts because no one plans how all the priorities of the administration can be met. Or, to say it another way, there is an
utter lack of coherent planning and even fairly decent administration.

The key to the solution of our planning and administrative chaos is to get the fullest participation in the determination of governmental policy by the citizens who are affected
by that policy, while at the same time achieving the economies
of large operation and the consistent coordinated use of city-
wide resources. I will do this by establishing administrative
and evaluation services reporting directly to me, and centralized
planning supplemented by up-to-date information from every
community in the City, made a reality by Departments given
authority commensurate with their responsibility.

Partnership between citizen and government at the local
level helping to shape City-wide programs is essential if we are
to move forward.

-2-

I propose six changes in the organization of our government which are predicated on simple principles of management and on an attempt to bring citizens into the decision-making process. If these changes are instituted and backed by the Mayor, they would constitute nothing less than a revolution in the administrative processes of New York City. They are:

1. Establish a Bureau of Program Planning and Budgeting to replace the present office of the Budget Director and create machinery for program analysis and planning, medium-term fiscal planning, and program evaluation. Such machinery, elementary to good management, has not existed at the top level.

2. Establish a Bureau of Administrative Management headed by the Deputy Mayor City Administrator concentrating administrative (in contrast to planning and budgeting) machinery in the hands of an administrative officer who would be, in fact as well as in name, the Mayor's chief administrative assistant.

3. Consolidate the multiplicity of departments, boards, commissions, et al., into a limited number of administrative departments, each equipped with adequate machinery for planning and managing its own program.

4. Implement the command of the Charter and use the City Planning Commission for land-use planning and creation of both a long-term and short-term capital improvement program.

5. Create Neighborhood Offices of the Mayor to solve citizens' problems, act as staff to Community Planning Boards, and to make more effective the services of government.

6. Involve each Community Planning Board in program analysis and operating and capital budget formulation and give them power over those administrative acts which effect them directly.

-3-

I. PROGRAM PLANNING & BUDGETING

The Bureau of Program Planning and Budgeting will prepare long-range projections and a comprehensive development plan
concerned with the whole range of economic, demographic and other
trends, and interpret their implications for City needs and hence
for City policies and programs; prepare a medium-term (four to
five year) fiscal plan to meet the City's upcoming needs, inaug-
urate a continuing evaluation of ongoing programs, and prepare
(in conjunction with the City Planning Commission) annual capital
and current budgets. Budget administration functions exercised
by the present Bureau of the Budget would be transferred in part
to the Bureau of Administrative Management and in part to the
operating departments.

The major function of this unit would be the preparation of a comprehensive development plan and a medium-term fiscal
plan to accomplish the purposes of the development plan. The
development plan would:

1. Set forth statements of goals and objectives of
    city policies, predicated upon studies of demo-
    graphic and economic trends and their implica-
    tions for city service requirements, an analysis
    of programs (levels and changes of ongoing pro-
    grams) required to meet the city's upcoming
    needs, and a medium-term fiscal plan (five to
    six years) relating programs to costs, both
    capital and current.

2. The medium-term fiscal plan should be, in
    principle, the most important of the city's
    fiscal policy documents; the annual capital
    and current budgets, now the foci of fiscal
    policy, should be regarded rather as instru-
    ments for fulfilling the long-term plans.
    There is nothing new or revolutionary about
    the concept of advance fiscal planning predi-
    cated upon analysis of future needs; it has been
    repeatedly advocated by the various management
    studies. Part of the process already exists in
    the form of the capital budget and five-year
    capital improvement plan, now prepared annually
    by the City Planning Commission.

reflect honest confusion or voter disinterest. Sometimes, in a three-way race, for example, the data will show that Candidate B, say, is the man whose challenge is strongest. If you therefore put Candidate C in the background and don't attack him, you may find that, near the end of the campaign, your final panel survey shows that C has gained considerable strength. It is then too late to recoup.* This kind of problem will occur more frequently as multi-candidate elections become more common. Research is necessary as a basis for informed decision-making, but intuition is sometimes absolutely necessary to anticipate trends before research data can fully document them. Professional-quality research is critical—but it cannot control everything. The creative campaigner and campaign manager use research, but they integrate it with their own well-developed political instincts. Sometimes you must take a chance before you have conclusive research results; if you are afraid of taking risks in a campaign, how can you expect to react promptly to emerging requirements as a government spokesman?

On other occasions, you may find it difficult to balance research results with your own view of what is right or prudent. About a decade ago, I set up a write-in survey for the challenger in a congressional campaign in the South Bronx, a formerly nearly all-white area into which large numbers of blacks and Puerto Ricans were beginning to move.† We received 2,000 responses which revealed, essentially, the middle-income white voters' fears of blacks and of increasing crime—each respondent seemed to want a private moat and a personal policeman. The candidate sincerely wished to minimize racial tensions and was therefore reluctant to issue a position paper on the subject, despite the research finding that race was a major issue. By now, he has been a congressman for some years and has sponsored bills to do crime control research. Ten years ago,

* This is precisely what happened in the Ottinger-Goodell-Buckley New York senatorial race in 1970. Ottinger made Goodell his main target and only at the very end turned his attack toward Buckley. The chance came too late; Buckley emerged the winner. Because of this race and others, the New York State legislature passed a bill in its 1972 session providing for a run-off election if no single city- or state-wide candidate received 40 percent of the vote.

† A "write-in" or "mail" survey is a commonly used device in which a post-paid envelope is provided and the voter is asked to answer questions on issues by mail. Such a study is not statistically reliable. It can be only suggestive. Don't make the mistake of using such a survey as a substitute for a sample survey.

however, he didn't feel the issue could be talked about from the campaign platform. Most politicians then shared his view.

There are times when you have to stop looking over your shoulder. Doing what you really believe may lose some votes, but people's respect for your honesty may also earn you votes that you might not have gotten otherwise. Senator Muskie's frankness in 1972 in indicating he would prefer not to have a Negro vice presidential running mate irritated many blacks and liberals. But some Negro organizations, noting that he was simply stating openly a fact of political life, supported him by admitting that, nationally, a Negro vice presidential candidate would hurt the chances of the Democratic party for victory.

Doing surveys yourself

In many campaigns, the candidate can't afford to pay a professional research consultant to do a sample survey. Often, when this occurs, campaign staffs attempt to do their own surveys. These surrogate "surveys" sometimes include postcard surveys, interviews with taxi drivers, a few telephone interviews, or reliance on press reports on the candidate's position in the race. These are not true probability surveys, and they have no reliability whatsoever.

Furthermore, strange things happen in campaigns when "bad" data are produced: Other people hear of the "study"—or are even told about it by members of the campaign staff—and comments are made to reporters. The data take on a life of their own, and staff people start believing them even when they are aware of their serious limitations. These surveys (and some professional ones as well) lend a magical cast to a campaign, much like the effect of magicians and astrologers in the courts of medieval kings. Good surveys are not magical, and inferior ones are magical only in their acceptance by unsuspecting politicians and in the great damage they can do. Good, professional-quality surveys depend on detailing, intensive training, and using quality-control routines from beginning to end.

Using inferior surveys in an attempt to manipulate public opinion is dangerous. After all, a full "survey" will be available on election day, and that is what campaigning must influence. Using unreliable data is not a good way to go about this job.

If you can possibly afford to have your surveys done professionally, by all means do so. If you must use your campaign staff for surveying, at least try to obtain the advisory services of a professional statistician. If you cannot afford a professional statistician, try to have the job done as close to professional standards as possible, as described in the course of this chapter, retaining consultants only for sample design and for computer tabulations.

The steps in doing a probability attitudinal survey were enumerated earlier, and the remainder of the chapter explains in detail how to take each step.

Sample designing is extremely difficult to do well without specialized training and experience. To approximate professional standards, the following rough guide is recommended when detailed information is needed on specific issues:

UNIVERSE	SAMPLE SIZE
Under 10,000 voters	150
10,000-24,999 voters	250
25,000-49,999 voters	400
50,000-99,999 voters	500
100,000-249,999 voters	750
250,000-499,999 voters	1,000
500,000 and more voters	1,500

Technically, the correct sample size is a function of the smallest "cell" for which your information must be reliable. A cell is a unit of information—for example, all the Negro families in the election district whose annual income is under $6,000. The sample size needed to provide adequate information if this were the critical cell would vary considerably from the sample size necessary to provide reliable data for a cell composed of all women in the area who are 35 to 55 years old and have been married at least once. To give another example, if for a city-wide sample you need reliable information on the views of divorced women 18 to 45 years of age who have children under 6 years old (which may make sense if you think day care might be a significant issue), your overall sample size would have to be considerably larger than if the smallest single group for which you needed reliable information was *all* women 18 to 45 years old (which might be adequate if you were interested in views on abortion reform). This example illustrates the basic principle that *the smaller the critical cell, the larger the necessary sample.* (The critical cell is the smallest group for which you need reliable information.)

Developing exact sampling routines is a highly technical process, and if you cannot afford to hire a professional, you should attempt it only after consulting, first, the U.S. Bureau of the Budget's *Household Survey Manual 1969* (available from the Superintendent of Documents, Washington, D.C. 20402, for $1.00; the U.S. Bureau of the Census's *Current Population Survey* methodologies; and, for specific statistical procedures, other texts that are listed in the bibliography in the back of this book.

In most political surveys, the sample should be picked from the voter registration books that are usually available from the local board of elections. State laws generally require that these books be published, and frequently they are available in local libraries. In a primary contest, of course, the sample is picked only from among those voters who are registered in a single political party. Names of voters in voter registration books are usually alphabetized by election district, with each registrant's party enrollment listed. If you have staff time available, it is preferable to select primary samples from a list of actual primary voters—usually 20 to 30 percent of all registrants. Since this requires checking each enrollment card in the district to see who has actually voted in a primary, it is thus usually a major piece of work and so expensive that it is not done as frequently as it should be. However, this single step can save more campaign monies than any other in primary contests.

If your district includes 8,000 registrants for your party, your sample control total from the table on page 107 is 150. An additional sample deck of 150 3×5 cards should be prepared for substitution purposes, since some voters move, die, get sick, or refuse to answer questions—and since, in some cities, as many as 20 percent of the telephones may have unlisted numbers. The usual routine is to attempt to interview the respondent (either by telephone or by household interview) at least three times during the course of the survey. If this fails for any reason, make a substitution. The new respondent should match the characteristics of the original sample respondent as closely as possible: woman for woman, election district for election

district, and even street for street if at all possible. The smallest
sample you should ever use is 100 interviews. The largest you'll ever
need is 1,500, for statewide or complicated city races. The Gallup
and Harris surveys use national samples of 1,500 respondents. The
U.S. Bureau of the Census household survey uses a base of 50,000
interviews, but it is designed to provide an enormous mass of detailed information for the nation as a whole as well as for individual
regions.

The proper way to select a probability sample employs tables of
random numbers which are available in basic mathematical statistics
texts. Since many registration books are arranged in columns, the
variables requiring random number selection are page numbers, line
numbers, and column numbers. Ideally, each of these variables
should be separately selected. To do this, for a sample of 150 voters,
you need 300 3×5 cards. The first 150 cards comprise your basic
sample; the second 150 cards are a substitute deck. Since, as noted
above, you have three variables, you go through 300 units of random
number series three separate times, so that when you finish, each of
your cards has three separate numbers on it. The first of these will
denote the page number, the second the line number, and the third
the column number of the name of the respondent associated with
that card. If you are running in a primary election and the name
designated by the random numbers is not of your party, you take the
first appropriate name following that one. This process is tedious
and time-consuming even for experienced people; it takes up to
three days for two professionals to do it properly for a sample of
500 to 700 (including a substitute deck).

With inexperienced people you may be better off sacrificing absolute professional accuracy and picking your sample in the following
way: Take the number of pages in the registration book and divide
by the total size of the necessary sample. For example, if you require
a sample of 100 and the registration book contains 300 pages, your
sampling guide would be one name for every three pages. Decide to
start on one of the first three pages. If you choose to start at page 2,
than one name should be selected on every following third page, that
is, pages 5, 8, 11, etc. The book may be divided into pages of three
columns containing thirty names each. Make an arbitrary decision
that your sample line will be the twentieth name in each second

column. The substitute deck sample can start on page 1 and use the tenth name in the first column of pages 4, 7, 10, etc. For technical reasons, this sampling method is not as reliable as using random numbers, but it will still produce useful results, and you may consider it a sacrifice of some quality which is made worthwhile by the saving of a professional consultant's fee.

There are other procedures for sampling beside the pure probability method just described. The "quota-sampling" method of sample selection allows the interviewers some discretion in choosing respondents. For example, the interviewer is instructed to interview any ten respondents residing in a specific block. When he has interviewed the ten of his choice, that part of the sample is complete. This method is cheaper and faster but considerably less reliable than probability sampling. Most interviewers are paid by the hour, and some may try to make their quota as fast as possible, sacrificing some quality in the process. It is more expensive, but far better, if you specify an address for each respondent. Sometimes, consultants pick an original probability sample and allow interviewers discretion for substitutions as needed in the field. In practice, this can be dangerous, since substitution must be exact if reliability is to be assured.

"Stratified sampling" involves selecting a sub-universe, perhaps males between 21 and 35 years of age, and selecting a sample from this group. Stratified samples are used when a candidate is interested in learning the opinions of only a given client group or client groups —for example, women or members of minority groups residing in his district. Stratified samples can be selected by either pure probability or quota sampling; the pure probability method is of course much more accurate.

After any sample is selected, it should be checked for consistency: proportions of men and women, geographic distribution, racial-ethnic distribution, etc. If there is a particular interest in one cell, you may wish to add to that portion of the sample to guarantee the reliability of data on that group's attitudes. For example, if one geographic area is important in developing your campaign strategy, that sample sector should be added to. This procedure really amounts to adjusting your sample for the critical cells necessary for making informed judgments and sensitive policy decisions. At the end of the process, you have a stratified probability sample that can be of enormous usefulness to the campaign staff.

Political sampling is filled with problems. In most metropolitan area and city samples especially, there are enormous sampling difficulties. The following technical remarks indicating the scope of the problem will be of interest only to those who are willing to do the background research and painstaking work that picking a quality sample requires. In some situations—particularly in urban areas, where unlisted telephone numbers can damage the reliability of a sample—sampling specialists use "random digit select" programs based on tables of random numbers taken from statistical textbooks. In this technique, a random series of seven-digit numbers is chosen, with the choices limited to those beginning with three digits that represent local telephone exchanges and the chosen numbers representing local telephones. Although this procedure eliminates looking up telephone numbers for respondents whose names have been selected from the election rolls, it has its own complications: You may have to call each number to find out whether the resident is a registered voter and, if so, in the case of a primary election, what his party is. (If your local telephone company makes available a directory of telephones arranged by number or by street address, you can check the names in the voter registration book—but you are stuck with the problem of unlisted numbers.) In my view, although more tedious, it is preferable to sample from registration lists or actual primary voter lists.

Short cuts can sometimes be discovered. In many cities and towns, for example, as well as in many rural counties, each registered voter is assigned a number. The numbers are sequenced in the order in which the people register. It is possible to work out a reasonably good probability sample based on these numbers. The only bias here is that older voters who have not moved are concentrated in the lower numbers and may therefore be underrepresented unless the sample is adjusted to allow for them. These problems are mentioned to indicate how much care has to be exercised in sample selection if the results are to be worthwhile.

Names chosen for the survey should be entered on 3×5 cards with election districts, assembly districts, and other details entered. The interviewers should be instructed to interview only the respondent listed and no other person in the family, or the sampling reliability of the work will be completely destroyed. The cards should look like the following example:

SAMPLING CONTROL CARD

Assembly District _____   Interviewer _____
Election District _____   Date of interview 1) _____
                                                       2) _____
                                                       3) _____
                                   Substitution _____

Name _____
Address _____
Telephone _____
Ethnic: Irish___ Italian___ Jewish___ German___ Russian___ WASP*___
         (etc.)
Race: White___ Negro___ Puerto Rican___ (etc.)
              Primary Voter? _____
Comments: _____
          _____
          _____

Questionnaire designing is best done by starting with a list of questions that you have to answer in order to make sensible judgments on campaign strategy and tactics—questions such as:

- How do voters react to your personality vis-à-vis that of your opponent and why?
- Whom would they vote for if the election took place at the time of the survey?
- Which issues are most important to them?
- How important are specific endorsements?

Other questions that research is frequently called upon to answer were discussed earlier in this chapter, and others that are specific to your campaign should occur to you as well.

On pages 114–15 and 117 are examples of telephone or household interview questionnaires that have been used in past campaigns. These should be taken as guides only, since each questionnaire was developed for specific reasons having to do with a specific campaign at a specific time in a specific locality.

As much as possible, the questionnaires you develop should be pre-coded in order to facilitate subsequent coding, editing, and

---

* WASP (White Anglo-Saxon Protestant) is used in many urban areas as a residual category—i.e., for voters who cannot be otherwise identified.

tabulation.* This is particularly important when inexperienced interviewers and editors are involved. The answers to open-ended questions such as "What do you think about . . . ?" must be looked at individually, are susceptible to misinterpretation, and are difficult for amateurs to code and edit.

Questionnaire design depends a great deal on whether you are using household or telephone interviews. You can do intensive probes in household interviews using both open-ended and associative questions, but this is much more difficult in telephone surveys.†

A good questionnaire is characterized by language so precise that each respondent clearly understands what is being asked. Each interview must be conducted the same way, with exactly the same questions. To emphasize: *The questions must be asked substantially as written in each case.* In practice, many interviewers change the wording slightly to fit their usual habits of speech. This is not particularly dangerous as long as each interviewer is consistent about the focus and basic wording of the questions. Some interviewers say, "May I also ask you about . . ." as a transition from question to question. Each interviewer must be trained so that only such minor changes in language occur. The wording should be as colloquial and as comfortable as is both possible and consistent with the need for precision. A successful interview is really a structured conversation, and it should not sound artificial. Proper, natural sequencing of questions is as important as the proper wording.

A questionnaire is most effective if it is designed around the appropriate focal question to which all other questions contribute. Too often candidates feel the focal question is simply "How well am I doing right now?" With thought and pre-testing, you can usually find a better focal question, which should then determine the logic of

* Pre-coding is a process of structuring the probable responses into multichoice questions. Such responses can be matched to "fields" (vertical columns) on IBM cards. Basically, an IBM card consists of 80 fields or columns, each of which can record up to ten responses. Designing a questionnaire in such a way that it can be kept to one IBM card can save significant amounts of time and money in editing and data processing operations.

† "Probe" is an instruction to interviewers allowing them discretion to rephrase the question and explore a respondent's first answer to a question.

An example of an associative question is: Which of these would you say best describes Congressman Jones? Energetic ___ Personable ___ Honest ___ Opportunistic ___ Incompetent ___ Represents us well ___ Means well but doesn't seem sure of what to do ___ Other___

December, 1971
Regular List Sample

I'm calling for Heiden Research. We're doing a survey of the opinions of Democrats in Bronx County. May I have a few moments of your time. (IF ASKED, NO, I'M NOT PERMITTED TO TELL RESPONDENTS FOR WHOM THE SURVEY IS BEING CONDUCTED. IT MIGHT AFFECT YOUR ANSWERS.) Thank you.

1. Are you satisfied with the rate of   Satisfied . . . . . . ☐
    troop withdrawal from Vietnam?   Dissatisfied . . . . ☐
                                                    Don't know . . . . . ☐

2a. Are you satisfied with the   Satisfied . . . . . . ☐
    Lindsay administration?   Dissatisfied . . . . ☐
                                                    Don't know . . . . . ☐
  b. (IF DISSATISFIED) Can you tell me why you feel that way?

    _____

    _____

3. Do you think that Mayor Lindsay   Yes . . . ☐
    should run for President?   No . . . ☐
                                                   Don't know ☐

4a. What is the most important problem facing you and your family in your
    neighborhood?

    _____

    _____

  b. What do you think should be done about this problem?

    _____

    _____

  c. Which elected officials in your judgment should provide leadership in
    dealing with this problem?

    _____

5. Which Democrat would you like to see run for Mayor in 1973?

    _____

6. Which Democrat would you like to see run against Nixon?

    _____

7. In your opinion who are the two leading Democrats in the City?

    _____   _____

8a. How would you rate Mario Merola as a Councilman?

Excellent ☐
Good . . . ☐
Fair . . . ☐
Poor . . . ☐
Don't know ☐

b. How would you rate Jonathan Bingham as a Congressman?

Excellent ☐
Good . . . ☐
Fair . . . ☐
Poor . . . ☐
Don't know ☐

c. How would you rate Oliver Koppell as an Assemblyman?

Excellent ☐
Good . . . ☐
Fair . . . ☐
Poor . . . ☐
Don't know ☐

9a. Which segment of the Democratic party do you feel best represents you?

(ROTATE) Reform . . . ☐
Regular . . . ☐
Independent ☐

b. Why do you feel this way? _____

10. Of the following Democrats which one do you feel best represents your interests and beliefs?

Robert Abrams . . . . ☐
Abe Beame . . . . . . ☐
Herman Badillo . . . ☐
Mario Biaggi . . . . ☐

Howard Samuels . . . . ☐
Burton Roberts . . . . ☐
Sanford Garelik . . . ☐
Edward Koch . . . . . ☐

11a. What do you think of the housing controversy in Forest Hills? (PROBE)

_____

_____

b. How do you think public housing should be provided?

_____

_____

12. How do you feel about the proposed purchase of Yankee Stadium?

_____

_____

CLASSIFICATION

13. Just a few moments for some statistical questions.

a. Are there any voters over 65 in your household?

Yes ☐
No ☐

b. Is your family income over or under $15,000?

Over ☐
Under ☐

the questionnaire. Often, such a question does not involve the relative standings of the candidates but, rather, why one issue is predominant among the voters and what they expect the candidates to do about it. In other instances, you may be able to establish that some aspect of the candidate's personality or television presence is disturbing to voters. On the positive side, you may be able to establish the basis for favorable reactions and try to maximize these in the campaign.

The design of good questionnaires is a technical skill requiring experience, judgment, and adequate pre-testing. This brief discussion cannot possibly cover all the particulars. For those, I recommend the U.S. Bureau of the Budget's *Household Survey Manual 1969* and Robert Payne's *The Art of Asking Questions* (Princeton, N.J.: Princeton University Press, 1951). Studying these works will help you design an adequate questionnaire. This is one more area in which an early start and wise pre-campaign investments of time can be critical in helping you to mount a professional-style campaign.

Pre-testing the questionnaire, which should be the prelude to any survey, enables you to "shake out" the questionnaire and to anticipate most of the problems of completing and processing it. Your people must be instructed to use the exact language of each question without modifications, to follow the sequence of questions as given, and, in the case of open-ended questions, to write down the respondents' answers in the respondents' own words as accurately as possible.

A minimum of twenty interviews by trained workers (or, lacking those, by your best available workers) should be carried out in the pre-testing process. A senior member of the campaign staff should be involved. New questions and revisions of others will probably occur as this staff member sees and hears the results of the pre-test calls. Any significant changes that he wishes to make in the questionnaire should be subjected to a new round of pre-testing. Generally, in pre-testing, questions can be profitably dropped as well as added or modified. Questions may be resequenced, and probing directives may be added. ("Probing" is defined in a footnote on page 113.)

After pre-testing has been completed and a final questionnaire decided upon, reproduce a sufficient number of questionnaires for the entire sample, plus about 20 percent to allow for mistakes and to provide copies for the records.

Training interviewers. Impress upon your interviewers that they

GOOD EVENING, MRS. _____, I'M MISS _____ FROM RESEARCH SURVEYS. WE'RE CONDUCTING
AN OPINION SURVEY OF DEMOCRATIC VOTERS ON THE SOUTH SIDE. MAY WE HAVE A FEW MOMENTS OF
YOUR TIME?

1. WHAT DO YOU THINK IS THE MOST IMPORTANT PROBLEM IN YOUR NEIGHBORHOOD TODAY?
   _____   6 –
   _____   7 –
   _____

2. WHAT KIND OF JOB DO YOU THINK THE MAYOR IS DOING?   WOULD YOU SAY.....
         Excellent   8–1   Fair   –3
         Good   –2   Poor   –4

2a. (If Fair or Poor) WHY DO YOU FEEL THAT WAY?   _____   9 –
    _____   10 –
    _____

3. DO YOU SUPPORT THE PRESIDENT'S VIET-NAM POLICY?   YES   11–1   NO   –2

4. IF THE ELECTION FOR PRESIDENT WERE HELD TODAY, WHO WOULD YOU VOTE FOR?
   _____   12 –

5. DO YOU CONSIDER YOURSELF A REGULAR, REFORM OR INDEPENDENT DEMOCRAT?
         Regular   13–1   Reform   –2   Independent   –3

6. IN YOUR OPINION, WHO ARE THE TWO LEADING DEMOCRATS IN ILLINOIS?
   _____   14 –

7. WHICH OF THE FOLLOWING NAMES HAVE YOU HEARD OF?   (Check)
         Politician A   15–1   Politician E   –5
         Politician B   –2   Politician F   –6
         Politician C   –3   Politician G   –7
         Politician D   –4   Politician H   –8

8. IF YOU WERE MAYOR OF CHICAGO, WHAT WOULD BE THE FIRST THING YOU WOULD DO?
   _____   16 –
   _____
   _____

I HAVE JUST ONE OR TWO MORE STATISTICAL QUESTIONS TO ASK YOU.
9. HOW MANY PERSONS IN YOUR FAMILY? _____   17 –
   (If more than 2, ask:)
9a. ARE THERE PERSONS OVER 60 IN YOUR FAMILY?   YES   18–1   NO   –2
9b. ARE THERE ANY CHILDREN UNDER 14 IN YOUR FAMILY?   YES   19–1   NO   –2

THANK YOU SO MUCH FOR YOUR TIME.
CLASSIFICATION: Sex: Male   20–1   Female   –2
                   Area: ED _____ 21–   AD _____ 23–
                                         22–   24–
         Ethnic: Irish   25–1   Italian   –2   Jewish   –3
                   Negro   –4   Yugoslav   –5   Polish   –6
                   German   –7   Other   –8

Name: _____
Address _____ Telephone Number _____
Refusal _____
Interviewer _____ Identification Number _____
Attempts: 1   2   3   Substitution made _____

are to seek objective responses and that a sample survey is not an appropriate opportunity to proselytize for your cause. Remind them that they are not to say they are doing the survey for you (your questionnaire will include a statement to the effect that they are doing it for the party or for a research bureau, a political committee, or some other such body), and be sure that they understand that "no response," "don't know," and even refusals to discuss an issue are legitimate responses which should be duly entered on the questionnaire.

The best way to train interviewers is to go through the entire questionnaire word by word and not leave anything to the interviewers' interpretation. Then give each interviewer the opportunity to play the role of interviewer and the role of respondent, and allow the interviewers who participated in the pre-test to discuss their experiences. Interviewers should also be drilled in entering responses on the questionnaire forms with particular emphasis on writing down open-ended responses in the respondents' own words, being careful to register at least the key phrases of the responses. Inexperienced persons should be allowed to interview only after a minimum of three hours of training.

Interviewing. The supervisor should check the results of each day's interviews to assure that responses are entered properly and that each interviewer understands the assignment. One interviewer may be found to be "prompting" answers while another one may be discovered to be omitting "don't know" responses from the form. Constant supervision must be provided to anticipate or at least stem these errors in order to assure something approaching professional quality.

Each interviewer should be reminded to write down any important information volunteered by the respondent, whether or not it relates to the questionnaire. Such information should be entered in the spaces left for comments. It may be something detrimental to the candidate that the respondent has heard in the neighborhood (whether or not the information reported has any basis in fact), or it may be a comment about something that happened during a walking tour. Bits of information gathered in this way are sometimes very important.

Coding, editing, and cross-tabulating. Coding consists of recording responses by category. Multi-choice questions are essentially self-coded—each question on the questionnaire has a blank space after each choice; when the interviewer checks the appropriate one, the response is coded—but at times new codes are needed for "other" responses. Editing, necessary for open-ended questions and sometimes for other types of questions as well, involves checking responses for obvious mistakes (for example, answers filled in on the wrong line of the questionnaire) and then putting similar answers into a single category for coding. Cross-tabulating is drawing up final tables that summarize the data, for example, "crossing" income by candidate preferred.

Just as your interviewing should be done by no more than five or six persons, only two or at most three should do the coding and editing. A member of your staff whom you trust to perform detailed work properly should set up the codes for the open-ended questions and should personally look at half the completed questionnaires. The codes that he sets up at this stage are extremely important. They will determine the quality and style of the cross-tabulations, and it will be from the cross-tabulations that you will make some of the most important decisions of the campaign. If at this late stage, your representative discovers that the questionnaires have not been prepared properly, it makes more sense to abandon the project than to make cross-tabulations on the basis of the possibly misleading data of the questionnaires.

Questionnaires generally include demographic data so that political client-group information can be obtained from the completed survey. For example, it is usual to ask the respondent's age ("Are you under or over 65 years of age?"), race, sex, and any other such identification question that might be locally important ("Are you a member of the chamber of commerce?"). The respondent's name itself can often provide an indication of his ethnic or religious group, questions that usually are not asked directly but are often critically important. These characteristics are usually important in the design of the cross-tabulations, which are usually cumulations of questionnaire responses compared with demographic data (for example, what percentage of people over 65 plan to vote for you) or of questionnaire answers cross-classified with other questionnaire answers (for example, what percentage of people who intend to vote for your opponent would be impressed by an endorsement from a certain local politician).

As a practical example, a question that is usually asked in surveys is: "If you had to vote today in the primary, whom would you vote for? Candidate A _____ Candidate B _____ Candidate C _____ Undecided _____." Demographic cross-tabulations of the replies to this question might take the following form:

INCOME	CAND. A	CAND. B	CAND. C	UNDECIDED	REFUSED
Under $10,000	%	%	%	%	%
Over $10,000	%	%	%	%	%
Totals	%	%	%	%	%
AGE					
Under 65	%	%	%	%	%
Over 65	%	%	%	%	%
Totals	%	%	%	%	%
GEOGRAPHIC					
Assembly Dist. 1	%	%	%	%	%
Assembly Dist. 2	%	%	%	%	%
Assembly Dist. 3	%	%	%	%	%
Totals	%	%	%	%	%

On pages 122–25 are examples of computer printouts of cross-tabs from a 1970 survey conducted to establish which client groups in a local area favored certain possible candidates for governor of New York. The survey was commissioned by a local candidate who wished to evaluate potential endorsements. (Incidentally, Governor Nelson Rockefeller's vulnerability was strongly established. It is often forgotten that the purpose of early polls is to examine objectively the conditions of the contest. The campaign is designed to change these early readings, and that is precisely what Rockefeller did, thereby beating Arthur J. Goldberg, the eventual Democratic nominee, by a large margin.) Note that computer cross-tabs normally provide both "raw" figures and percentages. In these printouts, the percentages appear below the raw figures.

The following six tables are from a survey I did several years ago. Using a sample of 600 voters and the procedures recommended in this book, I was able to predict with considerable precision the outcome of each assembly race in Manhattan. The survey was costly, since the sampling took five days of work—it included two substitute decks because of unique difficulties in Manhattan involving unlisted telephone numbers, single persons not at home, and high move rates

—but the results were extremely worthwhile. The possible cross-tabulations were in the hundreds, but I chose twenty-five—of which six are shown here—as being most useful for the purposes of the survey. Some professionals actually run hundreds of cross-tabulations—usually because the campaign staff are not certain what they are looking for—but I have never found more than thirty-five tables necessary even in the most difficult races.

Table 1 provides information useful in developing a profile of potential client groups that would react favorably to attacks on the administration currently in office.

Table 1

ETHNIC GROUP	TOTALS	VERY SATISFIED	SATISFIED	HALF SATISFIED	NOT SATISFIED
Irish	149	10	63	32	40
Italian	85	13	40	14	13
Jewish	262	6	91	57	81
Negro	178	11	91	32	30
Puerto Rican	54	7	35	1	6
Other	272	18	92	63	85
SEX					
Female	562	35	216	110	148
Male	438	30	196	89	106
Totals	1,000	65	412	199	255

Table 2 is a basic tool in political research—a measure of the endorsement strengths of various leaders at the time of the survey. Former Governor Herbert H. Lehman's endorsement was clearly the most important.

Table 2

ETHNIC GROUPS	FINLETTER	LEHMAN	RYAN	WAGNER	TOTALS
Irish	6	38	23	44	149
Italian	—	23	7	43	85
Jewish	16	128	28	34	262
Negro	—	68	7	78	178
Puerto Rican	—	7	—	33	54
Other	2	98	25	72	272
SEX					
Female	8	191	43	177	562
Male	16	171	47	127	438
Totals	24	362	90	304	1,000

PREFERENCE FOR GOVERNOR   Q-3

	TOTAL	JEW-ISH	IRISH	ITAL-IAN	NEGRO	PUER-TO RICAN	WHITE PROT-ES-TANT
TOTAL	153	78	36	18	9	1	11
	100.0	100.0	100.0	100.0	100.0	100.0	100.0

IF CHOICE WERE BETWEEN ROCKEFELLER AND SAMUELS

	TOTAL	JEW-ISH	IRISH	ITAL-IAN	NEGRO	PUER-TO RICAN	WHITE PROT-ES-TANT
ROCKEFELLER	18	4	5	7	2		
	11.8	5.1	13.9	38.9	22.2		
SAMUELS	46	25	10	4	2	1	4
	30.1	32.1	27.8	22.2	22.2	100.0	36.4
UNDECIDED	89	49	21	7	5		7
	58.2	62.8	58.3	38.9	55.6		63.6

IF CHOICE WERE BETWEEN ROCKEFELLER AND GOLDBERG

	TOTAL	JEW-ISH	IRISH	ITAL-IAN	NEGRO	PUER-TO RICAN	WHITE PROT-ES-TANT
ROCKEFELLER	14	3	5	5	1		
	9.2	3.8	13.9	27.8	11.1		
GOLDBERG	76	51	16	7			2
	49.7	65.4	44.4	38.9			18.2
UNDECIDED	63	24	15	6	8	1	9
	41.2	30.8	41.7	33.3	88.9	100.0	81.8

IF CHOICE WERE BETWEEN ROCKEFELLER AND VANDER HEUVEL

	TOTAL	JEW-ISH	IRISH	ITAL-IAN	NEGRO	PUER-TO RICAN	WHITE PROT-ES-TANT
ROCKEFELLER	15	6	3	5	1		
	9.8	7.7	8.3	27.8	11.1		
VANDER HEUVEL	30	16	10	2			2
	19.6	20.5	27.8	11.1			18.2
UNDECIDED	108	56	23	11	8	1	9
	70.6	71.8	63.9	61.1	88.9	100.0	81.8

IF CHOICE WERE BETWEEN ROCKEFELLER AND NICKERSON

	TOTAL	JEW-ISH	IRISH	ITAL-IAN	NEGRO	PUER-TO RICAN	WHITE PROT-ES-TANT
ROCKEFELLER	22	11	6	4	1		
	14.4	14.1	16.7	22.2	11.1		
NICKERSON	46	22	10	10	1		3
	30.1	28.2	27.8	55.6	11.1		27.3

--- SEX ---		----- AGE -----			--- INCOME ---			----- A D -----		
MALE	FE-MALE	UNDER 60	OVER 60	NO ANSWER	UNDER $10,000	OVER $10,000	NO ANSWER	80	82	84
63	90	104	42	7	42	98	13	57	11	85
100.0	100.0	100.0	100.0	100.0	100.0	100.0	100.0	100.0	100.0	100.0
12	6	17	1		6	10	2	11	2	5
19.0	6.7	16.3	2.4		14.3	10.2	15.4	19.3	18.2	5.9
18	28	37	7	2	10	34	2	18	1	27
28.6	31.1	35.6	16.7	28.6	23.8	34.7	15.4	31.6	9.1	31.8
33	56	50	34	5	26	54	9	28	8	53
52.4	62.2	48.1	81.0	71.4	61.9	55.1	69.2	49.1	72.7	62.4
8	6	12	2		3	10	1	7		7
12.7	6.7	11.5	4.8		7.1	10.2	7.7	12.3		8.2
30	46	61	12	3	13	59	4	25	1	50
47.6	51.1	58.7	28.6	42.9	31.0	60.2	30.8	43.9	9.1	58.8
25	38	31	28	4	26	29	8	25	10	28
39.7	42.2	29.8	66.7	57.1	61.9	29.6	61.5	43.9	90.9	32.9
9	6	14	1		3	11	1	7		8
14.3	6.7	13.5	2.4		7.1	11.2	7.7	12.3		9.4
10	20	23	6	1	4	24	2	12	1	17
15.9	22.2	22.1	14.3	14.3	9.5	24.5	15.4	21.1	9.1	20.0
44	64	67	35	6	35	63	10	38	10	60
69.8	71.1	64.4	83.3	85.7	83.3	64.3	76.9	66.7	90.9	70.6
9	13	20	2		3	17	2	8		14
14.3	14.4	19.2	4.8		7.1	17.3	15.4	14.0		16.5
24	22	33	12	1	14	32		22	2	22
38.1	24.4	31.7	28.6	14.3	33.3	32.7		38.6	18.2	25.9

WHO WOULD YOU LIKE TO SEE THE DEMOCRATS

--------- ETHNIC GROUP ----------

CANDIDATE	TOTAL	JEW-ISH	IRISH	ITAL-IAN	NEGRO	PUER-TO RICAN	WHITE PROT-ES-TANT
TOTAL	153 100.0	78 100.0	36 100.0	18 100.0	9 100.0	1 100.0	11 100.0
SAMUELS	14 9.2	10 12.8	2 5.6		1 11.1	1 100.0	
GOLDBERG	43 28.1	36 46.2	6 16.7				1 9.1
VANDER HEUVEL	4 2.6	1 1.3	2 5.6				1 9.1
NICKERSON	11 7.2	3 3.8	4 11.1	1 5.6			3 27.3
MACKELL	4 2.6		4 11.1				
NEGRO							
MORGANTHEAU	2 1.3	1 1.3			1 11.1		
SMITH	1 .7			1 5.6			
PROCACCINO	2 1.3			1 2.8	1 5.6		
UNDECIDED	72 47.1	27 34.6	17 47.2	15 83.3	7 77.8		6 54.5

NOMINATE FOR GOVERNOR Q-6

| | --- SEX --- | | ----- AGE ----- | | | --- INCOME --- | | | ----- A D ----- | |
MALE	FE-MALE	UNDER 60	OVER 60	NO ANSW-ER	UNDER $10,000	OVER $10,000	NO ANSW-ER	80	82	84
63	90	104	42	7	42	98	13	57	11	85
100.0	100.0	100.0	100.0	100.0	100.0	100.0	100.0	100.0	100.0	100.0
4	10	11	3		3	10	1	4		10
6.3	11.1	10.6	7.1		7.1	10.2	7.7	7.0		11.8
21	22	35	7	1	7	33	3	8	2	33
33.3	24.4	33.7	16.7	14.3	16.7	33.7	23.1	14.0	18.2	38.8
2	2	4				4		3		1
3.2	2.2	3.8				4.1		5.3		1.2
6	5	6	5		3	8		6		5
9.5	5.6	5.8	11.9		7.1	8.2		10.5		5.9
3	1	3	1		2	2		3		1
4.8	1.1	2.9	2.4		4.8	2.0		5.3		1.2
2		1	1			2			1	1
3.2		1.0	2.4			2.0			9.1	1.2
1		1			1			1		
1.6		1.0			2.4			1.8		
1	1	1	1			2		2		
1.6	1.1	1.0	2.4			2.0		3.5		
23	49	42	24	6	26	37	9	30	8	34
36.5	54.4	40.4	57.1	85.7	61.9	37.8	69.2	52.6	72.7	40.0

Table 3 relates party-faction adherence to ethnic group and sex, giving the candidate a way of learning which groups of voters are likely to be sympathetic to his faction.

Table 3

ETHNIC GROUP	REGULAR	REFORM	INDEPENDENT	TOTALS
Irish	68	28	32	149
Italian	46	11	10	85
Jewish	101	59	60	262
Negro	85	33	28	178
Puerto Rican	35	7	6	54
Other	108	41	58	272
SEX				
Female	258	88	96	562
Male	185	91	98	438
Totals	443	179	194	1,000

At the time of this study, New York City's fiscal problems were a critical political issue. Table 4 provides a sense of which solution was favored by voters in which geographic areas. Such information would be particularly useful in street campaigning and in preparing brochures for distribution on the street.

Table 4

	OFF-TRACK BETTING	INCOME TAX	STATE AID	FEDERAL AID	SALES TAX	CIGARETTE TAX	TOTALS
Greenwich Village	27	2	10	1	1	11	63
Lower Manhattan	58	6	10	5	—	10	106
West Side	113	5	26	12	5	23	212
Middle East Side	109	3	22	15	5	28	209
Harlem	184	16	22	23	3	12	280
Washington Heights	78	2	10	10	2	9	130
Totals	569	34	100	66	16	93	1,000

Table 5 provides information similiar to that in Table 4, except that it registers favored solutions by ethnic group and sex. This information would be useful in targeting mailings.

Table 5

ETHNIC GROUP	OFF-TRACK BETTING	INCOME TAX	STATE AID	FEDERAL AID	STATE TAX	CIGARETTE TAX	TOTALS
Irish	90	2	14	14	2	10	149
Italian	44	8	11	2	3	9	85
Jewish	135	9	46	15	2	32	262
Negro	118	4	7	18	2	9	178
Puerto Rican	37	6	—	2	1	2	54
Other	145	5	22	15	7	31	272
SEX							
Female	286	16	60	39	6	64	562
Male	283	18	40	27	10	29	438
Totals	569	34	100	66	16	93	1,000

Table 6 illustrates the frustrating but quite typical inconsistency of American voters. Many who expressed dissatisfaction with conditions in their neighborhoods liked the administration. The focus of the campaign would be to tie the voters' environmental dissatisfaction to the incumbent city administration.

Table 6

DEGREE OF SATISFACTION WITH ADMINISTRATION	ENVIRONMENTAL SATISFACTION		
	SATISFIED	DISSATISFIED	TOTALS
Very satisfied	20	43	65
Satisfied	176	233	412
Half satisfied	76	121	199
Not satisfied	81	165	255
Don't know or no response	35	28	69
Totals	307	591	1,000

Even if you have only limited amounts of money to spend on research, completed questionnaires of good quality would justify hiring a professional computer house for the tabulation process. It is possible to do tabulations by hand, but only with the probable loss of accuracy and only for a limited number of cross-tabulations. Since, as can be seen even from the single example given above, cross-tabulations can extract a great deal of potentially useful information from a questionnaire, it is clearly in your interest to have as many of them available as seem relevant and useful. Doing sizable numbers of cross-tabulations by hand is so arduous and time-consuming as to be practically impossible. This is probably the research investment that many candidates may find most advantageous for focusing any small amount of money they may have for outside consultants.

Key punching on IBM cards (with 100 percent verification—that is, checking each punched card for accuracy) and computing 50 basic tables should not cost more than $500 for most smaller sample sizes. If you can afford it, this is an extremely sensible investment.

Analyzing results. All the work you've done on a survey is worth nothing unless it is analyzed intelligently. In many instances, a candidate concludes from survey data that he is gaining on his opponent, and this may comfort him. The data, however, are really only a beginning and not a conclusion. The whole purpose of campaigning is to act intelligently to change the conclusion. (John V. Lindsay's victory over Mario Procaccino in 1969 and Nelson Rockefeller's victory over Arthur J. Goldberg in 1970 are only two of many examples in recent memory in which candidates have won elections after initial polls showed them to be certain losers.) Many facts and perceptions can be gained from or confirmed by cross-tabulations. For example, a candidate who finds he is gaining on his opponent may discover which groups still are not responding to his appeals and why they are not. Areas and groups in which undecided voters are concentrated and demographic characteristics of the undecided voters are other critical types of information that can be obtained by doing the correct cross-tabulations.

Professional research reports analyzing survey results run at times over 100 pages and include perhaps 40 to 50 tables. Often you have to be a professional yourself to know how it all relates to specific decisions. Many times the candidate depends on the analyst to make recommendations without really having time to examine the results himself. Many professional statisticians are only infrequently in campaign work and cannot be depended on for major decisions, since, in order to cover themselves, they will often qualify findings even if a major political crisis is staring them in the face.

Analyzing the results of surveys usefully will depend very much on the political and statistical experience of your advisers. As has already been pointed out, each survey should be designed to answer specific, practical questions and not academic considerations. The cross-tabulations should help you decide at least these basics:

- Which are the important issues?
- How to deal with the really hot issues?
- What are the characteristics of the undecided voters?
- Whose endorsement would be helpful?
- Whose endorsement would hurt?

The techniques of statistical analysis cannot be summarized in a few pages. Professional-level analysis requires experience in both statistics and politics; few professional statisticians are really talented campaigners. Sophisticated mathematical analysis is usually not required. Cross-tabulating responses about issues with race, ethnic characteristics, income, age, sex, and residence of the respondents is usually sufficient to isolate the problems of greatest concern to the voters. (For example, in the table on page 131 note that crime and drugs concern groups in almost every county.) Percent change and percent distributions are usually the only statistical devices used in professional analyses; the critical skill required is not so much statistical as it is a talent for combining the various tables to find the essential meaning of the voters' moods and opinions. Survey research in the hands of a talented, experienced man is a great blessing to a candidate; but the candidate still has to spend time to discuss results and devote some study himself to the data.

I would recommend not depending only on the most obvious data for decisions—for example, the percentage split between you and your opponent(s). Sometimes an issue comes up early in the campaign that at that time is statistically insignificant. Maybe, for example, 5 percent of the respondents don't like your "appearance." This would show up in associative questions; as a result, you may be advised to wear different ties and a more (or less) modern cut of clothing. A second poll may show that 8 percent are not pleased by your appearance. Since sampling reliability generally declines as the sample size decreases, the difference of 3 percent is statistically insignificant, but the matter may be worth looking into anyway. It may be that you sound too intransigent or talk too fast or don't look at the camera, or that something is bothering the voters that they can't articulate. It's only 5 percent or 8 percent, advisers may say. Keep in mind, however, that most elections are decided by less than a 10 percent difference between the candidates. What you must consider is how much of the other 92 to 95 percent may tacitly share the criticism of the vocal 5 percent.

In smaller campaigns, my recommendation is to have your survey consultant prepare the cross-tabulations on the questions most concerning you and then have his technician sit down with you and your advisers and discuss what the data mean. Often consultants will prepare handsome presentations, including tables, graphs, and charts and many pages of text in which people with limited political experience rehash the obvious. Top-quality consultants may charge $15,000 to $20,000 for doing 250 to 300 household interviews in depth and supplying a written report. You may save some money and get a more useful product by hiring them only to produce the interview data and having your staff contract directly with a computer house for the cross-tabulations you feel will be useful. The consultant should be willing to discuss the results with you for a fair additional fee.

DETAILED FINDINGS

PRIMARY QUESTIONNAIRE

% DISTRIBUTION

Question 2:

What do you think are the most important problems in your community (town)?

	County A	County B	County C	County D	County E	County F	County G	County H
Economic Issues (Inflation and Recession)	35	31	16	4	4	9	29	18
Youth	31	21	19	17	12	10	28	15
Drugs	22	39	40	49	31	16	34	53
Sanitation	6	1	3	6	8	7	1	1
Pollution	5	4	6	5	5	10	1	3
Transportation	3	6	6	8	4	3	3	-
Integration	3	6	6	1	-	3	8	3
Poverty - Welfare	3	4	5	1	2	3	4	1
Housing (Rents)	3	7	4	10	6	9	12	8
Crime	2	2	18	31	36	37	13	1
Other	3	1	3	-	2	4	-	3
Total (Including Duplication)	116	122	126	132	110	126	133	106

4 Campaign Problems

*In campaigns people don't develop a reasoned approach,
and the trouble with most analyses of political behavior by
political scientists is that they attribute a reasoned working out of things which are not worked out reasonably...*
—A VOLPE ADVISER*

Designing a campaign properly is a creative process that involves
intuition, experience, and some luck in personnel selection.† Some
observers of the process, however, come away disenchanted and
appalled at what they think is a deliberate, mechanistic effort, using
artifice and sophisticated technology, to manipulate the emotions and
predispositions of the electorate. Such a reaction is not always entirely rational: Some of the people who were favorably impressed by
Robert F. Kennedy's use of the media found Conservative James L.
Buckley's use of similar techniques somehow immoral and threatening.

The workings of the democratic process, in the final analysis, depend on the intelligence of the voting constituency. Although many
political scientists are disturbed by the small percentage of primary
voters and by the inferior information voters respond to, the American political process has nonetheless worked for the past two cen-

* Quoted in Murray B. Levin and George Blackwood, *The Compleat Politician: Political Strategy in Massachusetts* (Indianapolis, Ind.: Bobbs-Merrill,
1962).
† Every campaign needs a few breaks. The brilliant campaigner can force
some breaks, but no one can force them all. The Slavic maxim, "If you're
lucky, even your broom will shoot," has relevance in some campaigns. Yet
the role of "luck" in drawing the first position, in getting press and television
coverage at just the right time, for example, has never been scientifically
explored.

turies, and the American form of government has lasted longer than any other. The process, often irrational and wasteful, can offer no assurance that the best man will win. Indeed, many of the nation's best men have been denied elective office by their refusal to accommodate party leaders or by defeat at the polls. Over a period of time, however, the basic intelligence and sensibility of the voters have made the process work. The continued effectiveness of the democratic process depends to some degree on attracting able, independent men to public office. Such men will not allow themselves to be encumbered by campaign promises, so they will be able to respond freely and intelligently to the massive, seemingly insoluble problems facing our cities and the nation. For such men, the use of sophisticated campaign techniques may make more economical campaigns possible and therefore limit the necessity for making political contracts in order to raise sufficient funds.*

In order to compete while retaining most of their policy discretion, such men will need to use the techniques described in this book—techniques that are by no means Machiavellian and that have been used, in various forms, for decades. Television has changed the campaign context to some extent, but not as radically as some people apparently believe. A candidate can dissimulate on television, but he cannot do it for very long without the charade becoming obvious. In this regard, the public is becoming increasingly sophisticated and sensitized to the uses of campaigning artifice. One of the "slickest" campaigns in years was the effort to get voter approval for the New York State transportation bond issue in 1971. The campaign, costing $2.5 million, used computer letter endorsements, TV, newspaper

---

* The law of political contract is as binding as the law of business contract, although it generally is not based on written or signed documents. "Carrying a contract" is an important part of political life; it means delivering a job to a party regular or delivering construction awards to a major campaign contributor. It means trading endorsements or judgeships for jobs, future unspecified favors, and policy discretion. For example, a contributor may ask to name the commissioner of urban development or ask for the right to veto certain nominees for the job. The press naturally emphasizes the shady aspects of such tradeoffs, but that is how the business of government gets carried out and that is not so very different from the normal routines of American business. The process fails when taking care of friends and personal contracts results in the public's getting 70 cents on a dollar although they are entitled to, say, 95 cents (allowing for normal wastage), and when societal priorities are disturbed by the precedence given personal or political priorities.

ads, and virtually everything else in the advertising arsenal—but the bond issue was overwhelmingly defeated.*

Although each campaign has unique elements, almost all have similar characteristics as well. Fund raising, logistics, and certain other problems that candidates face are almost universally shared. Others are common but do not characterize all campaigns. These problems are the subject of this chapter.

Competitive fund-raising

The growing incidence of multi-candidate party primaries has caused considerable difficulty for candidates who share philosophical and political positions with their colleagues. They inevitably share the same fund-raising base as well. In the winter of 1971, for example, there were many press reports that some of the potential financial contributors to Senator Edmund S. Muskie's drive for the presidential nomination were waiting to see whether Senator Hubert H. Humphrey intended to make the race. Mayor John V. Lindsay and Senator George McGovern had similar problems until Lindsay dropped out of the competition.

Similarly, in 1969, Herman Badillo encountered financial difficulties in his primary race for the New York City mayoralty. He was said to have received former Mayor Robert F. Wagner's blessing and encouragement regarding the probable generosity of past contributors to Wagner's campaigns. Then Wagner decided he might make the race himself, and Badillo's sources dried up. It was rumored that Badillo finally spent $500,000 in his primary bid in a five-way race. His campaign manager, Steve Berger, was quoted in press reports as saying that, since Badillo lost by a very small margin to Judge Mario Procaccino, the availability of additional money for television might have made the difference.

There is no easy way out of this problem. You have to make potential contributors believe you have a better chance of winning, or offer more than your opponents in the way of "contractual" obliga-

* The major part of the answer to the question of why the bill lost "may be in the nature of politics which is supposed to be divisive. . . . In the American system . . . politicians are supposed to compete and dispute, and when two men [who are political enemies] . . . urge the public to vote 'Heck, yes,' the public's answer is more likely than not to be 'Heck, no!' " ("Talk of the Town," *The New Yorker,* November 13, 1971.)

tions. (See footnote, page 134.) Otherwise, you may have to recognize that you'll raise less money than you hoped for and plan your expenditures accordingly from the start. In the first instance, when it comes to money, a candidate should never count "possibles" as "probables." This is particularly important in budgeting. The budget should be as tight and as realistic as possible. For example, both Muskie and Badillo were reported to have maintained elaborate suites of offices, large staffs—25 to 40 full-time paid people in Badillo's case and hundreds in Muskie's national campaign—as well as other expensive appurtenances that may or may not have been absolutely necessary. Some commentators suggested that Badillo would have had the money for television if his overhead (including payroll) had been less costly. Running for city comptroller on the ticket headed by Badillo, State Senator Harrison J. Goldin leased a very small office (at the same hotel that housed the more extensive Badillo headquarters) and reportedly staffed it with an unpaid campaign manager and four or five unpaid workers. He was said to have spent three-fourths of his budget on television, and, although he lost, he still made an impressive showing.

Pooling resources with other candidates

This problem is one aspect of the financial difficulties that characterize many campaigns. If you're running with a ticket in a primary against another segment of the party or in a general election, you can pool your resources with other candidates on your ticket to reduce costs. For example, a shared mailing can be done so the 4.5 cents postage per envelope is shared two or three ways. Or you can get together and share the cost of developing the computer tape of primary voters, including the expensive process of taking the names from the election rolls and putting them on IBM cards.

The ethnication process—machine sorting of voter lists by ethnic or other characteristics—is expensive. There is no reason for each candidate on a slate to do this separately, but many do.

Costs of "finders' books" can also be shared. These books listing the election district and assembly district for any street address have been developed by various computer firms. In New York in 1972, for example, since the state had been extensively redistricted, new finders' books were especially useful in assigning the election and assembly districts to the addresses given by voters in signing candidates' petitions. Filling them in by hand would have been a laborious —and probably error-ridden—project. A computer house compiled finders' books, which it sold to various candidates for $300 to $500 per district. The firm would have been delighted to run all addresses in the entire city through a computer for a single sales order that could have been shared by many candidates on one party slate. It would undoubtedly have given a quantity discount for so large an order, and candidates for many offices would have saved money, effort, and time. Yet it was not done. Such sensible sharing of basic overhead expenses is rare and, in my judgment, is an important reason why many campaigns are needlessly expensive.

If two or three candidates share one telephone location, they can save significantly in supervision and rent for telephone campaigns. In smaller campaigns, using a service bureau to look up telephone numbers will probably cost 5 or 6 cents a name, yet I have repeatedly seen candidates, supposedly allied, duplicate efforts and expenses in looking up telephone numbers.

Surveys conducted for several candidates on the same ticket who share the expenses can also save each candidate money. It is even likely that combining research budgets may result in better research for all participating candidates. Unfortunately, in many campaigns, every candidate appears to be in business for himself. Many politicians jealously guard their prerogatives even at the risk of incurring considerably increased costs. Some candidates wish to have exclusive control over design of brochures and to whom they should be mailed. Some candidates running together as a slate may disagree about placement of their names on shopping bags or on a billboard. Sometimes these concerns are legitimate, but more often they reflect the insecurities and incompetencies brought about by campaign anxieties and the fact that everyone involved seems to regard himself as at least as qualified to make decisions on every aspect of campaigning as anyone else. These are very expensive conceits, indeed. If you are running for the first time, you'll have your hands full without spending money that could be saved by working with the other people who are on your ticket. Of course, there are times when there is no chance to come to any reasonable agreement with your fellow candidates. Arguing and discussing are a waste of time in such cases, and any concessions will cost you money anyway. In such situations, you are simply forced to go it alone.

Control of theme development

In many campaigns, media men or advertising men assume control of theme development, often without using sophisticated research even if that research happens to be available. Their concern is to put something on film or paper that has impact on the voter.

In some instances, you may be told by an advertising agency, after a few discussions lasting several hours, that such-and-such is the only logical theme. You and your campaign advisers are likely to be overwhelmed, since advertising is an area of expertise in which you may not consider yourselves competent. And once you commit the media theme, you'll find you'll have to live with it for good or bad and that it will directly affect other aspects of the campaign. It is much better to lay out the overall campaign strategy first, with or without media people, and then have them adjust their specific work to fit your strategy rather than let them decide on a theme perhaps quite arbitrarily and then design a campaign around this possibly peripheral theme. The agency's key decisions should include: specific media content illustrating the campaign theme, how many spots or ads to produce, their length, which stations to use, and how often to show the film or newspaper advertisements. There are specialists in this kind of planning and decision making, but since each is interested in maximizing the use of the medium or media he or his firm is involved in, you should bear this in mind and not rely exclusively on his judgment in setting up your campaign theme.

The advertising agency generally receives a commission or rebate based on volume. You may therefore decide to retain a specialist to purchase air time and let local advertising agencies produce the copy and/or films, paying them a consulting fee for this service. Some agencies may, in fact, prefer such an arrangement.*

---

* Some advertising agencies have a policy of not participating in political campaigns. For example, Doyle, Dane, Bernbach, a leading firm, instructed its staff several years ago to take leaves of absence if they wished to work in campaigns. Candidates may be able to hire individual advertising technicians rather than an agency.

Taking the first loss

The stock market saying that the first loss is the best loss applies to campaigning as well. You may, for example, plan to distribute a brochure that your staff regards as brilliant and that involved much staff preparation but that has drawn a measure of negative public reaction. Despite the fact that preparation of the brochure was costly and that 10,000 copies were printed, you probably should destroy all the remaining copies. Don't assume anything categorically or automatically. Listen to the voters' reactions to media. If they are negative, you may save yourself future grief by taking the first loss.

In a recent campaign, a candidate widely distributed a palm card with his photograph on one side and a list of convenient telephone numbers (fire, ambulance, hospital, pollution control center, etc.) on the other. His photographer had suggested that he looked handsome without his glasses, but since his strategy depended heavily on street campaigning, and since he always wore his glasses out of doors, the palm card did not contribute effectively to increasing his voter recognition. Nevertheless, he refused to have another card printed showing him with glasses, even though it would have accomplished what he intended. He should have suppressed the first card, written off his investment, and replaced it with one that showed him as he normally looked. Some candidates automatically assume that loudspeakers on cars and trucks can drum up interest, but many voters find them quite annoying. In some areas, a significant portion of the electorate may complain. Although you may have spent $500 or more to rent the equipment and the cars, it may be better to withdraw the equipment as soon as complaints begin to come in. Decisions such as these have to be made in every campaign; too often, the choice is made to gamble on an investment already made and hope for the best. Such a course is neither good business nor good politics. Refusing to acknowledge a mistake and throwing good money after bad are common weaknesses in campaigning. You should face up to your mistakes, and sometimes you may simply have to write off a substantial investment. By making staff changes or developing better staff coordination, you may possibly insure against a recurrence. If, however, you are the one who made the mistake, and you choose to repeat it, it is of course your option, but you deserve to lose, and you probably will.

"Improper" quotations and "dirty" tactics

Sometimes your opponent will attack you with one of your statements taken out of context. It is an effective tactic and often employed. If you defend yourself, he will interpret your defense as a confession of guilt. For that reason, some candidates ignore such incidents altogether, preferring not to give the statement any more publicity. A better response may well be to attack your opponent for unfair campaign practices, make a formal complaint to the fair campaign practices committee in your city or state, and publicly attack his lack of integrity and call attention to his use of gutter tactics.

To adopt a defensive stance in such a situation generally accomplishes little. As a number of campaign professionals have observed, the American public likes a good fight and becomes really interested in a campaign only if it senses one. However, many politicians today are advised to be cool, not to display emotion. It is pretty hard to put up a good fight and not display emotion. The trick is to use your emotions without affecting your judgment, allowing the voters to sense your dimensions as a human being, not only as a political party representative who wants their votes. Senator Muskie's public tears because of a newspaper's attacks on his wife were widely believed to have contributed to his relatively poor showing in the New Hampshire Democratic primary in 1972. On the other hand, Richard Nixon's emotional "Checkers" speech in his vice presidential campaign of 1952 put sentiment to his advantage. The lesson seems to be to avoid unreasonable or excessive emotion and to control your feelings, carefully picking the spots when and where you let your emotions show. Campaigns conducted on a completely even emotional level can be deadly boring to the voter.

Fairly often the press may quote you out of context or make harmful and inaccurate statements about you, but it is difficult to attack the local newspapers in the course of a campaign. Sometimes you may have to—as Mario Procaccino attacked the New York *Daily News* in 1969 for its public opinion polling procedures—but only as a last resort. It's wise to have a good working relationship with the men who cover your campaign. They tend to appreciate candor and some personal attention—informal meetings over a drink are probably good supplements to the usual formal press conferences in a campaign. Like everybody else, they would probably appreciate any interest you show in them as human beings.

Some campaigns are "dirty" and they can be unpleasant. In vendetta campaigns, for example, a candidate runs not to win but to kill off the chances of someone he doesn't like. In one such congressional primary in New York in the early 1960s, completely unfounded malicious personal rumors were started in local churches and synagogues, and boys giving out campaign literature were beaten by adults apparently paid by the opponent. It is hard to cope with such tactics dispassionately. When laws are broken, as they were in this instance, the responsible parties should be charged. Contacting the unfair practices committee won't help. You should bring civil and criminal charges where appropriate and get publicity for the reasons that compel you to make the charges.

Whispering campaigns are in questionable taste. The congressional primary race in 1972 between Bella Abzug and William Fitts Ryan was tragic for many reasons, not the least of which was that both were outstanding congressmen of the reform faction and one had to lose. Ms. Abzug's supporters were alleged to have used the slogan "The district needs a strong voice," making a clear although unspoken reference to the fact that Congressman Ryan, who had recently had a throat operation, was not physically strong. Ryan replied by issuing a brochure with the theme, "My work speaks louder."

Fighting back with equally dirty tactics is a natural and satisfying response, but it doesn't work and the public is apt to be sickened by the spectacle. There are no automatic solutions to this problem. In some cases, a brochure or a press conference counterattacking is effective. In others, when opponents claim endorsements that they have not received, you must get the "endorser" publicly to disown your opponent. When campaign literature is really malicious—for example, a 1972 Democratic primary handbill implying an opponent was supported by President Nixon, your only recourse is to try to get press and television attention to the incident; the public usually will be sympathetic.

In many theaters where the award-winning motion picture "The Godfather" was shown, the audience applauded when someone was murdered to avenge the murder of a member of the hero's family.

Revenge is a satisfying emotion, shared universally. Nonetheless, it has not yet become broadly accepted by voters as a reason to vote for or against candidates. Vendetta races may sometimes be impossible to avoid, but they are senseless and—perhaps more important—unattractive to most voters.

Newspaper polls

These polls vary considerably in quality depending on who does them and how they are done. *The New York Times* has a semi-exclusive contract with Daniel Yankelovich, one of the best market research firms in the country. Other newspapers also retain independent consultants, while many, in addition to subscribing to the Gallup and Harris national surveys and other syndicated polls, use write-in surveys, street sampling, and other non-probability surveys of doubtful professionalism and accuracy. Most voters are not statisticians, and an improper poll that newspaper readers assume is reliable can cost you votes. All other things being equal, voters don't like to vote for a sure loser. In the event a newspaper poll shows you losing by a large margin, you are well advised to criticize the paper's survey and challenge the procedures and the results. In no event should your campaign strategy be based on the results of a newspaper poll of demonstrated non-professionalism; the newspaper's methodology, interviewing techniques, and sampling design should be checked out thoroughly before using its results as substitutes for polls you can't afford to conduct. If you can't afford professional consultants to make this appraisal, someone on your staff who has market research or statistical experience should be assigned to do the checking.

In Canada, the danger of newspaper polls is generally recognized, and they are not permitted by law, although private (that is, unpublished) polls are, of course, allowed.

Disassociation from the ticket

Many election ballots still consist of party slates; that is, all candidates of one party or one segment of a party are listed on one vertical line. In situations like this, a strong candidate on top of the ticket can carry his colleagues with him. But the opposite happens as well—a weak candidate at the top of the ticket can neutralize much work and expenditure. The defeat of many local Republicans in

1964 on tickets headed by presidential candidate Barry M. Goldwater is an example of this.

When your research shows that you're running stronger than the top of the ticket, you may have to disassociate yourself as well as you can. Some candidates exclude the party name from their advertisements and emphasize their own name, giving the voters a reason to look for the name, not the party, on the ballot. In recent New York primary elections, reform candidates ran as independents, regular candidates avoided identifying themselves with this faction, and many voters were completely confused.

On the other hand, as a new candidate, you may have trouble getting yourself identified in a way that strengthens your candidacy. Some national movements have local followings with which you can identify. Current or recent examples of such groups are Ralph Nader's consumer advocates, John Gardner's Common Cause, the Eugene McCarthy presidential campaign, and ecology-oriented private groups such as the Sierra Club and Friends of the Earth.

Reversing the field

If you use basic research to make decisions, there are usually occasions when the results of that research force you to consider changing your strategy, assuming that the campaign is not so advanced that all options are precluded. Reversals of field, sometimes involving changes in media emphasis, sometimes changes of themes, campaign managers, or endorsements, all have an element of danger.

In his race for the Senate in 1964, Robert F. Kennedy refused to participate in a public debate with the incumbent, Kenneth B. Keating, because the polls showed that he was ahead. But Keating gained strength as the race proceeded, and Kennedy decided to change his strategy and debate Keating about three weeks before the election, reportedly against the advice of his staff. Kennedy, however, was a consummate politician and sensed the necessity for this decision.

You'll have to balance the risk of introducing something new against the damage resulting from your present strategy. There is usually time for only one major reversal. Such a decision, therefore, deserves careful consideration. Research is helpful, but in my experience, this is one case when research must defer to emotion and political instinct.

Third candidates

Sometimes one of the major candidates deliberately plants a third candidate to pull the votes of ethnic, racial, or religious minorities from his opponent. In 1971, for example, Queens County Democratic Leader Matthew J. Troy candidly admitted having done that in a New York City Council race. Troy's attitude was, "Well, doesn't everyone do it?" This tactic (so common that *The New York Times* gave the Troy story only a few paragraphs) is usually adopted to split the opponent's voter base. The ploy is based on the political reality that, all other things being equal, a given percentage of voters will vote for a name suggesting a religious, ethnic, or racial affinity. The only possible defense is to appeal directly and forthrightly to the group the third candidate hopes to split, indicating that a deliberate manipulation of ethnic or religious or racial ties is being attempted and that a vote for the third candidate cannot serve the group but only the politician trying to manipulate the group for his own purposes.

Name identification problems

Deliberate splitting, as described above, relies on voters' recognizing a candidate's faith, ethnic group, or race from his name. Such identification is probably worth 10 to 15 percent of the total ethnic vote, depending, of course, on the ethnic makeup of the district. A candidate may have difficulty if his name is not easily identifiable as belonging to the politically dominant group. Such a situation may be agonizing—you can't go out and advertise that, although your name is Brown, you're really Italian. In one case, a candidate, pushing the matter to excess, wore a Star of David medallion on his street tours in a Jewish area to identify himself as Jewish. One way to handle this is to use civic group associations, indicating your background in your literature, and taking "ethnic" sides of issues *if* your research and your convictions make this seem to be the proper thing to do. In his race for a judgeship in the Bronx, a Jew whose name did not sound Jewish considered using the slogan, "Put a *mensch* on the bench," to establish his religious ties in the voters' minds.*

Judicial races

In special political races, such as those for judgships, you can't really hit hard: Dignity and dispassionate discussion are expected pre-

---

* *Mensch,* a Yiddish word meaning a decent man.

requisites for judicial candidates. Many judicial races are arranged by a consensus of all the political parties beforehand, and judgeships may be parceled out, in agreed-upon quotas, to Italians, Jews, Democrats, Republicans, and others. Judicial races of this kind may be empty formalities and can hardly be described as open. Candidates who render substantial services to party leaders make their wishes known years in advance, eventually being given a judicial post as a reward for long service in carrying contracts, raising money, and other critical party tasks. The outright purchase of judgeships is not unknown.

Nonetheless, there are judicial contests for which prior arrangements have not been made. In recent years, judgeship campaigners have used direct mail, posters, and newspaper ads, but without the complete hoopla spirit of personal criticism of opponents that characterize elections for other posts. The necessary strategy is to bring some philosophy and/or emotion to the race and still appear credible. Judicial candidates can discuss the law as it operates to respond to or to thwart societal or community needs. For example, in a judicial campaign in which I was involved, the candidate developed a program that related to neighborhood problems. He wanted jurors' fees raised from $12 to $20 a day, since working men lost a day's pay when forced to accept jury duty; he asked that small claims courts try cases up to $1,000 instead of $500; and he advocated the trying of landloard-tenant cases at night so that tenants would not have to sacrifice their salaries to gain their day in court.

Reapportionment: the salami and the knife

Redistricting or reapportionment of election districts takes place at various intervals—usually after the results of a decennial census are announced, and sometimes more frequently than that. The need for redistricting arises from population increases and decreases.

State and federal laws require that districts be balanced in a reasonably equitable manner. As people move away from some areas into other areas, redistricting is required to assure equitable representation. For example, each congressional district is now supposed to contain a population of about 450,000. In practice, the party that controls the state legislature, which is responsible for drawing election districts, is likely to enact a redistricting plan with lines drawn in such a way as to be favorable to the interests of its own members, while technically including approximately equal members of citizens in each district.*

In a process known as gerrymandering, districts are drawn—sometimes in preposterous shapes—to suit not public equity but the needs of the party in power.† Tradeoffs are sometimes arranged between political parties so that leaders and other senior people of both parties are assured "safe" districts.‡ Many election district maps look distinctly artificial because natural boundaries and existing neighborhood lines are completely ignored.

What does reapportionment mean for a new candidate? In the first instance, an examination of past voting behavior is particularly important if redistricted lines have just been drawn. The party in power assigns technicians to assure as many "safe" districts as possible for loyal party men. They occasionally make mistakes, but they are paid to know their business. If you are considering a race in a newly drawn district, examine the area's voting data very carefully. In some instances, you will find that it is better not to make the race there, and it may be wiser to try to find a district in which you have a better chance or simply not to run at all.

As a consequence of reapportionment in 1972, two congressional seats were eliminated in New York City, with tragic consequences for

---

* "In New York, a legislative employee long noted for his artistry at drawing district lines greeted with joy the U.S. Supreme Court decision requiring the smallest possible deviation from district to district. He noted that from then on it depended on how you 'slice the salami,' and that his party had control of both the salami and the knife. In Ohio a leading political figure openly acknowledged that political party registration and past voting habits had been fed into a computer to assure that the majority party could get the maximum benefit from the forthcoming congressional redistricting. . . . It is not too surprising that the legislature invariably 'sees fit' to give maximum protection to incumbents and to assure that the majority party continues and, if at all possible, expands control. New York has a new district which slices two sections out of Bronx County and fits them together. The state claims they are 'contiguous by water,' which a minority leader has likened to the contiguity of East and West Pakistan." (Editorial, *National Civic Review,* January 1972, pp. 4–5.)

† "Gerrymandering" is named for Elbridge Gerry (1744–1814), a Massachusetts governor who redistricted the state to give his party a number of state senators in excess of their voting strength, and for salamander, the animal whose shape Essex County, Massachusetts, resembled after Gerry redistricted it.

‡ Tradeoffs are a type of political contract. For example, in 1971, the Bronx borough president wanted New York City to rehabilitate Yankee Stadium at a cost of $24 million. According to rumor, the true cost to the city was probably much higher, since tradeoffs to other borough presidents for voting for the Yankee Stadium project would involve several other major capital facilities for their boroughs.

to-house canvass in the areas of the district where interest is highest. Direct mail has little impact—written appeals generally don't work well here—and television, radio, or newspaper advertisements are out of the question. Keep lists of those who are favorable to you and try to have each favorable potential voter on election day contacted by someone in your family or canvassed in person by a volunteer.

Outside "campaign doctors"

In the theater, if a play or musical show encounters difficulties during its preview period, the producer may bring in an outside consultant or "show doctor." However, when a politicial campaign seems to be going badly, the usual procedure is to call together the consultants, the "kitchen cabinet," the campaign manager, and the candidate's family to define what's going wrong and to develop remedies. Sometimes this works, but more often the result is confusion or reinforcement of the original problem. If you are in such a situation, you may have to ask for advice from a political leader of your party or a political consultant from outside your area—one who has had no direct involvement in your campaign and who can be more objective about the options that remain open to you. Do this, however, before the campaign is half over, since after that point almost all major resources are usually committed. Check with local politicians and local political reporters for the names of possible campaign doctors. Such local campaign mechanics are not usually well known, and men with national reputations may be unavailable or too expensive. Dan Nimmo, *Political Persuaders* (Englewood Cliffs, N.J.: Prentice-Hall, 1970), lists consultants who may be available, as does *The Political Market-Place,* edited by David L. Rosenbloom (New York: Quadrangle, 1972).

Debates

Since the Richard M. Nixon-John F. Kennedy televised debates, which were widely regarded as a turning point in the 1960 presidential campaign, interest in the debate as a campaign device has been high. As television has assumed a major role in the campaigning process, political debates (and refusals to debate) have become particularly important. As a candidate, you have three options:

Debate as much as possible; debate only under stated conditions; or avoid debates altogether.

In some situations, such as the Robert F. Kennedy-Kenneth B. Keating senatorial race in New York in 1966, or the Kevin White-Louise Day Hicks mayoral campaign in Boston in 1971, one candidate considers himself so far ahead that he believes debate can only help the challenger. In this event, many stalling devices may be used, such as disputes over the format of the debate, who answers the first question, who is the moderator, whether the debate will be live or filmed, and which reporters should be present. Such tactics can delay the debate, either indefinitely or so long as to permit only one or at the most two debates to take place. (An example of this, in another arena, was the behavior of the delegates to the organizing meetings for the Vietnam peace talks in Paris. They spent months arguing over the shape of the table and delayed substantive talks while the fighting and bombing went on in Indochina.) The challenger, however, may, in turn, buy television time and debate an empty chair.

Your strategy should be guided by what the voters want as expressed in probability sample surveys, tempered by your judgment of how well you can handle yourself in public debates. By and large, most voters do want to see the candidates in a personal confrontation.

In the debate itself, the usual technique is to talk to the audience and avoid answering your opponent's charges, while sounding confident and well informed.* But voters like a fight and have become somewhat turned off by the obvious artifice and sweeping generalities that have come to characterize most political debates. Try to turn the debate toward the questions that your research shows are of interest to the voters. Talk about them with conviction and in the most concrete terms possible. Address your opponent directly and with as much emotion as is appropriate. Viewers will respect you if you act like a concerned human being, not an emotionless marionette —but no matter how strongly you feel, stop short of name-calling or displaying open contempt.

---

* Murray B. Levin describes this tactic in *Kennedy Campaigning: The System and the Style as Practiced by Senator Edward Kennedy* (Boston: Beacon Press, 1966).

Relationships to political clubs

Most candidates start their campaigns on the basis of their membership in or endorsement from a local political club. Such a base is important to provide a semblance of party blessing, as well as campaign workers and occasionally funds. Often, however, the club leadership will expect the candidate to pay for some club mailings, furniture rentals, signs, or other club expenses. If such costs and other club demands seem excessive in relation to what the club offers you in the way of workers or facilities, you may be better off campaigning independently.

Club sponsorship is less critical than it used to be. Efficient mechanical and electronic means—computerized direct mail, radio, television, newspaper advertising, and professionally manned telephones —can effectively replace large numbers of workers. Also, a candidate can usually attract campaign workers from other sources. Relatives, friends, business associates, and fellow members of civic groups often are willing to volunteer their services.

In some situations, you may get your club's endorsement simply because you have waited your turn in the club; and then you cannot turn your back on your sponsors. In other situations—for example, if the club needs a candidate to run for a given office and you consent to fill the void—you may be able to run the campaign with only token consultation with the club.

When to announce your candidacy

There are many views on the question of when to announce one's candidacy. Some candidates, particularly those who aspire to high office, prefer to "play it coy," to develop momentum and then announce—or accept a "draft"—at a suitable time and place. I am personally convinced, however, that once you've decided to make the race and are assured adequate funds, your best course is to announce as soon as possible. If you delay, there is a strong possibility of leaks to the press that you're looking for campaign funds or otherwise preparing to become a candidate. If you are confronted with a situation like this and still wish to delay your announcement, your best course is to state that you are considering making the race and will announce your candidacy when you have made a final decision.

For a June primary, you will probably wish to have an announcement ready by Easter or shortly thereafter. If you're going into a September primary, you may want to be ready to announce before people leave for their summer vacations. Examine local precedents by checking newspaper coverage of previous campaigns. (Back issues of local newspapers are normally available at the public library as well as at each newspaper's offices.) Ask previous candidates why they announced when they did, and see whether you agree with their thinking.

Try not to make your announcement on a holiday when people are not home to read the local paper. If there is an influential weekly newspaper in your area, make your announcement on a day when it can report the news.

When the time comes, simply find a convenient meeting place—a local press club, or your campaign office if you already have one. If you anticipate television coverage, be sure to choose a place which has adequate electrical wiring and outlets for television equipment. The television station will tell you what is necessary. Then telephone the radio and/or television stations and the local newspapers to inform them that you are having a press conference. At the conference, make the announcement in a businesslike way, stating the theme of your campaign, explaining why you have decided to make the race, and mentioning any major supporters and endorsements that you have. You can also announce that you welcome contributions and volunteers, giving an address and telephone number where they will be welcomed. Have copies of your statement available for the reporters who cover the meeting, and be prepared to answer any questions they may have.

The carpetbagger issue

In many campaigns the fact that a candidate doesn't really live in a district (whether or not he has an official residence there) is made much of by his opponent. The public usually disregards the residency issue unless other more emotional and solidly negative factors are related to it.

In my home district in lower Manhattan, carpetbagging was made the cardinal issue in a district leadership race in 1971. The front-runner's opponents had the facts clearly on their side: They circulated photographs of his suburban home with his listing in the suburban telephone directory superimposed on the picture. Additionally, while he still maintained an official address in the Manhattan district, they reported that his children went to school in the suburb in which the house was located. The evidence appeared to be irrefutable and was made known throughout the district. Nonetheless, the carpetbagger won the election by a large margin. (After he won the election, the new district leader, who held a responsible city job, was publicly accused of seriously mismanaging hundreds of thousands of dollars in connection with his job. It is interesting to speculate how the election might have turned out if, rather than spending all their time belaboring the carpetbagging issue, his opponents had made an effort to investigate his performance as a city employee with discretion over large amounts of money.)

My advice would be never to key an attack on the carpetbagger issue alone—the voters don't always buy this approach. However, the residency issue can be used effectively if it is made part of a larger theme with emotional impacts that the individual voter can feel and relate to. An effective way to use the carpetbagger issue against an opponent is *not* to start with it. Instead, start with something like "Last year Assemblyman Jones voted against Propositions A, B, and C—all of which would have benefited our district. Apparently he doesn't have our needs in mind. Maybe it's because he doesn't live here; he doesn't know what it's like here every day."

If an opponent uses the carpetbagger issue against you, your wisest course is probably to let your record speak for you and not to address the issue directly at all. If you need moral support in this position, simply remember how far the incumbent Senator Kenneth B. Keating got using the carpetbagging issue against Robert F. Kennedy in New York in 1964.

5 Political Advertising and Public Relations

Nothing can be more annoying than to be òbscurely hanged.

—Voltaire

Political advertising is a major component of any campaign, both in energies consumed and in monies spent. Recent press reports sometimes give the impression that this is a new phenomenon, or that it is somehow undemocratic. As a matter of fact, however, American political advertising has a long if not always noble history. Campaign broadsides from the eighteenth and nineteenth centuries and nineteenth-century campaign buttons can be found in many museums. Thomas Paine's *Common Sense,* which is now read in some literature courses, was a very effective political advertisement in its day.

What is new in political advertising is its potential for effective saturation. Broadsides were distributed to perhaps a few hundred people; a television commercial in a major city may reach millions of people simultaneously. Also, while political advertising broadsides generally took the form of ideas on paper that were aimed at the readers' minds, political advertising now makes use of many other stimuli: a candidate's television appearance or his statesmanlike voice appeal to the emotions of voters at the same time that his ideas appeal to their minds.

Joe McGinness's best-selling book *The Selling of the President 1968* focused on the harshest characteristics of the process and made the sophisticated advertising techniques of Richard Nixon's 1968 campaign appear to represent a dramatic transformation in campaigning. Actually, however, the change in the process (not to mention the expense) of political campaigning—particularly in campaigns involving larger districts with hundreds of thousands of voters—began in the mid-1950s, when television ownership became common. Television made a new, effective medium available to politicians and merchandisers alike. Its use by candidates simply made obvious the long-standing fact that campaigning depended partly on merchandising and that candidates were "sold" in much the same way as consumer products. McGinness's phrase "the selling of the president" struck home to many as a recognized, shared truth.

Despite the techological revolution in political advertising, the time-honored techniques of newspaper advertisements, brochures, mailings, stickers, and giveaways remain a significant aspect of campaigning at all levels, and in fact are the only ones in use in the vast majority of elections for local offices, where television is usually neither desirable nor affordable. This chapter reviews the use of these classical techniques as well as those made available by recent technological developments.

The importance of consistency in advertising themes

Too many campaign managers or campaign committees waste money, and lots of it, by making expenditures based on the apparent assumption that one medium has nothing to do with another and that, without retaining what has been said in previous advertisements, the voter hears only one message at a time. For example, in his radio advertising one candidate emphasized that he could listen patiently to all groups in his state and work out solutions carefully; however, his billboard advertising featured his ability to get things done expeditiously. As a consequence, the two contradictory appeals probably canceled each other out and lost him at least as many votes as they gained.

The basic question in political advertising is what to say. Whatever you do, if you use more than one medium, make sure that each one reinforces the other. If you have nothing new to say, don't waste your money saying it; you'll only irritate some voters, and you'll pay dearly for that privilege. Whatever media you use, map out the basic structure of your advertising campaign as early as possible. If you are using radio and television, early planning is an absolute necessity, since you must buy the right spots well in advance, with careful choice of day and hour—for example, following certain popular shows. To do this effectively, you will have to have some idea of the different ways in which you wish to utilize the various media in your theme development. You will therefore wish to lay out your basic themes as soon as possible. Be sure, however, to leave some degree of flexibility to enable you to take advantage of developing opportunities that cannot be anticipated and to be able to respond to your opponent's attacks.*

Basically, most campaign themes focus on two or three weaknesses of the opponent(s) while maximizing the candidate's own strengths. From the time that you and your campaign manager delineate the basic themes of your campaign, all advertising expenditures should be keyed to implementing them. All forms of advertising you use should reinforce each other by illustrating the same themes and appeals.

Different media are appropriate for different situations. In a small community you might rely on press coverage, street campaigning, mailings, and buttons and forget radio and television, since the costs would be excessive in relation to the number of people to be reached. In even smaller campaigns, you might rely entirely on personal canvassing and distribution of brochures. In certain communities, it may be possible to depend mainly on street campaigning, while in others, that could result in certain defeat. Each situation varies somewhat, and the response must be based on public-opinion research combined with experience in the area, political judgment, and an objective evaluation of your actual abilities. Some candidates, for example, are wonderful street campaigners, while others lose votes every time they conduct a walking tour.

A campaign theme can consist of a phrase like Franklin Delano Roosevelt's "New Deal," Harry Truman's "Fair Deal," or Adlai

---

* Some campaigners (including Clifford White, a Republican campaign manager who has worked for Barry M. Goldwater and others) do not agree with this strategy. They believe that every campaign should be conducted positively and that response should not be made to opponents' attacks, since if a candidate responds to an opponent he presumably no longer fully controls his own campaign. This theory sometimes underlies the strategy of refusing debates. In my judgment, no absolute of this sort is applicable to campaigning. Political campaigns involve many variables, and an inflexible response cannot always be right.

Stevenson's "Let's Talk Sense." It can be a phrase or a characteristic you want to emphasize—ability, experience, ideas, youth, honesty. A combination of research and intuition is necessary to provide a good theme. But regardless of its derivation, the theme must relate to the problems that are important in your district and the way the voters feel about them, and it should appear consistently in all your advertising.

Impact of news coverage

Newspaper, television, and radio news coverage are at least as important as direct advertising.* Most experienced political mechanics agree that newspaper and radio-TV news coverage together can influence at least one fourth of your vote. This estimate is based on the observation that undecided or independent voters often tend to make up their minds on the basis of news reportage. Some of these voters are also influenced by the editorial recommendations of their local newspaper.

My experience indicates that the cumulative recollection of television, radio, and newspaper coverage of the campaign will affect at least as many voters as will ethnic, racial, or religious ties. Because of this, getting television and newspaper coverage is a very serious consideration. In the larger cities and states, merely running for office will not assure you of receiving press coverage. Some county and township newspapers, on the other hand, find primary and general election fights very interesting and often will go to the candidates for news. In larger states and cities, however, elections for Congress and local offices take place in districts, each of which represents only a small fraction of the newspaper readership or the radio and television audience. The mass media can't possibly give full coverage to all these races. There are so many primary fights in the New York metropolitan area, for example, that even *The New York Times,* which prides itself on being a newspaper of record, can give com-

---

* The dollar value of such free coverage has not gone unacknowledged by some candidates. There have been rumors in many campaigns that some newspaper reporters were on a candidate's personal payroll to guarantee coverage and a friendly interpretation of events. Such payoffs are not uncommon in American business, and it would not be surprising if they sometimes occurred in campaigning. Besides being immoral and possibly illegal, however, this tactic can backfire if it is discovered and made public by an opponent. I don't recommend trying it.

prehensive coverage to only a fraction of the races in the metropolitan area that it serves. In such a situation, the candidate has the problem of making news—he can't assume that the press and television will come to him.

Controversy creates news; emotional confrontations are interesting to the public; accusations and actions invite attention. One politician, seeking to dramatize the pollution crisis, made headlines and the six o'clock television news in New York by taking a brief swim in the Hudson River, whose filth is of legendary proportions. Issue papers hardly ever get press and television attention unless they include examples of corruption by the opponent or his party. Public service law suits—for example, a suit charging a public utility with polluting a river—are increasingly popular as a way of getting public attention, but they are expensive, and you run the risk of losing both the lawsuit and some credibility if you don't have a very strong case. If you plan on such a suit, your budget should include at least $5,000 for legal fees. The injustice must be a real one; to make it politically worthwhile, your cause should be one that already has significant public sympathy.

Television and press interviews may be an important source of free publicity in congressional, county, city, and statewide races; and Sunday discussion programs, innocuous as they usually are, cumulatively can be very significant in a campaign. Many technicians believe that a large proportion of undecided voters watch these programs and are influenced by them.

Many managers advise candidates not to say too much on specific issues on interview programs in order not to irritate too many client groups.* If you're an incumbent, the advice generally is to emphasize

* Stimson Bullitt, a two-time candidate for Congress, advised: "Without sacrifice of the public interest, a compromise can be struck between saying nothing about anything and letting the chips fly. A man's duty demands candor, while his survival demands discretion. As much as possible, a politician must refrain from criticism of individuals and groups, except by inference; such talk is the main source of antagonisms. . . . When asked about a pending issue, he has the duty to speak out clear and straight. But one may mitigate the rancor of those who feel the other way by phrasing one's declaration in terms which accommodate the audience. General answers of opinion are more likely to inflame than specific answers of fact. Arguing the merits of a specific solution to a problem is safer than asserting controversial principles, which may antagonize whether understood or misunderstood, and more useful than asserting principles on which everyone agrees." (*To Be a Politician* [New York: Doubleday, 1959], pp. 58–59.)

your legislative achievements, particularly the construction of new facilities, as much as possible. If you're a challenger, regardless of which questions you're asked by a television interviewer, the most widespread advice seems to be to criticize your opponent's record. Candidates usually do not answer publicly asked questions in a straightforward manner. Yet some politicians, such as New York's outspoken Bella Abzug, have made reputations as sensational news-makers by habitually speaking their minds.

Radio and television advertising in smaller campaigns

There are situations when it may be worthwhile to advertise on radio or television, even though for congressional and smaller campaigns you may be paying to reach many times the number of voters you really want to reach. If your research shows you're still not getting full recognition after half the campaign is over, or if you feel you must answer an accusation that the press or public seems to be accepting, or if you wish to attack your opponent with something you believe will be conclusive, you might consider a radio or television saturation even though it is uneconomical. But usually, television advertising for smaller-area campaigns is not advisable, as it takes money from effective, more economical techniques such as mailings, brochures, paid professional campaign aids, and telephone canvassing.

Radio advertising is usually cheaper than television and in the hands of creative technicians can be very effective. Sixty-second spots dramatizing a theme by simulated voter conversations, with some taste and humor, are more productive than the candidate's voice solemnly praising his own virtues. For obvious reasons, some media experts recommend scheduling these shots before or after evening news programs.

Television advertising in larger campaigns

Television campaigning has become almost a necessity in city-, state-, and nation-wide campaigns. In many larger-scale campaigns, according to Walter Diamond, an experienced New York campaign manager, "the image coming out of the box controls almost everything." Most politicians acknowledge the importance of television in large-scale campaigns, and it commands a large proportion of the campaign funds of most candidates for major offices.* Nonetheless, spending the large sums of money that television requires is not by itself a guarantee of victory; the match-up between the candidates, their personality and drive, and the experience and judgment of their staffs still count for a lot.†

When you decide on expenditures for television, as well as for all other media, always try to determine your costs on the basis of cost per thousand voters reached. If you must choose among types of expenditures, make sure you're choosing among the *net effective costs* —that is, the costs per thousand voters actually reached. Viewing the situation in this way, it is easy to see, for example, that television in primaries has a very high net effective cost because you pay to reach the entire viewing public while only perhaps 10 percent of the viewing public at most are primary voters.‡ (There may, of course, be other reasons—not the least of which may be your opponent's heavy use of television—that cause you to decide to use television in a primary despite its relatively high cost per voter.)

In planning your television budget, keep in mind the fact that if you buy television or radio time through an agency, the agency will receive a 10 to 15 percent rebate from the station in addition to the fee you pay for the agency's services. If you book your own radio and television time (which may be feasible in small areas), you yourself should be able to get the discount from the station.

* However, in recent elections candidates use TV spots more and more to simulate news, since many voters seem to distrust political commercials, and their impact has appreciably diminished. That is one reason why news coverage is so valued by candidates.

† In their major 1970 campaigns, leading political television consultants had won-lost records on the order of 4–3, 3–3, and 5–4. After John V. Lindsay met disaster in his presidential bid in the spring of 1972, many commentators noted that the various television campaigns in the primaries had canceled each other out. Garth, Lindsay's own media man, was quoted as saying that the role of television and media generally had always been exaggerated. In *The New York Times* of May 2, 1972, Warren Weaver, Jr., reported, "So far in the 1972 primary season, most of the Democratic candidates who made heavy investments in television and radio campaigning have failed, raising the question whether commercial use of the broadcast media still has a political impact on voters."

‡ That is why primary campaigns so frequently use the more focused mechanisms of direct mail and telephones, which can be designed to reach the primary voter only and thereby minimize wastage.

Television consultants

General advice on choosing consultants will be found in Chapter 1. Each of the television specialists has his own approach. David Garth, for example, shoots unstructured and unrehearsed *cinéma vérité* footage and then uses the political instincts he has developed over the years in many campaigns to select appropriate segments from thousands of feet of film. Other television mechanics study survey research, discover reactions, and try to expand on the favorable reactions to find a theme the candidate can be comfortable with, and then shoot their films. In some instances, advertising agency men may go out on the street with the candidate and question people's reactions to try to find a potentially successful approach for a television campaign.

There is no general agreement on the best approach to television advertising for political candidates. Garth, who, before the 1972 Lindsay disaster, was considered one of the best television consultants, uses 30- or 60-second spots to illustrate the campaign theme; indeed, most of the money spent for all radio and television ads in the 1970 campaign—some $47.9 million out of a total of $50.3 million—went for ads a minute or less in length. Other specialists, however, attacking the 30-second political television ads, point out that oversimplification and distortion necessarily characterize such short spots and that the ads, therefore, mislead, rather than inform, the electorate and are not helpful to the democratic process. Senator Adlai E. Stevenson III of Illinois told the U.S. Senate, "These short spots are the ones offering the greatest potential for superficiality and demagoguery." *

Naturalism and credibility are the qualities most sought after by

* Writing in the *Wall Street Journal*, March 9, 1972 (p. 12), Alan Otten observed: "Perhaps more influential with the politicians and practitioners than this moralistic type of criticism is evidence suggesting [that] spots may no longer be as effective as they once were, and perhaps [are] even counterproductive. Some of the slickest (and most expensive) recent campaigns didn't win. . . . The viewing public has gradually been raising its guard, more suspicious of politicians generally and particularly alerted by books and articles to the abuses of political commercials. . . . *The Ticket Splitter*, by Walter De Vries and Lance Tarrance, actually rates paid TV ads 24th in influence on the critically important ticket-splitting group, voters well informed on issues and highly distrustful of politicians. . . . This year is seeing a trend towards . . . direct, issue-oriented spots."

television consultants.* In the first Lindsay mayoral campaign in 1965, for example, Garth focused on Lindsay's natural good looks and television presence, drawing his short spot ads from thousands of feet of candid footage of Lindsay on the streets with his collar open, his hair a little windswept.

Since his firm term as mayor had not been a shining success, Lindsay was the underdog in his second mayoral campaign in 1969. He used two themes: (1) Being the mayor of New York City is the second toughest job in the United States; and (2) I've made mistakes, but now I have more experience and can do the job better.† In the judgment of many experienced political observers, the key television commercial, the "I've made mistakes" theme—one characterized by Lindsay's inner circle as the "Lindsay eats shit spot"—made the campaign. This commercial, done in cooperation with the advertising firm Young & Rubicam, showed Lindsay saying:

> The school strike went too far—and we all made some mistakes; but I brought 225,000 new jobs to this town and that was no mistake; I fought for three years to put a fourth platoon [of police] on the streets and that was no mistake; and I reduced the deadliest gas in our air by 50 percent and I forced the landlords to roll back unfair rents, and we didn't have a Newark, a Detroit or a Watts in this city— and those were no mistakes. The things that go wrong are what make this the second toughest job in America. But the things that go right are what make me want it.‡

* Credibility has become an increasingly important theme in television advertising since continued exposure to political commercials appears to have made a significant number of voters skeptical. The *Wall Street Journal* pointed out on January 28, 1972, that many candidates were attempting to give their commercials the appearance of straight news, apparently to counteract the "credibility gap" of political commercials.

† The first theme was designed to make the voters think about Mario Procaccino, Lindsay's Democratic opponent, in the "second toughest job," and Procaccino didn't look the part. Appearance counts heavily in big campaigns, especially in those using television.

‡ Quoted by Terry Galanoy in *Down the Tube, or Making Television Commercials is Such a Dog-Eat-Dog Business it's no Wonder They're Called Spots* (Chicago: Regnery, 1970), pp. 235–36. As Galanoy points out, the Lindsay commercials were based on a smart advertising principle which has also has been used to sell such products as bad-tasting mouthwashes: "If your product has a fault, don't try to hide it—try to make it an asset."

Garth's influence isn't limited to the television aspects of campaigning—it is felt throughout any campaign he is involved in. His staff has come up with brilliant "one liners" that have keyed campaigns. Examples of such Garth-inspired slogans are "Ottinger Delivers" (New York); "Vote for Specter and Gola because you need these guys to watch those guys" (Philadelphia); and for Lindsay, a subway and bus poster ad in striking white and black declaring, "This air conditioned car is brought to you by Mayor Lindsay, a man who's been in the hot seat too many times to ignore the sufferings of others." For John Tunney, the son of the famous boxer, Garth coined the slogan "John Tunney is a fighter. You need a fighter in your corner."

Joe Napolitan, who, like Garth, normally works for liberally oriented Democratic politicians, uses a different approach in political advertising.* He favors 15- or 30-minute narrative documentaries developing empathy, understanding, and acceptance of the candidate first as a human being, then as a political person.

Nelson Rockefeller's television campaigns have been widely and justly admired by many political observers. In his 1970 campaign, at a time when Rockefeller's popularity as reported by the polls was low, his advertising firm chose to keep his image off the screen. Instead, his voice was heard (a technique known as "voice-over") while his achievements were portrayed on film.

Other leading television political packagers are listed in *The Political Market-Place* (New York: Quadrangle, 1972). Each consultant works differently but, to the best of my knowledge, none is inexpensive. The exact amounts of professional consulting fees are kept secret, but Garth's has been estimated to be $50,000 per campaign. In addition, many television consultants also act as their own advertising agency and thus supplement the fees candidates pay them with the usual 10 to 15 percent rebate on radio, newspaper, and television costs. The rebate alone can amount to $150,000 for a million-dollar campaign.

---

* Some political professionals, television consultants included, prefer to work for a single political party or only for a wing or segment of a party. Many began as volunteers who worked in politics out of ideological conviction; eventually their hobby became a profession.

Newspaper advertisements

Newspaper ads are to some small campaigns what television is to large ones: They are the means by which the candidate can reach a mass audience. Generally, each newspaper ad dramatizes one concept or one criticism of the opponent. Newspaper advertisements should be coordinated with other campaign publicity, and ads in series should reinforce each other. Sometimes, a series of ads appears on successive days in the same place in the newspaper, usually in a section, like the national news section or the radio-TV section, which is thought to be read by voters of all special interest groups. Series of this type are intended to be seen in sequence and to have a cumulative effect on the person who reads more than one of them. Some candidates prefer to run series of short, so-called bullet ads in different parts of the paper and direct them at different audiences— for example, placing an ad about food and drug legislation or about abortion reform on the woman's page. If you have a relationship with an advertising agency, the agency should help you to decide what space to buy to give your ad campaign the maximum effect. Otherwise, a trusted member of your staff who is involved in writing the ads will have to make these decisions.

It is traditional to include a photograph of the candidate in political ads; this is particularly useful if you plan to do any street campaigning and if your face is not already known to the voters. A candid photograph dramatizing the content of the ad—for example, one showing you conversing with an older person in an ad on medical benefits or social security, or hiking in a park or visiting a recycling center in an ad on conservation of natural resources—is likely to be more effective than a formal one. Family photographs are much used and may appeal to some voters; whether you use them will depend on both your family and your constituency.

All your newspaper ads should include an address where volunteers may come and where you may be contacted if readers have further questions about your candidacy.

Pay attention to the appearance of the ad on the printed page. If it appears cluttered or if the type is too small, few people will read it. In a recent district leadership race, I spent a great deal of time working with the candidate, an experienced politician, to develop a series of newspaper advertisements that formed the basis of his campaign. The ads were carefully written to build upon each other in successive issues of the local weekly newspaper, which was widely read by the residents of the district. The first ad was relatively successful, and no change in format was contemplated for the rest of the series. The newspaper layout man, however, changed the typeface in the second ad without consulting the candidate or his staff, and used a small face that was difficult to read and that undoubtedly diluted the effectiveness of the ad. This small but serious fiasco illustrates a basic theme of this book: most campaign accidents can be avoided by proper detailing. When the copy for the third ad in the district leadership campaign was delivered to the printer, the typeface was specified explicitly.

Successful newspaper advertisements can be reproduced on good-quality paper and distributed throughout the district, either in conjunction with walking tours or street rallies, or by volunteers standing on street corners. Additional visual material—for example, a sample ballot showing the candidate's name in red type or boldface or the campaign slogan in large type—can be included with the ad on such a flyer.

Political brochures

Preparing and distributing brochures accounts for a considerable portion of campaign activity. New candidates are often surprised at how much printing and mailing brochures can cost. In many campaigns that do not use television, this cost, including overhead (paid staff, rent, etc.), may account for 70 percent of all campaign expenses.

The largest investment is likely to be in mailings—which now run between 12 and 14 cents a letter. To justify the cost of printing (where unit cost decreases sharply with increases in quantity), mailings must be on the order of tens of thousands. Sending out a professional mailing requires: (1) an advertising agency to prepare copy; (2) a printer; (3) a group of volunteers or a computer for addressing and labeling. (The use of a computer can result in a net saving over hand addressing, since returned letters are entered into the computer file and the addressees, who include people no longer living at a given address, are removed from the computer file, saving on future mailing costs. The computer can also combine the same surnames at a single address, resulting in an additional saving on mailing costs.) Other necessary steps are bagging and delivery to the post office. All these cost money, and there is no way to substitute for them unless you risk a loss of quality by preparing the copy yourself.

Professionally managed campaigns normally do three mailings in addition to the sample ballot mentioned on page 172: one introducing the candidate and his program, another attacking the opponent, and a final one, two or three days before the election, reinforcing the basic appeal. The best way to save on costs here is to send mailings only to areas where your research shows "undecideds" living in considerable number and to the swing districts where voters are usually independent.* Another economy comes from using pretested themes in these mailings, so that their appeal is maximized. Don't cram too much copy into these letters, and don't use too much "hard sell" in your appeal.

Some practical considerations can greatly increase reader receptivity to your campaign mailings. Voters nowadays receive so many mail appeals from political and other sources that they often do not even open the envelopes. Anything you can do to personalize your mail will increase the likelihood that they will at least go that far. If your funds permit, you may wish to consider sending your letters first class, with the stamps affixed by hand rather than stamped by a postage meter. This adds about 3½ cents to the cost of each letter—assuming that volunteers do the stamping. Bulk-rate letters can also be stamped by hand, but a first-class letter is much less likely to remain unopened. For the same reason, hand addressing is a good idea: people are much more likely to open a hand-addressed envelope than one with a duplicated label.† Hand addressing is very tedious, however, and your volunteers may not stay around to finish the job.

---

* If you can afford to do so, by all means attempt to reach all the significant client groups. In most campaigns, however, this is a luxury, and a priority ordering for mailings becomes important so that limited funds can be used in the most effective way. A reasonable order of priority might be undecided, independents (general elections only), selected ethnic groups, and then the favorables. A few campaign professionals advise spending your time and money where your "sure" votes reside; see, for example, Stephen Shadegg, *How to Win An Election* (New York; Taplinger, 1964), p. 98, on using this approach in scheduling Barry M. Goldwater's appearances. I believe this is an inefficient use of resources.

† There were a number of press reports in late October 1972 that the Nixon campaign committee was launching the largest personally-addressed mailing in American political history: 12 million hand-addressed envelopes were to be sent to voters.

VOTE THE BOTTOM LINE FIRST

Professional office service firms will do hand addressing (on envelopes with the return address printed on them) for about 3½ cents an envelope.

In my first state assembly campaign, after spending a full week working up a basic piece of campaign literature with a designer, we had the text printed on expensive paper, and we paid extremely careful attention to the typeface and the colors of the ink as well as to the description of the legislative program. But all this was so expensive that we had enough money to print only 10,000 pieces for a single mailing. In the last week, the opponent came out with several mailings through the district, and our single mailing was buried. You can't count, I've learned, on only one piece or theme; a vote on election day results from a cumulation of impressions in the voter's mind, and a single mail contact is not likely to win his vote by itself, without some reinforcement. As we have seen, mailings are expensive, and mistakes are both common and costly. If you make intelligent decisions and spend your money carefully so that your mailings reinforce your campaign themes, you can give yourself the best shot possible.

Selecting the right day to do your mailings can be critical. For example, many people subscribe to popular magazines such as *TV Guide, Time,* and so forth. In New York, most of these magazines arrive in mailboxes on Wednesdays and Thursdays. It is clearly not advisable to compete with these. Note which days of the week popular magazines arrive in your area, and try to time your mailings to arrive on a different day.

Similarly, all candidates commonly release a barrage of mail and literature two days before election day. If you hear that ten pieces are going out for competing candidates and candidates for other offices, I would recommend your sending your last piece a week before, if that is necessary to guarantee that yours is the only political piece of mail the voter receives that day.

In my judgment, the only piece that is mandatory two days before the election is the sample ballot displaying the slate you're running with and showing where your name appears on the ballot. A complicated ballot can destroy even the best campaign. In a recent New York election, the ballot was so complicated that people took ten minutes to vote even though the legal maximum was three; to

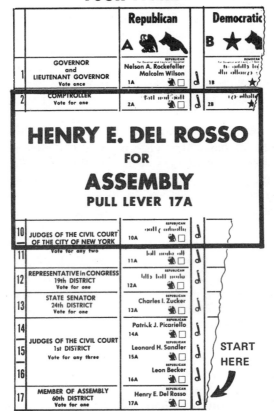

FIRST VOTE **ROW "A" LINE 17**
FOR **ASSEMBLY**

THEN GO BACK AND
VOTE THE REST OF

YOUR TICKET

		Republican	Democratic
		A	B
1	GOVERNOR and LIEUTENANT GOVERNOR Vote once	Nelson A. Rockefeller Malcolm Wilson 1A	1B
2	COMPTROLLER Vote for one	2A	2B

HENRY E. DEL ROSSO

FOR

ASSEMBLY

PULL LEVER 17A

10	JUDGES OF THE CIVIL COURT OF THE CITY OF NEW YORK Vote for any two	REPUBLICAN 10A	
11		11A	
12	REPRESENTATIVE in CONGRESS 19th DISTRICT Vote for one	REPUBLICAN 12A	
13	STATE SENATOR 24th DISTRICT Vote for one	REPUBLICAN Charles I. Zucker 13A	
14		Patrick J. Picariello 14A	
15	JUDGES OF THE CIVIL COURT 1st DISTRICT Vote for any three	REPUBLICAN Leonard H. Sandler 15A	START HERE
16		Leon Becker 16A	
17	MEMBER OF ASSEMBLY 60th DISTRICT Vote for one	REPUBLICAN Henry E. Del Rosso 17A	

"TIME FOR A CHANGE"

YOU MAY CARRY THIS CARD WITH YOU
TO YOUR POLLING PLACE

E.C.I., 1970   711

accommodate all the voters the polls remained open in some precincts until 1:00 A.M. instead of closing at the scheduled hour of 10:30 P.M. Some ballots—including those in the New York election just mentioned—list so many candidates that they must contain multiple columns, so that the voter must read up and down as well as the normal left to right. In such cases, confusion often occurs, and candidates for lesser offices tend to lose votes owing to fatigue, as well as confusion, on the part of the voters. The best aid for a candidate in such a situation is a well-designed sample ballot such as that shown on page 171. A palm card (see page 173) usually spots the candidate's name, but a sample ballot shows the design of the entire ballot, with your position highlighted in color or by the use of a device that calls attention to it. In districts with particularly complicated ballots, a sample ballot can be the most critical piece in the campaign.

Another factor that is often overlooked is targeting the distribution of brochures. Mailing, of course, is the most important means of distribution, since it enables you to choose the recipients. Computer-assisted ways of working up a mailing list are discussed on pages 000–000. But masses of literature are also distributed on the street, stuffed under doors and in mailboxes, and placed under windshield wipers of parked cars. In my experience, much of this is wasted effort and money, since many of the recipients may not be registered voters and, in a primary, a majority may not even be eligible to vote in your party's primary. Very little care is exercised in distributing handbills in most campaigns. One candidate I know took advantage of his opponent's laxity in this regard by simply sending his workers to the opponent's headquarters asking for literature to give out. The headquarters staff complied with the requests gladly. At 500 brochures per visit, the workers collected—and presumably destroyed—thousands of the opponent's brochures.

Even if care is taken in brochure distribution, few handbills are likely to be read or make an impact on the voters unless they contain extraordinary copy or they are printed on cardboard stock which voters tend not to discard so quickly as lighter paper which is easily wadded up and thrown away. Incidentally, if you do intend to have brochures distributed under doors, you might enlist your children for the job. Older children are likely to be happy to contribute their services, and adult backs frequently give out after bending over to stuff a hundred brochures under doors.

Examples and critiques of campaign literature
Original campaign literature includes both mailings and brochures to be given out in person. To be effective, literature must always have these characteristics:

- good copy, illustrating the key campaign themes, simply stated, without extraneous material
- careful design, including good paper, attractive and easily legible typeface, effective use of color, and the proper fold, so that the basic message is on top, in case the voter doesn't open the brochure—a not unlikely event
- absence of conflicting or confusing themes or emphases

Try to create literature that can be used in various ways. Designing and printing a piece of campaign literature costs money, time, and effort, and if you can use the piece later, in another way, you've saved some money that you may need for something else.

In Nathan Straus's congressional campaign in the Bronx in 1968, his campaign manager Walter Diamond produced imaginative copy in close cooperation with the campaign advertising agency and under very tight deadlines.

A brochure designed for mailing used the campaign theme "Send Straus to the the House of Representatives." Another key theme, "A man like Bingham"—developed from campaign research that showed that Congressman Jonathan B. Bingham, who had been redistricted out of the area, had built up a considerable following there—was designed to transfer some of Bingham's reform strength to Straus. The brochure, printed on heavy paper and using red ink on a white background, was quite effective, but the multiplicity of themes—the two just mentioned plus (on the reverse; see page 176) "The bosses have done it again" and "The tradition of three generations of service"—was probably too much for one piece of literature. Usually, it is best to stress one basic theme and illustrate and orchestrate it in various ways. Too many themes in a brochure tend to neutralize one another.

The bosses have done it again.

To save the last Congressman of the discredited Buckley-McDonough machine, they have gerrymandered Congressman Bingham out out of your district. They think you will buy a "used" Congressman from them. DON'T BE FOOLED!

Vote for

NATHAN STRAUS

**Democratic Primary
June 18th for Congress**

A MAN LIKE BINGHAM.

Nathan Straus discusses community problems with local resident.

This is what the New York Times said about Nathan Straus in 1966:

As your Congressman, I will want to know
your views on all issues, from local
neighborhood problems to major international
questions. This questionnaire introduces a regular program
I will conduct, seeking your opinions and advice.

NATHAN STRAUS

LOCAL ISSUES

1. What do you think is the No. 1 problem
in the Bronx today? ....
....
....

2. Is police protection adequate in the
Bronx?
Yes ☐   No ☐

3. Are recreational facilities in the Bronx,
such as parks and playgrounds,
adequate?
Yes ☐   No ☐

4. Many believe the Bronx needs more
housing. What is your opinion?
We need more rehabilitated housing ☐
We need more middle-income
housing   ☐
We need more low-income housing ☐
There is no need for additional
housing   ☐

5. Do you favor the present plan for decen-
tralization of the school system? (Putting
the school system under community
control.)
Yes ☐   No ☐

6. Do you favor a guaranteed annual income?
Yes ☐   No ☐

NATIONAL ISSUES

1. Do you think the poverty program
☐ has changed the conditions in your
neighborhood?   ☐ has done nothing?
☐ has caused dissention?

2. Do you favor lowering the voting age to
18?
Yes ☐   No ☐

3. Would you be in favor of a tax increase if
the money were going to be spent on
alleviating poverty?
Yes ☐   No ☐

INTERNATIONAL ISSUES

1. Do you think our government policy in
Vietnam should (check one)
Increase our troops ☐
Decrease our troops ☐
Withdraw immediately ☐

*If you would like to hear from Nathan
Straus on these matters, please sign
with name and address. But whether
you sign or not, please answer the
questions and return questionnaire.*

NAME ....
ADDRESS ....
....
....

This woman's place is in the House the House of Representatives

A short personal note about BELLA ABZUG

Everything Bella Abzug is and does in public life is a reflection of her background. Her upbringing and her family life today.

A native New Yorker and the long Democrat, Ms. Abzug is a graduate of Hunter College (where she was President of the student body) and of Columbia Law School (where she was an editor of the Law Review).

She also studied at the Florence Marshall Hebrew High School and the Jewish Theological Seminary.

In her law practice, she is considered an outstanding expert in labor law and civil rights.

Mrs. Abzug lives in the district with her husband Martin, a stockbroker. They have two teen-age daughters, Eve and Isobel.

Citizens for Abzug 37 Bank Street, NYC

BELLA ABZUG talks woman-to-woman:

"Isn't it time we shared in the power we create? I want to take the cause of women, the real Silent Majority, to the halls of Congress. I want to fight the discrimination that condemns most working women to low-paying jobs. This gives them less of an income then eases them out of the professions. That means them day care facilities, Headstarts their children, and gives third rate health care to black, Puerto Rican and poor women. And I'm not talking about being less womanly. I'm talking about being more womanly. We have potential. Not to use it is sheer waste. And a real woman hates waste.

BELLA ABZUG talks as a friend of Israel:

"With my whole heart, I'll support all measures necessary for the defense and survival of Israel. But I won't stop there, settling for promises as too many politicians have. Since Israel can't survive in a permanent state of war, I intend to organize a lobby in Congress to press for face-to-face negotiations between Israel and the Arab states, and a political solution that will guarantee Israel's territorial integrity and end the Mid-east arms race.

Let's Look at Her Record.
BELLA ABZUG IS...

Chairman of "Taxpayers Campaign for Urban Priorities" (fighting to put New York's tax money to work here, instead of pouring it into Vietnam)

Founder and National Legislative Representative of "Women Strike for Peace" (one of the earliest, most effective peace movements in America)

Executive Committee Member of the "New Democratic Coalition" (of both national and New York State NDC)

Member of Mayor Lindsay's Advisory Committee

Lawyer for minority rights and labor rights

Spokesman for the real Silent Majority (women)

Wife and Mother (two teen-age daughters)

BELLA ABZUG for Congress.
The People of New York for Bella Abzug

BELLA ABZUG FOR CONGRESS
51 (???) STREET
NEW YORK, NEW YORK 10014
(212) 691-0540

SIX REASONS TO KEEP BINGHAM IN CONGRESS

THE BRONX NEEDS A CONGRESSMAN FOR THE BRONX

KEEP BINGHAM IN CONGRESS. WE NEED ALL THE HELP WE CAN GET.

Democratic Primary Tuesday June 20th

Keep Jonathan Bingham in Congress Committee,
2453 White Plains Rd., Bronx, N.Y. 10462

REASON TWO:
CONGRESSMAN BINGHAM WORKS FOR THE BRONX IN THE BRONX

Jack Bingham has helped thousands of Bronxites with Social Security, housing, Medicare, Veterans and other problems. When you need Congressman Bingham's help, call his office: WE 3-2310.

Despite the Lindsay-Rocky feud, Jack Bingham got Federal funds for many projects including:

- A new veterans hospital.
- An educational park in the North Bronx.
- Building code enforcement programs.
- Library development.
- $1,139,973 for Montefiore Hospital.

In a letter to Jack Bingham, one constituent wrote, "I feel that if all Congressmen cooperated with their constituents in the same way you do, it would be a better country."

REASON FOUR:
CONGRESSMAN BINGHAM IS A CRIME FIGHTER

Congressman Bingham

- convinced the City to assign additional scooter and foot patrolmen to protect the North and West Bronx.
- led the fight for gun control legislation.

Jack Bingham is the author of

- the Citizens' Anti-Crime Patrol program.
- the Safe Schools program.

Jack Bingham knows that the Federal government must help make our neighborhoods, our streets, our schools and our homes safe again.

REASON ONE:
CONGRESSMAN JONATHAN BINGHAM

Jonathan Bingham is a leader.

As a former Ambassador to the United Nations, with Adlai Stevenson and former chief advisor to Governor Averell Harriman, Jack Bingham has spent the last 8 years fighting for the Bronx and the people of New York in the United States Congress.

Jack and his wife June have lived in the Bronx for the last 19 years and raised their children here.

June Rossbach Bingham is no newcomer to public life. An author, she learned her politics from her greatuncle, Governor Herbert H. Lehman.

REASON THREE:
CONGRESSMAN BINGHAM IS A LEADER IN THE SEARCH FOR WORLD PEACE

President John F. Kennedy said "Jack Bingham is a valued spokesman for our country."

Viet Nam:
Jack Bingham is fighting to end the war in Viet Nam and bring home our young men.

He feels that the money spent on the war should be spent in the Bronx on better schools, better housing, safer streets, better health care and lowering local taxes.

Bingham was the chief House sponsor of the McGovern-Hatfield Amendment.

Northern Ireland:
Jonathan Bingham has urged an end to internment and withdrawal of British troops. Permanent peace will come only when Ireland is free and united.

Israel:
In 1952, Jack Bingham, as Deputy Director of the Point 4 program, helped get Israel its first $40 million loan. At the U.N. and now on the House Foreign Affairs Committee, Bingham has consistently fought for full U.S. commitment to Israel. Bingham knows that a strong Israel means peace in the Middle East.

Jack Bingham is the chief House sponsor of the Soviet Jewish Refugee Act of 1972—now on its way to passage in the Congress.

REASON FIVE:
CONGRESSMAN BINGHAM LEADS THE CRUSADE FOR FAIR TREATMENT FOR SENIOR CITIZENS

Jack Bingham's tireless efforts on behalf of senior citizens earned him the Council of Senior Citizens' "National Award of Merit."

Bingham sponsored:
☐ the first Medicare bill.
☐ the "Meals on Wheels" program.
☐ the Senior Citizens' Service Corps.

Bingham's program includes:
☐ 25% increase in Social Security benefits with an automatic cost of living increase.
☐ special tax exemptions for senior citizens.
☐ a housing allowance for citizens under Social Security—these programs would assure dignity, justice, respect and fair treatment to all senior citizens.

REASON SIX:
CONGRESSMAN BINGHAM'S OPPONENTS MUST BE DEFEATED

Jack Bingham's real opponent in this race is not James Scheuer. It is the Rockefeller Machine and the political bosses in Albany. They redistricted New York—They want to dictate which Democrats should go back to Congress.

The new 22nd Congressional District contains 60% of Jack Bingham's old district, 26% of Congressman Biaggi's old district and only 14% of Scheuer's old district.

We cannot allow the big power interests in Albany to push Jack Bingham out of Congress.

Ted Kheel, the man who led the fight against the Lindsay-Rockefeller-Ronan alliance last year is now leading the fight to KEEP BINGHAM IN CONGRESS.

Another Straus brochure (reproduced on page 177) was a questionnaire on local, national, and international issues that the voter could fill in and mail. Diamond arranged for each returned questionnaire to be acknowledged by personal letter. That isn't done in many campaigns, but voters like personal attention, and the word of mouth was good from people who got a response. Attention to details and to opportunities such as these is extremely important. At the same time, however, it must be emphasized that you and your staff should not regard mail response of this type as the same as a probability sample survey. Although it is much more than a public relations or advertising gimmick, since it suggests what's on the voters' minds, it should be only helpful, not controlling, in developing a sense of the issues and priorities. Results of mail questionnaires can be expeditiously hand tallied by your staff; the low reliability of the sample does not justify additional computer expenses.

The Bella Abzug for Congress brochure (reproduced on pages 178–79) was suitable for mailing and for personal distribution in public places. It contained endorsements, concise backgrounds and stands on issues, and a simple text explaining why she was running. The typeface and wide margins made it easy to read, and the use of photographs and their placement were most professional. The piece was folded so that the campaign theme—"This woman's place is in the House / the House of Representatives," in yellow against a white background—was on top. The brochure, each folded section of which measured 8½″ × 3⅝″, opening out to 14½″, was mostly black on white, but the campaign theme and several other highpoints appeared in yellow. My only criticism is that perhaps too many subjects were included for an eight-page fold. A hand-stamped office address was used since there were several campaign offices in Ms. Abzug's large, oddly shaped congressional district. If she had had a single headquarters, her office address should have been printed rather than stamped, since the hand stamp, in addition to requiring staff or volunteer labor, might suggest an afterthought. Political literature should normally contain a printed address and telephone number for people who would like to volunteer, contribute, or work in your campaign.

Jonathan B. Bingham's 1972 brochure (reproduced on pages 180–81—another excellent example of an eight-page fold-over multipurpose piece—focused on issues of specific concern to his new congressional district. Effective use of photographs and white space helped persuade the voter to read the text, which was brief and to the point. As the voter unfolded the brochure, the "six reasons to keep Bingham in Congress" appeared in numerical order, with the main points printed in large, clear, blue type. The brochure, each folded section of which measured 9″ × 3⅞″, opening out to 15⅜″, was mostly black on white, with a blue background on the outside fold.

See, by contrast, another brochure (pages 184–85) citing six reasons to vote for a candidate—in this case, Arthur J. Goldberg, whose gubernatorial campaign in 1970 against Governor Nelson Rockefeller of New York was generally regarded as a disaster. Goldberg's personality was bland, and his political literature didn't help. The unexciting text of the brochure, which indicated only the candidate's legal and judicial experience, and the campaign theme, "Integrity, Experience, Concern" (printed on the front cover), were not sufficiently vigorous to carry this basically dull handout. The piece was printed in two versions: with and without a picture of Basil Paterson, a Negro who ran for lieutenant governor on Goldberg's ticket. (Various versions of brochures are sometimes printed for distribution in different areas or to different client groups.)

The 1968 reelection mailer of Senator Jacob K. Javits of New York (part of which is reproduced on pages 186–87) is a fine example of brochure layout. Although each page measures only 4″ × 5″, the copy is highly legible. Every statement is illustrated by a photograph, and white space is used effectively. The outside covers (printed in white against a blue background) and the first six of the brochure's thirty inside pages are shown here. The final seven pages, printed in smaller type and without photographs, contain Senator Javits's legislative record, with items divided by topic for easy reference. A brief biography of the candidate appears on the inside back cover. An expensive brochure of this sort should be mailed selectively, not given out on the street where many copies are likely to be wasted on passersby who throw it away without looking at it.

Campaigning deadlines don't generally allow time for perfection. The Nathan Straus piece shown on pages 188–89, produced in only 72 hours, was quite successful on balance, although it may have irri-

6 Reasons For Making Arthur

1. The Man

Arthur J. Goldberg . . . son of immigrant parents . . . one of nine children . . . worked his way up, in the years when the labor movement was changing America, to become one of the nation's top labor attorneys. A confidant of President Kennedy, he worked at Kennedy's side in the critical years when Kennedy was changing America. Goldberg is married to the former Dorothy Kurgans. Their son, Bob, practices law in Alaska and their married daughter, Barbara, lives in Chicago. The Goldbergs are proud grandparents of three grandchildren.

2. The Working Man's Lawyer

Arthur J. Goldberg began practicing law at 21 and today's polarization is not a new experience for him. He was the mediator, the negotiator and, when needed, the forceful spokesman for the labor movement in the critical years when the working man carved out his fair share of America's prosperity. With over 4 million Americans unemployed and inflation prices, these Goldberg talents can be put to work for New York.

3. In The Cabinet

The early sixties were exciting years. President Kennedy was turning America towards tomorrow. Large corporations were brought into tow, wages and labor conditions were stabilized, and depression-like unemployment was brought under control. Arthur Goldberg sat in the President's Cabinet and, as Secretary of Labor, helped solve these critical issues. He was an excellent administrator of large Government programs.

4. On The Supreme Court.

Secretary Goldberg became Justice Goldberg when President Kennedy appointed him to the Supreme Court . . . a seat formerly occupied by Holmes, Cardozo, and Frankfurter. There he participated in, and often wrote for the Court, decisions on issues which covered the span of American life, winning praise as one of the Court's outstanding legal minds. His work was to make the Constitution live, and so it did, on racial questions and the rights of the indigent, on capital punishment and the right to travel, on free speech and the right to dissent.

Goldberg Your New Governor

5. In The United Nations

Justice Goldberg became Ambassador Goldberg when the world threatened to erupt into nuclear war and President Johnson asked him to become Ambassador to the United Nations and America's spokesman to the world. He participated in the decisions which changed the course of history. He fought against the escalation of the war in Vietnam, and for a complete stopping of the bombing of North Vietnam, and for a negotiated settlement without concern about "losing face." He fought for the protection of Israel's integrity. He negotiated the space treaty and the nuclear non-proliferation treaty through the General Assembly. He convinced President Johnson to reject advice from the generals to invade Cambodia. When he spoke, the world listened.

6. Integrity, Experience, Concern

As Governor, citizen Arthur J. Goldberg will bring the talents of a lifetime to bear on the problems which plague, confuse and anger New Yorkers. He is, at first, a mediator, a conciliator, a peacemaker, a finder of a way to justice through the maze of anger and violence. But he is also an aggressive leader when the time and the issues demand. He is a man of judicial restraint, but he is also a tireless advocate and a tough adversary to those who would deny justice.

He is what New York desperately needs in Albany.

A Distinguished Running Mate

Senator Basil A. Paterson is a forceful counterpart and partner for Arthur Goldberg.

Like Goldberg, he is an attorney, and like Goldberg he worked his way up from the ghetto to become a compassionate attorney, a university professor and a State Senator.

In the State Senate, he served with distinction, leading the fight for a progressive Democratic Party. He has served on the Judiciary, Banking, Labor and Industry Committees . . . committees which served all New Yorkers. In April, 1967, he was selected as one of the two outstanding legislators in the State.

A Roman Catholic, Senator Paterson is married to the former Portia Hairston, a teacher. They have two sons.

WHAT I'VE DONE.
WHAT I'M DOING.
AND MOST IMPORTANT,
WHAT I AM GOING TO DO.

Jacob K. Javits
U.S. SENATOR

VOTE FOR THE SENATOR.
RE-ELECT JAVITS.

IF WE WERE ABLE
TO REBUILD WESTERN EUROPE,
WE CAN REBUILD OUR OWN CITIES.

I have met American soldiers who felt they were better off in Vietnam than they were in Harlem.

I have seen American citizens loot and burn their own neighborhoods.

I understand the hopelessness with which these Americans face life. I also understand the frustrations of all who live and work in our deteriorating cities. And why many families and businesses are being driven out.

That is why I call for massive economic redevelopment of our cities.

My idea is not for just another urban development program. It is a plan which would call for 10 to 15 billion dollars a year for 10 years. Mostly from private sources.

Like the Marshall Plan which rebuilt war-torn Europe, it is a total program. One which enlists both self-help and self-determination.

It is a program which relates the human problems—such as jobs and education—to the physical problems like housing, transportation and pollution. In short, it treats the total environment.

The difficult task of revitalizing our sick cities must begin now.

And when it is done, we will see more than cities rebuilt. We will see cities reborn.

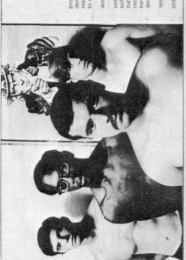

I THINK EVERY QUALIFIED STUDENT SHOULD GO TO COLLEGE, WHETHER HE HAS THE MONEY OR NOT.

The Federal Government has a program guaranteeing loans to students. For millions of youngsters it means the difference between going to college or not going.

I authored that program and worked successfully to expand it.

But our students weren't the only ones who needed money. Our schools did. So I saw to it that our nation's colleges and universities received federal assistance to build new dormitories, new classrooms and new laboratories.

But my fight for education isn't limited to the college level.

In 1965 I helped break a 10-year-old deadlock in Congress. The result was passage of the first federal program for aid to elementary and secondary schools.

Last year I cosponsored the Bilingual Education Act. It enables Spanish-speaking students to receive instruction in their native language. And helps them adjust more effectively to their new environment.

And this year Congress enacted my program to provide millions of dollars worth of free school lunches and breakfasts for the children of poor families.

My philosophy on the subject is simple. Education should be based on a child's ability to learn.

Not on his parents' ability to pay.

THE SOLUTION TO POVERTY ISN'T WELFARE. IT'S JOBS.

Last year we established a day-care center program.

It provides care for the children of poor families. So their mothers can afford to go out and look for a job.

The program was one of 12 amendments I wrote into the anti-poverty law.

Another amendment provided government aid for business to train the hard-core unemployed. This program will take 100,000 more people off the unemployment rolls by the middle of next year.

Right now I'm pushing hard for a project I call the Domestic Development Bank. By using both private and public funds, it will supply money to help the poor go into business for themselves.

At the same time, I'm working to establish locally-owned development companies in depressed areas. The government would hire these companies to perform community services like housing rehabilitation and rat control.

But more jobs are still needed. And my plans for the future include working for tax incentives for industry to provide the training as well as the jobs.

Finally, the entire welfare system must be reformed. Because welfare can only make poverty bearable.

Jobs can end it.

YOU PAID YOUR INCOME TAXES on April 15th like all the rest of us.

THIS is what JACOB GILBERT did with some of your money.

THIS was delivered to 155,000 mailboxes, including every:

Congressman Gilbert sent his self-glorifying biography into our district free

Bar

Poolroom

Pet Shop

This cost you approximately $11,000.00.

Congressmen are given this privilege of free mailing for official communications.

When you go to work, your boss expects a full day's work for a full day's pay.

Every Congressman is entitled to a paid staff for his New York and Washington offices. Only 8 out of 11 of Congressman Gilbert's employees work at all. They are:

GILBERT wastes taxpayers' money while the community suffers!

If you agree with the New York Times

incumbents deserve renomination. Representative Jacob H. Gilbert, last survivor of the Buckley regime, is opposed in the 22d by Nathan Straus. Mr. Gilbert's retirement to private life is overdue, as is that of Paul A. Fino, the reactionary Republican incumbent in the 24th, who is also the Bronx County G.O.P. leader.

VOTE FOR THE MAN WHO CARES NATHAN STRAUS
PRIMARY DAY, TUESDAY, JUNE 18th, 3-10 P. M.

tated thoughtful voters. Based partially on the well-known 1040 income tax form, the front of the piece implied that the incumbent congressman, Jacob Gilbert of the Bronx, had used his franking privilege to mail his campaign biography without charge to 155,000 addresses, including bars, poolrooms, and pet shops, in his new constituency (new as a result of a redistricting), at a cost to the taxpayers of $11,000. (Every congressman has the franking privilege, but it is supposed to be used only for official business, not for campaigning.) The front of the piece, with its large red panel and contrasting black text, was visually effective in dramatizing the issue, and it did the most difficult thing in brochure design: it got the voters to read it. However, the back was cluttered and crammed with too much copy. The critical themes—Gilbert (the incumbent) wastes taxpayers' money while the community suffers; and "Vote for the man who cares"—were somewhat obscured by many other important textual details. A secondary theme, "Only 8 out of 11 of Congressman Gibert's employees work at all," might have been more effectively used as the theme of a separate piece.

Since most political handbills distributed on streets are thrown away within one block, your basic problem in designing your brochures will be to make them attractive and distinctive enough so that perhaps at least 50 per cent of the voters who receive them read them. Careful use of photographs and space, using cardboard stock or lighter paper of good quality and attractive, readable type, and perhaps using colored paper or bright inks—or white ink on black paper—will all contribute to the receptivity of your literature. Brochure design remains an art.

A final word of caution is in order: Candidates whose funds do not permit them to hire an advertising agency to design their brochures are naturally tempted to try to adapt or emulate a political brochure that they have seen used successfully by a candidate in another area. In doing this, they run some risk. A really good piece is designed in response to a specific local situation, and someone else's situation may not be applicable to you.

Reprinting literature from other sources
Not all your campaign literature need be original. You can—and should—reprint favorable newspaper publicity, editorials endorsing

you (see page 193), and statements by local civic clubs, chapters of the League of Women Voters, or other prestigious organizations that may have a positive impact on the voters. These should be duplicated soon after the endorsement and preferably delivered by volunteers to the voters' residences. Preparing a mailing, in addition to being expensive, needs a certain lead time, and delay takes away some of the beneficial impacts of the endorsement.

Whatever you do, don't take extracts from an endorsement or newspaper article, as movie and other entertainment ads do when they carefully select complimentary words out of a basically unfavorable review. Use the whole text even if it contains a few negative or neutral statements. If you use the selectivity artifice, it may soon be found out and used effectively against you.

Negative editorial comment or unfavorable news articles about your opponent can be reproduced and distributed in the same way, in the style of the political broadsides of the eighteenth and nineteenth centuries.

Printed matter of this sort can be reproduced inexpensively by photo-offset. Design elements, paper quality, and the use of color and white space are basically the same as those applying to original literature. You may wish to superimpose the material to be reproduced on your letterhead or add a photograph or campaign slogan at the top or bottom of the page.

The recognition compulsion (or the name game)

Probably because candidates, like other human beings, have strong ego needs, billboard and poster advertising often gets an undeserved emphasis. Many candidates enjoy seeing their names and pictures all over the district; they are gratifying, and they provide physical evidence of expenditures.

In some campaigns, billboard and poster activity becomes absolutely frenzied. For example, in a county campaign on the East Coast, the senior men of the campaign staffs wasted their time ripping each other's posters down. There were fist fights, and one group went to the extreme of carrying baseball bats as defense weapons. When the going became really rough, one team was accompanied by an armed off-duty policeman, the brother of one of the participants. Each evening they presented their candidate with trophies: stacks of the opponent's posters which they had torn down. These forays at night are conducted by so-called phantom squads.

Despite the frequency of such occurrences, posters are very popular. They are tied on telephone poles and pasted on U.S. mailboxes, telephone booths, and anything else in sight. They literally disfigure areas and remain years later as shabby silent memorials to the campaign. Many candidates nowadays, realizing that permanently glued posters deface neighborhoods and may arouse negative reactions for that reason, put up posters with string or otherwise assure that they can be removed easily. At the bottom of each poster, it would be wise to print the line: "Not to be posted on telephone poles or public property."

There is controversy about the beneficial impacts of billboards and posters; there are reasons to believe that few voters determine their choice on the basis of this type of advertising.

Many members of political clubs insist that posters be used since putting up posters is an activity they're used to and understand, and a way for them to make a direct contribution. In any case, don't allow the poster-billboard mania to seize your staff. It isn't worth concentrated effort and can be destructive if it takes attention and money from more productive activities.

It is also common in campaigns to have large signs painted and placed in front of campaign headquarters. These are expensive to prepare and to have mounted and then removed, and they give almost no return in votes for an investment of about $500. If you face pressure from club members and other candidates to have such signs, you might consider using bunting or flags on which your name is stencilled in different colors: It is cheaper and pleasing to the eye, although it is no more likely to win voters to your side than is a conventional sign.

Other devices to gain name recognition are bus and subway posters, car stickers, and car aerial pennants. But posters are usually purchased for placement in all the buses from one city garage. In larger cities this may be a problem, since the routes from a garage may not be coterminous with your district. Outside bus posters, although more expensive, may be a better value, since they are larger and can be seen by pedestrians as well as passengers.

Comparison of media impacts

In only a few campaigns, even when a great deal of money is involved, does anyone bother to investigate the relative impacts and effectiveness of the various media approaches being used.* One reason for this obvious deficiency is that each medium is usually assigned a specialist, and coordination among the specialists is generally restricted to message content alone; there is hardly time to think of developing the most effective role for each. Each technician or consultant has a vested interest in encouraging investment or expenditures for his own medium. It is up to you and your campaign staff to do a comparative evaluation of the impacts of the various media and decide the emphasis to be given each one in timing and expense.

The campaign staff of Governor George Romney of Michigan was reported to have developed some excellent evaluatory devices. James M. Perry notes that in 1966 the Romney staff, focusing on certain Michigan counties where vote-splitting was probable in the gubernatorial campaign, used a recorded telephone message campaign followed by market research evaluation of impact.† When they discovered the technique was successful, they went into a saturation campaign.‡ Evaluations cost money, but it makes considerable sense to spend several thousand dollars on research to make certain that it will be worth investing $50,000 on a particular campaign appeal. Evaluation techniques should also be applied when analyzing the impacts of direct mail versus telephoning or radio versus television, for example, in small campaigns as well as large ones. They involve marginal increment analysis and cost benefit analysis, techniques long in use in American business, and don't really require enormous technical expertise. Figures showing what it costs to reach a thousand

* There is not any absolutely accurate measure of exactly how much more effective one medium is than another. In commercial advertising, it is usual to test impacts of magazine advertising versus phone advertising or radio and television. Such a study is usually done by an independent research agency. But in political advertising time is very short and the variables—costs, criteria (unaided retention, recall, etc.), and continuity in motivation—are complex and constantly changing. Timely recommendations are, therefore, unlikely.

† Some technicians think that recorded messages are effective, while others—including myself—regard them as having very limited impact.

‡ See James M. Perry, *The New Politics* (New York: Potter, 1968), for a good objective comparison of specific media in actual campaigns.

people are generally available from the advertising directors of local radio and television stations and of newspapers and magazines. If you lack these figures, or wish to supplement them, there are other ways of evaluating relative effectiveness:

1. If you are doing public opinion research, a question on media impact can be included in the survey questionnaire: Where did you hear of _____? Which source did you find most helpful in deciding whom to vote for?

2. Midway through the campaign, you can ask the same questions in a spot telephone check of 200 voters chosen at random (in primaries, only registrants of your party, of course), perhaps concerntrating your survey in the swing areas or in the areas where the voters you're not sure of are concentrated, and keeping in mind that by this time up to 75 percent of the electorate have made up their minds. Your media allocations should then be revised to maximize cost effectiveness.

Buying time and space

It would be prudent as early as possible for you and your staff to make a comprehensive evaluation of media impacts in your own area and decide on the basis of your study what percentage of your investments you wish to allocate among the various political advertising techniques, in the following fashion:

TYPE OF EXPENDITURE	1ST HALF OF CAMPAIGN	2ND HALF OF CAMPAIGN
Television	%	%
Radio	%	%
Newspaper ads	%	%
Brochures	%	%
Mailings	%	%
Telephones	%	%

It is also important to get some idea of the best phasing of these expenditures by analyzing past successful campaigns in your area and, if possible, discussing them with the successful candidates and/or managers. If you are a new campaigner, you may decide to hit television hard in the beginning to get recognition and awareness and then rely on news breaks, discussion programs, etc., later on, while emphasizing direct mail in your own budget at that stage.

In his 1966 gubernatorial campaign, Nelson Rockefeller's strategy was to run a quiet, low-keyed television campaign. It was reported that his campaign staff bought television and radio time months in advance, concentrating on day and late evening hours. His staff had decided what audience they wished to reach, found that it could best be reached at non-prime-time hours, and then bought the time well in advance when the spots they wanted were still available. The point here is that if you are using radio or television you have to decide your schedule early because you will have to compete with other commercial and political television and radio advertisers for the times and days you want. Other people also know which times are effective with which audiences, and time is sold on a first come, first served basis. This is not to say, of course, that you should make all your radio and television commitments far in advance. Some leeway must remain in your plans to allow for modifications midway through the campaign, as discussed in the previous section.

Time buying is an art in itself. Political television consultants, like David Garth, retain specialists whose job is to match the character-istics of the voters you want to reach as closely as possible with the characteristics of the listeners and viewers who are tuned in to a particular program at a particular time. Some politicians like radio time on serious music stations, assuming that listeners to those stations include proportionately more undecided voters, who tend to vote in higher proportions. (Similarly, some campaign managers prefer to place certain newspaper ads on the sports pages, where male voters are most apt to read them, and to use different copy on society or women's pages.) Other politicians emphasize television ads immediately before and/or after the 10- or 11-o'clock evening news. All these slots are popular and must therefore be reserved early. If you retain a specialist, you should go over these choices very thoroughly with him. If you staff are to perform this function, they should educate themselves in the options by talking to the advertising managers of the local radio, television, and newspaper offices, and by examining the back files of the newspapers. In addition, you ought to ask your party's best campaigners and their managers about their experiences with the effectiveness of the local media.

Giveaways

Almost every campaign features some type of giveaway. The most popular giveaways are of course buttons, which are produced by the thousands and hardly ever worn. William J. Pfeiffer, one of Nelson Rockefeller's campaign managers, was quoted as saying in 1966, "Somewhere around this city [New York] there are two million Rockefeller buttons. Where are they? You can stand all day on the busiest street corner and not see one of them. On the other hand, if you didn't have them, you'd hear from every county chairman in the state that you weren't doing anything for them. Some day, somebody's going to have the guts to throw the buttons out." * Pfeiffer is right, yet most campaigns have buttons because that's the way it's always been done. Pfeiffer has also been quoted as saying that 25 percent of the money in any campaign is leaked right out the window. In my experience, the percentage is often higher than that, and buttons and other giveaways are responsible for a significant proportion of the waste. If you have fiscal constraints in a campaign, it's silly to spend funds for giveaways just because everyone else does, particularly if the potential return in changed votes is not great.

Joe Napolitan is among the big-name campaign managers who doubt the utility of gimmick giveaways. Combs, bookmarks, ballpoint pens, rulers, rain bonnets, nail files, shopping bags, and balloons are expensive and rarely change a significant number of votes.

Two giveaways, in my experience, do seem to be effective. One, used by Walter Diamond in the 1968 Straus congressional campaign, consisted of a small ballpoint pen enclosed with a thank-you card that was sent to every voter who had signed the nominating petitions. Purchasing the pens, handling, mailing, and printing the thank-you card all cost money, but it was a focused investment, a thoughtful gesture that pleased many people and could not offend anyone. Relatively inexpensive plastic shopping bags are in continued use and, unlike campaign buttons, are highly visible.† Costs run about 5½ to

---

* Robert MacNeil, *The People Machine: The Influence of Television on American Politics* (New York: Harper & Row, 1968), p. 233.

† Shopping bags have become the current obsession. In the Bronx Democratic primaries of 1972, an estimated 2.5 million shopping bags were given out by congressional, judicial, and other candidates. There are only 150,000 Bronx Democratic primary voters. One Bronx voter told a candidate that he had collected twelve hundred political shopping bags; when he had five thousand shopping bags, he intended to have his name entered and run for office himself.

over 10 cents apiece when the bags are ordered in lots of 10,000.

To provide maximum effectiveness for your money, shopping bags should be well designed from both an artistic and a functional point of view. They should be attractive, with an uncluttered pattern and with clear colors that do not rub off, they should be convenient to carry, with handles that do not break or stretch out of shape, and they should be strong enough not to burst when they are full. They need not be the largest size available. Some New York department stores now provide relatively small (11×11 inches) plastic shopping bags, which are used over and over again judging from the frequency with which they are seen on the street. Whatever their size, the bags should be easily recognizable as yours and they should be convenient, attractive, and durable enough that people will carry them frequently.

In his 1970 senatorial campaign, Richard L. Ottinger had silk scarves and ties designed to be given to larger contributors as souvenirs. On a mass basis, however, scarves, balloons, rulers, or lighters are not really effective, in the judgment of most professionals. They are frequently used on the basis of "why not?—it's not that expensive," but the money could be better spent elsewhere.*

Street campaigning

In local campaigns, and to a lesser degree in national campaigning as well, meeting the voters on the streets remains an important part of campaign public relations. It is the most direct and often the best advertising technique. National candidates visit large factories or make lunch-hour speeches in areas where office workers are concentrated. In local campaigns, half of a candidate's energies may profitably go into street campaigning and personal door-to-door campaigning.

Some basic rules do exist for this. If you're using telephones or direct mail in your campaign, employ these media to give some advance notice that you will be in a given public place at a given hour and day. You may wish to have workers with bullhorns advertise your presence in the neighborhood. Some candidates prefer to use

---

* In Milwaukee, for example, political candidates still give out blotters, despite the fact that most people now use ball point pens which do not require a blotter. In West Virginia, candidates provide liquor, since that is the custom. Now, *that's* sensible.

cars equipped with loudspeakers that cruise the area indicating where you are and what your walking schedule will be. Other candidates prefer to be accompanied by a coterie to give out campaign literature or by members of their families to develop voter rapport. Stop and talk to groups of people if possible, but don't impose on them. Many voters will be cordial even if they have no intention of voting for you; do not make the mistake of thinking, as greater men have done before you, that a warm reception on the streets assures you a victory at the polls.

Obviously, street campaigning works out best in areas where there are clusters of voters. In major cities, campaigning at subway stops is popular. (In New York City, this is now automatic. I had something to do with initiating the custom in James H. Scheuer's congressional campaign in 1961.) Parks and shopping centers are also important. If you can find a place where voters are clustered and where other candidates are not campaigning, by all means use it. For example, one candidate running in a suburban New York district campaigned very successfully at the New York City terminal of the express bus line serving his area; soon his opponent, sensing a good idea, began doing the same thing.

In small campaigns—for assembly or district leader—the most effective campaigning is probably done door-to-door. Properly, you should start three to six months before election day, since you can cover only a few voters per evening. Meeting the voters in their homes is time-consuming and exhausting, but it is most effective not only in gaining votes immediately but also in setting up a base for direct mail, telephone calls, and newspaper ads if you can afford these reinforcements.

Loudspeakers

Many candidates send sound trucks through their districts blasting away with their endorsements and their qualifications. Some of these broadcast recorded cassettes, but usually the loudspeaker is manned by a campaign worker accompanying the driver. In some areas, this technique offends many voters and is not worth the investment. In my judgment, loudspeakers are seldom helpful except in special situations. In a recent four-way race for a judgeship, for example, *The*

New York Times endorsed one candidate three days before the election. For the next three days, the endorsed candidate, Stanley Danzig, used loudspeakers to announce that he had been endorsed by the *Times* and selected as most qualified by a lawyers' screening committee. He won in a 4,000–2,000–1,000–1,000 break, despite the fact that he had not used direct mail, street campaigning, or telephones, while his opponents had put posters all over the district and put literature under multitudes of front doors. He won very handily and very economically as well.

Used purposefully—for example, manned by a celebrity or putting a last-minute endorsement before the largest possible audience—loudspeakers are a useful public-relations tool. Used indiscriminately, however, they are a blight to the ear, just as last year's campaign posters are blight to the eye, and they are likely to lose as many votes as they gain.

Personal mailings

The use of computer letters as described on the following pages has become so common that a simple but effective approach is frequently overlooked. The device of having a candidate's friends send letters to their professional colleagues or fellow members of a fraternal order, school board, etc., making a personal appeal to vote for him, has considerable impact. The candidate supplies the prepared letters, stamps, and blank envelopes, and the friends supply their signature and their personal mailing lists. To stay in keeping with the personal effect that makes them effective, these letters should be hand addressed and hand stamped.

Sometimes, a candidate can be embarrassed when a friend writes such a letter on the letterhead of an organization to which he belongs, thereby suggesting a nonexistent official endorsement from the organization. This usually offends many members and can cost you votes instead of increasing your support. Friends can also do you unwitting harm by supplying lists that are years old, without removing the names of colleagues or members who have died or have simply lost contact. Caution friends who offer you mailing lists about this problem and ask them to prune their lists so that letters are sent only to those whom they will not offend. Offer to provide staff assistance in this task if there is any way your staff can contribute to updating the lists.

Using computers in campaign advertising
The use of computers in political campaigning is often referred to in a derogatory manner as the professional engineering of election campaigns, which permits candidates who can afford the technology to win elections regardless of their merit. This is simply untrue. Computer technology has merely given a new speed and efficiency to the old methods. (If you can afford a car, you don't ride a camel. Riding a camel is neither more nor less moral than riding in a car.) As far as I am concerned, it always makes sense to take advantage of whatever technology is available, if you can afford it and if the net results are more efficient or otherwise beneficial. This is certainly true in campaigning, where competition is tough and time is very short.

Over the last decade, I have frequently done voter profiling and analysis of a district's election returns by laborious hand processing. These operations were arduous but not uncommon and did not appear "threatening" until computers, with their supposed depersonalization, were introduced. As a matter of fact, the computer has simply made it possible for me and others to do the same job with less effort and a greatly reduced margin of error. This applies equally to computers used in research and to those used in direct mail campaigns. As a practical matter, my experience leads me to predict that your main worry will be paying the bills for computer-related services rather than responding to adverse press and public reactions to your doing so. The remainder of this chapter summarizes the ways in which computers may be useful to you in the political advertising process.

Warren Weaver, Jr., cited the reversal of a governor's stand on an issue because of a computerized vote simulation done by Decision Making Information, a public opinion analyst in Los Angeles.* The governor had changed his position to attract the approval of younger, relatively liberal Republicans. Weaver wrote, "Increasingly, candidates are coming to rely on [political technology] for guidelines, inspiration, and in some cases, preservation." He noted that "a good deal of the new technology has become semi-secret and controversial. Few candidates want to be observed shaping their views to conform to the public prejudice of the moment, and it tends to make the voters uneasy to learn that their prejudices can be so easily identified

* Warren Weaver, Jr., "Computers Counseling the Candidates," *New York Times,* October 30, 1970, p. 1.

and copied." But opinion polls were common long before computers came into use in politics. Computers—the "new technology"—have simply made it less time-consuming to tabulate the same results.

Weaver also described the use of computers to provide lists of voters who tend to swing back and forth between parties by Nelson Gross of New Jersey, who wished to direct recorded telephone messages at the "swing" voters identified by the computer. According to Weaver, the firm of Bailey, Deardorff and Brown used computers for Gross's campaign as follows: (1) analyzed the last four elections for 5,000 election districts to ascertain where liberal and moderate Republicans did well and why; (2) produced a list of 1,200 swing districts that were sometimes but not always carried by Republicans; and (3) isolated areas for special mailings and for the candidate's schedule of personal appearances. Jobs like this can be done by hand and are still done that way in smaller areas.

Weaver reported that Decision Making Information had a broad range of services for political candidates providing professional judgments based on computer-processed data. It offered a system of advising candidates how best to reach any one of 21 voter groups, each classed by degree of party affiliation and level of political interest. The service included advice on which media could best reach which voter group and whether ads would be more effective in the sports section or in the news section. Costs as of 1970 were based on a fee of $600 an hour for computer use; the comprehensive advice just described cost in the area of $2,000 to $3,000.

William E. Roberts of Decision Making Information told Weaver that he didn't see anything particularly sinister in a candidate's scientifically determining the interest and opinions of the electorate; rather, he felt that "this enables the candidate to talk about issues which interest the public and not about those on which the public disagrees with him." *

Increasingly, the financial and political logic of a large-scale campaign forces such uses of the computer. The techniques are relatively elaborate and usually expensive. At a scale less than a congressional district, you may not need them, but you can put the same logic to

* I believe this fairly common approach can backfire; many voters may disagree with a specific position of a candidate but so respect his integrity and courage that they will vote for him despite their disagreement on the issue.

work with less sophisticated instrumentation and obtain similarly good results.

Computer-assisted direct mail advertising. Direct mail is perhaps the most important use of the computer in current campaigning on any large scale (over 50,000 voters). Governor George Romney's campaigns in Michigan were a relatively early example of the sensible use of this device.† Computers can also be used economically in small campaigns, but some computer firms will not accept smaller jobs since they involve fees of only several hundred dollars.

As a beginning, computers can save you considerable mailing expense by combining members of a single household (actually all voters with the same surname and the same address) onto a single card. There is an error margin of 5 to 8 percent on these combinations, since the computer will not combine the same surname at the same address if, for example, one card spells "Street" in full and one spells it "St.," or if apartment numbers don't match exactly. Such elimination ("suppression") of duplications alone can produce important savings, particularly in larger campaigns sending out several mailings, since otherwise the same household might receive two or three duplicate pieces, one for each registered voter. Some firms give political clients a choice among several options for suppressing duplications within a household and making other possible suppressions.

Computers can also economize on mailings after the first mailing by eliminating cards of voters whose first mailing was returned as undeliverable—usually deceased voters and those who have moved since the registration list was published. Such "nixies" can account for up to 20 percent of registration lists. But some companies will not do this since it costs them some of their business volume by reducing the number of labels, envelopes, and other items they provide a candidate.

Alvin L. Steinhart, the president of Datatab, Inc., a New York company, described to Philip Dougherty of *The New York Times* how "letters can be specifically designed to do such things as send private home owners messages on property taxes and slum dwellers

† Romney's methods are described by James M. Perry in *The New Politics* (New York: Potter, 1968).

messages on crime in the inner city." "These letters," Dougherty reported, "are constructed from a number of paragraphs programmed into the computer and drawn forth in the proper combination for the proper voter." *

Several computer houses, largely concentrated in New York and Los Angeles, serve the needs of political campaigners and use computers in direct mail. Among them, in addition to Datatab, are Bonded Mailings and Computer Services. Typical, perhaps, is O.S.I., Inc., of New York, whose Democratic and Republican clients in New York and New Jersey have included Governor Nelson Rockefeller. One of O.S.I.'s most useful developments is Jeff Barrett's ethnication or ethnic-select program, which identifies the religious and/or ethnic origin of voters and enables the client to direct focused appeals at the group or groups of his choice. The file was made by selecting specific names and name endings known to be common among certain groups. For example, thousands of names were stored in the memory file as probably Jewish. As a check, another file was prepared to remove names that didn't belong on the list for each ethnic group.† Construction of the files for New York City was done by hand and took three weeks. With the hand work done, the computer can go through its tape file and pull out the names in any category it is instructed to select. The charge for the process early in 1972 was $10 per thousand names searched, with a $250 minimum fee for congressional districts and $100 for assembly districts. Considerations of economy require pre-selecting the geographic areas to be searched (on the basis of census and historical data) rather than searching an entire large district.

Many mailing firms use the Cheshire machine, which glues computer-typed labels onto envelopes, at a cost of about $3 per thousand labels plus $3.50 per thousand for mounting. The Cheshire system makes it possible to produce carbon copies of labels—a considerable

---

* *The New York Times,* March 12, 1972, Section 3 (Business and Finance), p. 17.

† No ethnic-select program of this type can be absolutely accurate, of course, since, for example, some Jewish people change their names, some Jewish women marry non-Jews and thereby acquire non-Jewish surnames, and some people with Jewish surnames have given names that indicate non-Jewish origin. (There are ways of matching common given names by ethnic group, but this increases the expense more than proportionately.) All told, however, the error margin is only on the order of 10 to 15 percent.

KEVIN BRINKWORTH
645 ELLICOTT SQUARE BUILDING
BUFFALO, NEW YORK 14203

October 26, 1971

Mrs Evelyn ~~Brockey~~
675 ~~Delaware~~ Ave   708
Buffalo   NY   14202

Dear Mrs ~~Brockey~~:

When a candidate asks for your vote, his responsibility should be to tell you how he sees the problems.
He should avoid political sniping. I am asking for
the votes of you and your family as 10th District
Candidate for our County Legislature. Why? I feel our
major problems are welfare, drug abuse and crime.

Welfare. Our system does not help people become
productive. The fault lies with State and Federal
officials playing politics with public dollars. For
instance, my opponent, as Assemblyman, voted against
the one-year residency requirement; a vote for spiral-
ing welfare cost.

Drug Abuse. We must wipe this filth from our door,
now. I will fight for: One-legislation to hit hard
drug suppliers, to get at the source; Two-a new county-
wide program to teach our children about the horror of
drug abuse.

Crime. We fear to walk our streets or in our parks
at night. And now even our children are not safe walking home from school in daylight. Crime is increasing.

These problems demand new solutions. I intend to
deliver them.

As a Republican, I believe you feel as I do. We
cannot afford the kind of indecision we saw on the
Stadium question. I ask your support for myself and
for Ned Regan.

Sincerely,

Kevin Brinkworth
Kevin Brinkworth

saving. Another process that has been commonly used consists of putting on adhesive labels by hand—usually with volunteer labor—at a cost of about $3.50 per thousand; but no carbons are available for future mailings. Some computer firms avoid the labeling problem altogether by inserting a computer-prepared card into an envelope with two cellophane windows side by side. In addition to eliminating labeling costs, this process is extremely useful for sending out attractive palm cards with the voting place marked in the first window and the voter's address in the second window. In this way, part of the message reaches the addressee even if he does not open the envelope. Window envelopes can, of course, be utilized without using computers, but computer personalization (mentioned below) adds great appeal to the mailing. Computer printing combined with offset typography costs some $45 per thousand, including printing but not postage. Early in 1972, O.S.I. was producing such pieces using an IBM 360-30 computer, which printed the addresses on continuous-form envelopes—envelopes connected to each other that are "burst," or separated, after processing—at a rate of 1,100 lines a minute, and it was planning to obtain an IBM 370 computer with a capacity of 2,200 lines a minute. There can be problems with continuous-form envelopes, since a printer has to add the bulk rate stamp and return address; and some coordination is required between the printer and the computer house in selecting the right envelope—for example, flap in or flap out, size, etc.—to avoid foul-ups. Such coordination should not be assumed to be automatic. Most of these problems, however, can be avoided by allowing enough time—for example, the bulk rate stamp can be preprinted.

A useful campaign device is the computer letter that looks like a personally typed letter, individually addressed and signed with a facsimile signature (see example on page 205). (In smaller campaigns, the candidate should sign these letters by hand, and it is probably advantageous to have the letters addressed by hand as well; the voter is more likely to open such an envelope.) The costs for this run $75 to $130 per thousand, including postage and stuffing and addressing envelopes. Richard L. Ottinger used this approach to thank people for their interest as he traveled through New York State in his 1970 senatorial race.

Another effective computer piece is a mailer that resembles

BULK RATE
U. S. POSTAGE
PAID
Hackensack, N. J.
Permit No. 2521

SPECIAL ELECTION INFORMATION

REPUBLICAN
PRIMARY
TUESDAY
SEPTEMBER 14

TELEGRAM
FROM
MIKE COFFEY

3
City Councilman

3 A
Michael A.
COFFEY

YOU SHOULD VOTE FOR MIKE COFFEY IN THE REPUBLICAN
COUNCIL PRIMARY. BECAUSE, MIKE IS A DYNAMIC YOUNG
MAN WHO IS NOT AFRAID TO SPEAK OUT ON THE ISSUES.
MIKE HAS THE EXPERIENCE IN COMMUNITY PLANNING
SERVING AS PRESIDENT OF THE NORTH BROADWAY ASSOC-
IATION.

AS COUNCILMAN MIKE COFFEY WILL REPRESENT OUR
BEAUTIFUL CITY WITH A SENSE OF HISTORICAL PRIDE.

YOUR VOTE FOR MIKE COFFEY WILL BE APPRECIATED AND
MEANINGFUL.

SINCERELY YOURS,
WHITE PLAINS REPUBLICAN
CITIZENS COMMITTEE

A CHOICE FOR A CHANGE

a telegram envelope with the machine-printed telegram form inside. It can be used in many ways, for many purposes. A study conducted in New Jersey found such a piece to be 9 percent more effective than any other computer letter, largely because voters opened it, thinking it might be a telegram. The envelope might bear a legend like "Special Election Information" (see page 207). Telegram-style pieces are generally partially done by photo-offset and cost approximately $55 to $60 a thousand.

Other uses of computers in campaign advertising. In addition to producing advertising mailings, computers can also be used to keep records of which voters have received which mailings, which voters have received telephone calls and what responses they gave, and which voters have met the candidate personally, called headquarters for information, volunteered to help, *ad infinitum*. In this function the computer is used as a memory bank. It is very expensive to program such a memory bank, but the expense may be justified in a large, close race. Additional uses of computers in campaign publicity are limited only by available funds and by the ingenuity and creativity of campaign and computer-house staffs.

6 Using Telephones in a Political Campaign

In a campaign, effective phone calls are like a marksman's bullets; posters, signs, radio and television are like a sweeping barrage of artillery—maybe they'll hit some of the right voters, but the odds are they'll hit mostly the wrong ones. But at least an incompetent campaigner doesn't kill anybody.

—A POLITICAL MECHANIC

In early political telephone campaigns, a simple canvass call was usual—for example, "Come out and vote on election day for Candidate A." Later, because many candidates were charmed by sophisticated technology, recorded messages had a period of popularity. Currently, professional campaigners use telephone calls to try to ascertain which voters are favorable, unfavorable, or undecided. In 1972, telephones were used to establish which issues concerned undecided voters, and a computer letter on the appropriate issue was sent to each undecided voter. Despite all the possible approaches, however, the effectiveness of telephoning depends on the quality of the message and the individual caller's ability to gain rapport with the voter being called.

An organized telephone effort is a feature of most political campaigns. It may be directed by amateurs or by professionals and may range from the candidate's relatives and friends making random personal appeals, each different from the other, to campaigns such as the Ottinger-Buckley-Goodell senatorial contest in New York in 1970, in which hundreds of professionally trained interviewers made several hundred thousand structured calls.

Telephone campaigns by paid or volunteer callers are useful if organized under experienced, professional direction and if the message content and method of delivery are supervised intelligently. Unplanned and unsupervised telephone campaigns can have negative effects. A voter insulted or annoyed by a telephone canvasser may tell his friends and relatives, and several such occurrences can adversely affect a tight election.

A telephone campaign must be kept within the context of the overall campaign. Calls should present the same themes as other advertising media used in the campaign, but they should be focused on groups that cannot be reached by the other media. They should be used when it is felt that conversation can make a more effective impact.

Telephoning should be regarded as a form of canvassing, for many of the same principles apply to both procedures. Whether contacting voters in person or by telephone, the caller is the candidate's personal representative and must be sufficiently well acquainted with the candidate's stands on issues of particular concern to the voters to be able to answer reasonable questions immediately and sensibly. A telephone call or personal visit in which the worker recites a memorized statement and is not prepared to answer questions is not likely to be effective. Engaging a voter in conversation and answering his questions in a forthright, friendly manner can have considerably greater impact.

Basic requirements

Institute a comprehensive telephone campaign only if you or your campaign committee are convinced significant benefits will accrue and not because your opponent is using telephones. The benefits may consist entirely of "firming up" friendly voters and proselytizing new voters, or they may also include research spin-offs, such as establishing just who the undecided voters are and how they may be reached through theme or issue development or through media. (To emphasize an important principle discussed at greater length in Chapter 3, the undecided are the 20 to 25 percent of the registered voters who do not make up their minds until late in the campaign. A few of them don't vote at all, but the group as a whole frequently casts the "swing" or determining vote in elections. Since the margin in most elections is usually under 10 percent of the total vote, and the undecided —usually well educated and knowledgeable—tend to vote in larger proportions than other groups, they are critically important. Establishing their characteristics and number is worth money and time.) If the conversations are carefully structured, information gathered in your telephone canvass can provide a valuable supplement or "input" to your campaign research, as well as serving an advertising function.*

In some situations, calling every voter in a district—for example, in a district where research indicates that 90 per cent of the vote is yours—is pointless and possibly harmful, since you may alienate voters who become annoyed at what they consider too many irritations in the course of a political campaign. You could spend the money more profitably in districts where you are not too popular. On primary or election day, however, brief calls usually should be made to remind "favorables" to vote.

Use telephones only when you can guarantee proper supervision to provide some control on message development, message delivery, and message follow-up. There are people whose telephone voice or manner is so bad—and even worse without direction—that, with all the good will in the world, they can cheerfully destroy your candidacy. Each voice on the telephone is the voice of *the* candidate for the 100 to 500 voters who hear it. In the judgment of many political professionals, a woman's voice and telephone presence are much more effective than a man's, particularly in areas where nuisance or obscene calls are common.

Use telephones when demographic and voting-pattern analysis and comprehensive, organized pre-testing indicate that worthwhile results are probable and that other techniques will not be more effective or less costly. Some areas have been so inundated by advertising and market-research telephone campaigns that if you add your political calls, you can expect to arouse considerable irritation—and your money will have been wasted. In some areas, the local, state, and national parties and candidates all do telephone campaigning; in such a situation, your call, one of many, tends to have minimum impact unless it is done with very experienced people, who tend to be quite

---

* "Input," like "impact" and "parameters," was a trendy word for politicians in 1972. Such words don't mean much—they are often used to avoid the necessity for original thinking—so they change almost every year.

expensive. Consider the impact carfully, after pre-testing several hundred calls in various areas, before you launch a telephone campaign.

Ideally, telephones should be used only in those areas where substantial numbers of voters live whom you wish to appeal to and whom your research shows to be at least 60 per cent favorable or undecided. In selected cases, you may feel you have to call into areas where your opponent is strong to try to get some of his supporters to your side, but then you run the risk of reinforcing his vote rather than increasing your own. These are not simple decisions, and you should discuss the problems with experienced politicians and with other persons of mature judgment before deciding what to do.

Do not attempt to conduct a comprehensive telephone campaign (over 50,000 calls) unless professional supervision can be assured at each central location and some flexibility built into the calling procedures. In many campaigns where continuous professional monitoring and supervision are not used, the telephone message is frozen early and never changed, although issues and voter responses may change drastically during the campaign or may differ significantly in different areas.* Unless there is constant professional supervision of the operation to assure that the message meets the current demand, a great deal of money and motion will be wasted. If you can't retain a professional consultant but still wish to have a telephone campaign, give someone with mature judgment from your personal staff full-time responsibility for the telephone operation.

Calls should be made only from central locations. You can't provide supervision economically if you have numerous scattered locations or if calls are made from individual homes.

Use professionals as interviewers, if possible. Volunteers can't be properly supervised and they don't always show up when scheduled. According to William J. Pfeiffer, Nelson Rockefeller's former campaign manager, one professional is usually worth five or ten volunteers.† I've seen campaigns that used both volunteers and professionals, and overall, I would advise employing professionals, who

* Even professional phone consultants sometimes freeze the message quite early—some, because it reduces their costs considerably; some, because they have no understanding of the overall campaign. These consultants believe their function is simply to manufacture a given number of calls.

† James M. Perry, *The New Politics* (New York: Potter, 1968), p. 126.

arrive on schedule and will accept direction. Even with volunteers, telephone campaigns involve expenditures for rent, furniture, telephone installation, food and refreshments, message development, and often miscellaneous items like transportation and babysitting. You can probably bring off a small-area campaign involving 5,000 to 10,000 calls with a few reliable volunteers, but in sizable telephone campaigns, volunteers tend to be inefficient and more costly than usually anticipated.

When to call

Telephone campaigns should start no sooner than four weeks before election day. If the time span is longer than that, the average voter tends to forget. Set-up work—looking up telephone numbers, obtaining computer printouts by election districts, developing the message (or messages) and the voters' probable questions and desired answers, and renting space, furniture, and other facilities—should start ten to twelve weeks before election day.

Calls should be made between 6 P.M. and 9:30 P.M. weekday evenings in order to get as many voters as possible at home. Don't call on public and religious holidays or weekends.

Costs

A major telephone campaign runs to money. If it is done without relation to the central theme and without quality-control considerations, the net effective costs can be catastrophic, since the results from the investment will be substantially diminished.

Costs range from $5,000 to $10,000 for a modest campaign in state assembly or city council races to hundreds of thousands of dollars for gubernatorial, senatorial, or presidential races. In many cases, a major campaign may be designed around the telephone component. That seemed to be the case when Congressman Jacob Resnick of New York State ran for U.S. senator in 1968. It was reported that his telephone campaign cost almost $500,000. Virtually every registered Democrat in the state was said to have been called to hear a recorded message from the candidate. Resnick lost badly, and in the judgment of many observers, the telephone campaign was of little help. Recorded messages, sometimes delivered with the help of computers, have been used in many campaigns, but their usefulness or lack of usefulness, as in the case of many other campaign techniques, has never been conclusively established. However, if everyone in a political party or in an area is called, a significant portion of the money goes down the drain.

In some campaigns, $1,000 spent on telephoning is too much, but in others, $100,000 can be too little. The proper amount can be determined only as a function of overall campaign strategy and from establishing which groups (and how many people) you must reach that you can't get to in any other way. A full saturation telephone campaign is never worth what it costs.

Some advance thought and careful use of research can save you money by indicating which areas and client groups need not or should not be called. In one campaign in which I worked professionally as a telephone campaign consultant for a reform candidate, I recommended that the campaign staff provide me a list of election districts in the order of reform strength. (That was to be determined from past voting patterns, as described in Chapter 3.) Just developing the list eliminated the districts, amounting to one-third of the total, which were clearly strongholds of the opposing party faction from consideration for calling. Determining the sequence of election district priorities was particularly important since we were working with volunteers and there was therefore no way to guarantee that every productive district would be called. Clearly, if there is any significant possibility that all your calls will not be completed, the most productive areas (however you wish to define them on the basis of your research) should be called first.

As a rule of thumb, in campaigns of over 100,000 voters, telephone campaign costs should not exceed 20 to 25 percent of the total, particularly if a television emphasis has been decided upon. (Television can account for two thirds of the entire campaign budget in larger campaigns). In smaller campaigns (city council, town supervisor, state assembly), telephone cost allocations can go as high as one third, again with the caveat that well trained, intelligent interviewers, with a reasonably prepared message, call the right people.

Budgeting for a volunteer telephone campaign
If you want to organize your own telephone campaign, your estimates of cost should take the following factors into account, adding 10 percent for contingencies.

Space rental. The space used for the telephone operation should not be located in or near your campaign headquarters. Usually a motel or hotel suite is fine, but cheaper space is frequently available in storefronts and office buildings. You must assume you'll need 50 to 60 square feet of space per caller (for furniture, telephone setup, aisle space, etc.). If you have ten women and one supervisor (to make 15,000 calls) you'll need 600 to 700 square feet, depending on how the room is laid out. If the climate is hot and humid, you may need to find a place with air conditioning. Five dollars a foot, or $3,500 for 700 square feet, would be reasonable for a year's lease. Short-term leases are naturally more expensive on a pro-rated basis. For a six-week campaign, you'll need at least a two-month occupancy—it takes the telephone company about a week to set up, especially if new cable has to be installed. The rental charges for two months may thus amount to one-sixth of $3,500 plus a few percentage points for a short-term lease, amounting to about $750 for decent space.

Maintenance of space. Most landlords don't follow through on provisions of services for short-term tenants. If you make certain the place is clean, garbage is picked up, coffee is prepared, your costs may amount to an additional $25 a week, or perhaps $150 for the campaign.

Furniture rental. Chairs and tables can be rented, shipped, and picked up at a cost of perhaps $200 to $250 for a month. Many furniture renters require a deposit to guarantee return of the equipment in good condition. Tables run about $12 each and chairs $30 a dozen, plus delivery charges.

Telephone installation charges vary but average about $15 to $25 per telephone, and about $50 for the "call director" (the instrument used by the supervisor to monitor the quality of the calls). Installation for a ten-telephone operation with a call director will come to approximately $250. Touch-tone telephones cost about $1.75 per month more per unit. The extra cost is more than compensated for by the increased speed of dialing.

Cost of telephone calls. In some areas, an unlimited number of calls may be made for a flat monthly fee, while in others the cost may be on the order of 6.5 to 8.2 cents per call, plus extra charges for calls over three minutes in length. If about 15,000 voters will be reached, we can assume that about 18,500 calls will actually be made.

(First, about 20 percent of the persons listed in the telephone directory will have moved within a year, and some calls will be to the wrong person at an old number. Second, often a voter in a primary may have one party registration, but the family member who answers the telephone may be of another party and you will have to call back. Finally, some interviewers will call home or their friends after a while to break the monotony of the calls.) The total cost of calls may run about $400 in communities with flat-rate telephone billing and about $1,600 in communities with message-rate telephone billing systems.

Insurance for personal injury. It's a good idea to take out an insurance policy for injuries to cover people working in the campaign and visitors so that you're protected from law suits. Estimated cost: $500 to $700.

Development of message and pre-testing calls. One of your full-time paid staff or your advertising agency men will generally develop a message and arrange to pre-test it. You may not be charged directly, but eventually this will cost, either in your own payroll or in consultant's charges, about $500 for a small-scale test of various messages for different areas and voter constituencies in advance of the full-scale telephone campaign.

Training expenses. For full-time staff, materials, cards, and refreshments, plan on spending about $200.

Looking up telephone numbers and preparing cards. This is the simplest step involved in the telephoning process, but even it can become complicated. Commercially, looking up numbers in large quantities costs about 4 to 6 cents per number. In some areas, the local telephone company may actually help you to do this for small jobs, but you can't count on their assistance.* At a minimum, you would have to have these things done:

(*a*) On 3×5 cards list alphabetically, by street address, all voters to be reached.

(*b*) "Buy" (really rent, in most areas) the telephone company's reverse telephone book, which lists all numbers (except those un-

---

* In emergencies you may find it necessary to call Information. In many cities the operator will provide three numbers on one request. In a recent primary, there were twenty amateur and professional phone campaigns in one county. By the last week of the campaign, Information provided only one number at a time.

listed) by street address, with all at a single street address listed alphabetically.

(c) Enter on the card the numbers of the assembly and election district, the name and address and telephone number of the voter.

(d) Scan the deck to combine family names at the same address. (This is also useful in saving on mailing expenses.)

If these chores will be done by volunteers, estimate that cards, reverse telephone book rental ($60 to $75 for that alone), and space and refreshments for the volunteers doing this very time-consuming job will cost about $500.

If your local board of elections has a list of voters on computerized tape, you may be able to reduce the cost of preparing the 3×5 cards by having a computer transfer the basic information from the tape to 3×5 cards, leaving only the telephone numbers to be entered by volunteers. This may save around $100 in volunteers' expenses.

Preparation of message-supporting statements. So that the callers can answer questions intelligently, the background of the candidate, issues statements, questions and answers have to be prepared, which require the use of campaign staff and possibly professional advertising people. This will cost, including typing and reproduction, perhaps $150 at a minimum.*

Refreshments. Provide coffee, cold soda, cake, and other refreshments to give the telephoners a break each night from work that can become very tedious. If you budget 50 cents a person a night, the total cost for 30 nights of calling would approximate $165.

Supervising expenses. The supervisors, at least, should be paid. A minimum fee of $100 a week for 25 hours of work would amount, over a four- to six-week calling period, to between $400 and $600 each.

Babysitting and other expenses. Some volunteers will need babysitters on certain nights. Anticipate a total of about $400 for this. Adding up the items listed above produces a total cost of $5,000 to $6,000 (or more) for a campaign that comprises 18,500 calls

* The best such issues book that I have seen was a printed pamphlet prepared for Senator George McGovern's presidential campaign in 1972. A model of its kind, it was used for distribution to campaign staff and potential contributors, and as background for chairmen of volunteers. The preparation cost was considerably in excess of $500.

attempted, including 15,000 completed calls—not much less than a consultant would charge. Clearly, a telephone campaign requires a significant investment, even if you do it yourself. Since overhead and fixed costs, such as message development and insurance, are so expensive in telephone campaigns, the unit cost decreases significantly as the number of calls increases. In most cases it is uneconomical to do a small-scale telephone campaign.

In areas with unlimited message units, where it is certainly sensible to emphasize telephone campaigns, costs may average 15 to 20 cents a call in volunteer-staffed campaigns of 20,000 calls and over. In other areas, where each call or message unit is separately charged, average costs may run between 18 and 23 cents a call.

Making a contract for a professional telephone campaign
Professional telephone firms charge approximately 25 to 32 cents a call for 50,000 calls or more. Your staff and legal representatives must make certain that the contract stipulates which services you are to receive. If you have the telephone campaign done professionally, make sure that the contract states that you will pay the telephone bill directly. One campaign manager told me that a well-known political advertising man had charged him for 10,000 telephone calls he had never made. The candidate discovered this after the campaign was over, when the telephone company billed him instead of the advertising man, and he realized from the message unit count that the advertising man had charged him for 10,000 calls that could not have been made. In negotiating with a telephone consultant, ask for two prices—one in which the consultant performs all services and one based on your office's paying for the telephone installations and the message units. Some consultants may be available to provide advice on procedures and message development for a flat fee.

Another useful service that should be in the contract (in large-scale campaigns) is the provision by the consultant of daily counts of telephone calls made by areas called, by numbers of favorables, unfavorables, and undecideds, and by developing issues in each area. If a campaign has a number of installations around a state, preparing such data and calling them in to headquarters can cost $1,000 a week. If this type of service is not explicitly required in the contract, consultants are unlikely to volunteer it. You will be charged for this extra service, but it is often well worth it.

Ask the consultant the percentage of unlisted numbers in the locality, which groups are receptive to phone appeals and which not, and how many completed calls he thinks likely. A reliable consultant will give you an estimate for nothing more than is honestly possible. The prices are usually estimated on the total number of voters that you want to attempt to reach. If you have 50,000 unduplicated voter households that you want to contact, the probabilities are that only 35,000 to 38,000 can actually be reached.

Whom to call and what to say

In many professional telephone campaigns, with investments of several hundred thousand dollars, no research at all is done on the basics: Whom to call? What to say? In some campaigns, a junior staff member may make this determination and never bother to check it with the research or polling staff member. In the heat of campaigning, many basic decisions may get rushed through without your knowledge. For your telephone effort, no less than the rest of your campaign, *it is critical to do as much advance planning as possible before the actual campaigning begins.*

There is no simple, magical way to make these determinations. Research is needed to protect your investment in the telephone operation. Either you should insist that your consultant demonstrate how he came to recommend a message, or you should have a mature staff member research the matter for you, concentrating on the three areas indicated below. In no case should you or your manager allow the message to be frozen before you or your representative examine the research and listen to recordings of calls made to pre-test the proposed message. In my own campaign work, messages are never completely frozen because experienced interviewers are constantly finding new and better ways of presenting the candidate's advantages within the structured routine.

Whoever you make responsible for the telephone operation should:

- analyze past elections by individual election districts to locate the favorables, unfavorables, and undecideds
- analyze client-group voting patterns

- correlate these analyses with demographic analysis—the distribution of the voters by age, sex, income, race, and ethnic group. These procedures are described in Chapter 3.

After some preliminary hypotheses are made on the basis of this information, pre-test calls *with varying message contents* should be made to the client groups you want to reach. These calls should be made by experienced supervisors. The message starts to become finalized at this time. The campaign policy group should be involved here if in no other phase.

Training telephoners

Several days in advance of the beginning of the telephone campaign, each telephoner should be provided with a copy of the candidate's biography and a list of questions and answers on his stands on issues that the staff anticipates will come up in the telephone conversation. (Examples of these materials will be found on pages 221–22.) By the time they arrive for the training session on the first night of telephoning, they should have read and mastered the information in the biography and the questions and answers so that they will be able to refer to it comfortably and will not have to read it to respond to most questions which come up in the course of their work.

At the training session, the candidate should make it his business to talk to the telephoners briefly and then answer any additional questions they may still have after having read the questions and answers. The supervisor or a member of the campaign staff should then pass out copies of the message and review it with them. Finally, the callers should be carefully instructed about the information that is to be registered on the card—usually an indication of whether the voter was favorable, unfavorable, or undecided, plus any special information gotten from the call such as "aged, needs help voting" or "has questions about grandson in jail."

If the campaign staff is prepared to follow through with it, it is a good idea to instruct the callers to answer all reasonable questions to the best of their ability based on the biography, the questions and answers, and any other materials provided by the candidate's staff, and to offer to have a member of the campaign staff call the voter back or send him literature if he has a question that the

Biography of Irwin Silbowitz

Candidate for Civil Court Judge

Irwin Silbowitz is 38; he and his family (his wife, the former Eleanor Kaufman; daughter Donna, 13; and son Mitchell, 9) reside on the Grand Concourse in the Bronx. Since working his way through New York Law School he has had many years of legal experience in all phases of the law. At present he is Senior Law Advisor to all the Justices of the New York State Supreme Court. His official title is Deputy Chief Law Assistant of the New York State Supreme Court-- First Judicial District; he has worked in this section for ten years.

His experience includes:

1. Acting as Supreme Court Referee

2. Trial Counsel to the Appeals Court

3. Special Adviser to the Justices on matters of court procedure

4. Specialized legal adviser on all matters currently before the court

5. Participation in thousands of civil and criminal cases

6. Performance of legal research

7. Before his present post he was in private practice (Markewich, Rosenhaus & Beck) and was Law Clerk to Sidney H. Asch, presently a State Supreme Court Judge.

Mr. Silbowitz is the only candidate for Civil Court Judge who has developed a specific program for necessary court improvements and reforms. This program includes:

1. Neighborhood night courts to settle many disputes now clogging court calendars. These will also make it unnecessary for working people to lose a day's pay to get their day in court.

2. These courts would resolve landlord-tenant disputes.

3. These Neighborhood Night Courts would include small claims court; Mr. Silbowitz proposes to increase the limit on small claims cases from $500 to $1000 to help settle disputes quickly without the claimants having to lose a day's pay to settle their claims.

Silbowitz Questions and Answers -- Page 2

6. Why does he feel the present court system is mismanaged?

The system is too centralized and filled with red tape creating endless backlogs. Silbowitz thinks that there should be more rotating judges, and that some courts should be open weekends as well as nights for the convenience of the working public.

7. Why is Silbowitz running?

He has a program that will work, and he can't make it work unless he is elected. He has the experience and understanding to be able to have insight into the community's needs.

8. Why would he be a better judge than his opponent?

a) More experience in all phases of the court system

b) Experienced as a trial referee, i.e. one who renders advisory decisions for judges

c) Experienced in legal research in all areas of the law

d) Has written hundreds of decisions

e) Experienced as trial counsel in Appelate Division of New York State Supreme Court

9. He went to New York Law School. That's not a great school.

He had to work his way through school and attend law school at night. N.Y.U. and Columbia are both daytime schools. He had to work days at the Post Office to support his family.

10. Why did the Liberal Party endorse him? They don't usually, do they?

Both candidates were interviewed by an impartial panel, and Silbowitz was found more qualified.

caller cannot answer or that she feels is too sensitive for her to handle. This course should emphatically not be followed if the campaign staff is not prepared to follow through, since it is much worse not to follow through on such a promise than not to make it in the first place.

The following general advice should be included in the training session and repeated if necessary as the campaign progresses: (1) Never argue, and don't spend too much time on supporters of the opponent if there is little or no hope of bringing them over to your side. It is more productive to thank the person for his time as quickly as possible and go on to a voter who might be convinced. (2) Listen to the voter. Listening often has a more positive effect than talking. The call is too often treated as a recited message instead of a conversation. Not only is the conversational approach more effective, it can yield research spin-offs that are usually helpful and sometimes critical for the campaign's success. (3) Don't spend too much time talking with favorable voters. Thank them and go on to another voter who might be brought into your camp. (4) Always maintain a friendly, interested tone.

Professional or amateur telephoners?

I would advise you to have your telephone campaign done professionally. As Jesse Unruh said, "You can't control what you don't pay for." When you work with amateurs in a campaign, you learn the true dimensions of anarchy. It can, and usually does, become community participation to the nth power, with each participant doing the job as he or she sees fit rather than as you want it done. This is true of telephone operations no less than of other campaign activities.

If you cannot afford to have a telephone campaign done professionally, my recommendation is that your campaign policy committee sharply delineate the areas and groups to be called. Someone of maturity and judgment should be made responsible for the orderly development of research, message content, and training. Volunteers can be used to list voters' names, addresses, election districts, and assembly districts on cards; others should be assigned to look up telephone numbers and enter them on the cards. Pre-test calls may be made by carefully trained volunteers; questions and answers as well as a biography and issues position of the candidate should be prepared by the regular campaign staff. In no case, however, even in the smallest campaigns, should a telephone canvass be attempted unless you can afford to have at least ten telephones in a central location, with the telephones manned at given hours under some type of supervision. Since the operation is expensive, even with volunteers, considerations of economy of scale suggest the need for 10,000 calls as a minimum to make the effort worthwhile.

Research spin-offs

An advantage of a telephone campaign is that you can get major research findings at little or no extra cost. Keeping daily counts of results—favorable, unfavorable, and undecided—by district and by subpopulation group can be enormously informative about how the campaign is going and about how specific groups are responding to television, radio, and newspaper ads and to positions on issues.

In one recent campaign, the telephoners clearly established that the candidate's television saturation was starting to backfire in certain areas. But, as in many major campaigns, the channels of information and communication were blocked, and no one wanted to hear this finding, because it conflicted with the point of view of the policy committee. There was no coordination between policy strategy and data obtained from the telephone effort. Hence, the television campaign continued unabated, costing large sums of money and possibly actually losing votes. This not uncommon situation illustrates a principle of effective campaigning: To maximize his investment in the telephone operation, the candidate must assign one of his immediate staff, with operational and policy discretion, as telephone liaison.

In a similar instance, the telephoners received complaints that the candidate was too sedate in televised debates with his opponents. The information was sent on to the headquarters staff, which in this instance passed it on to the candidate, who attempted to make some modifications in his speaking style. On another occasion, the telephoners picked up a complaint in a middle-class white district that Black Panther literature was being developed and mimeographed in one of the candidate's offices. The information proved to be true, and the potentially explosive situation, of which the candidate had been unaware, was quietly remedied.

Election day telephone canvassing
Telephones can be used to advantage as a substitute for personal canvassing on election day. Most of the principles of election day canvassing described on pages 70–72 apply equally well to telephone canvassing. If you have had a telephone campaign preceding election day, you should already have cards for the voters whom the telephone campaign identified as favorable to your candidacy. Ideally, these cards should be divided according to election districts. Your campaign staff can determine the order of priority in which the favorable voters are to be called; this order can be altered during the day, if your poll watchers report particularly light turnouts in areas that your research shows are largely favorable to you.

The message for election day telephone calls is brief—15 to 30 seconds. Your callers need only politely remind the voters that today is election day and that their vote is important to you and will be appreciated. However, if many candidates are making pull calls, you may be wise to cancel yours, to minimize voter irritation.

7 Non-Political Elections

Don't run too slick a campaign. People will think you're a politician.

—NAT SORKIN

Although the precise number of private organizations conducting elections each year in the nation is not available, the order of magnitude can be estimated. There are over 180,000 incorporated and unincorporated communities in the nation. Most of these communities have parent-teacher associations, men's and women's social clubs, and religious institutions; and many also have League of Women Voters chapters, businessmen's groups, economic development associations, alumni organizations, a Rotary club, a Masonic lodge, and other fraternal orders, labor unions, a chamber of commerce, bar associations, medical associations, a junior chamber of commerce, and various other organizations.

Most of these groups have boards of directors whose members are elected. An estimate of over a million private elections per year is probably conservative, even assuming that many organizations have *pro forma* elections with a nominating committee in effect controlling the outcome of an election.

Many of these elections do not directly concern the public, although, cumulatively, the civic groups significantly influence the course of public affairs. Public policies are modified, and sometimes changed entirely, as a result of pressures brought to bear by these groups.* Yet, public drama resulting from these elections is likely to be minimal, owing to lack of interest on the part of the communications media; but for the people involved, and the communities and interest they serve, these elections are very important. This chapter suggests which political techniques may be appropriate in private-election campaigning and shows how they can be used.

The reasons people seek private office are not dissimilar from the motives of those who seek public office. The need for recognition, for ego gratification, for a sense of public purpose somewhat larger than the satisfactions of a job or of family life are major reasons motivating many people to run for office. Anger and frustration at complicated bureaucratic response—when non-response becomes the anticipated response—lead people to seek redress by working in community organizations. Some of the most effective local organizational campaigning has been done by housewives banding together to get a traffic light installed on a corner where a child has been killed by an automobile, or to picket a store having higher than usual prices, or to form an ecological interest group. People express their sense of impotence as individuals by joining together in community and civic groups which provide a vehicle for direct action and some accomplishment. For varying reasons, many people find political clubs distasteful, so special-interest groups or general civic groups become attractive alternatives. Couples whose marriages are faltering join civic clubs to develop new common interests; other people join for purely social reasons. Retired people find civic clubs interesting and have leisure time to invest in their activities. Many business people (lawyers, insurance men, and others) regard civic clubs as valuable places to meet prospective clients or customers. Leadership potential originates from all these groups as people become knowledgeable, develop new ideas, and find that being president or chairman is a satisfying means to express and implement their ideas.

Semi-public groups serve many useful functions in a community. They dramatize local issues and develop alternatives, and they often

* For example, the powerful consumer and ecology movements originated from such private groups, not from public officials. Such privately based groups have changed public priorities and policies, demonstrating that they have real political power. The political significance of these groups is only now beginning to be properly understood.

provide training for people who later seek public office. Frequently, such clubs can be more candid on critical, controversial, and emotionally charged issues than can elected officials whose sensitivities and insecurities are naturally exacerbated by the necessity of running for reelection after relatively short terms of office, or whose friends, political allies, or contributors may be involved in activities that deserve critical attention.

With certain modifications, the political techniques described earlier can be applied to elections in these groups. Fortunately, the scale of these private elections is much reduced from that of elections for public office, and an individual interested member can more readily afford the costs both in time and in money.

The following steps should be taken:

1. Read and know the constitution or by-laws of your organization, including which offices are elective, when the elections are held, and how nominations are secured. In addition, learn the organization's procedural rules—often a modified form of Robert's Rules of Order.*

2. Know the history of the organization, its purposes, and its non-elected key cadre, the group that has provided organizational continuity. Has the organization taken stands on public issues? What were the results? Which issues are important to the membership now? Are there conflicts on matters of policy? How do members line up on these issues? Answering these questions usually involves reading the minutes of the meetings for the last few years and checking the voting pattern.

3. Learn which committees are called for by the constitution. How many members serve on a committee? Who appoints the committee chairmen? (This can be critical, because these offices provide a natural transition to running for organizational office.)

4. Find out who controls the way the organization operates. Who controls the membership and finance committee? Who provides

* Robert's Rules can be used for making meetings productive; they can also be used obstructively. See Pete Hamill's marvelous article in *New York* magazine, August 8, 1972, for a description of reform Democratic clubs and how these rules can bring everything to a standstill. Having been a member of such clubs, I can vouch for the accuracy of the article.

most of the organization's funds if membership dues are not enough to make ends meet?

5. Learn which persons control the policy formation activities. What is the source of their power, and what type of following do they have?

6. Establish whether preventive defenses are necessary. For example, most organizations will not allow "stacking"—a candidate's paying for voting memberships for friends and family members—but you should make sure that this hasn't happened; if it has, get ready with a counter-tactic. Just before a club nominating vote, one idealistic, reform-minded club president, anticipating what his less idealistic and more "practical" opponent would do, paid for 40 club memberships for personal friends. The presumably more practical opponent had never even considered such a course of action, and he lost. The reformer simply bought the nomination—an occurrence that is not uncommon in American organizational life.

7. Know the membership's voting background—information on the past voting behavior of the club membership is most important. How many people vote, and how is the vote usually divided?

After six months or so of active membership in a small club, you should have a pretty good idea of your potential, and you'll know the protocol—for example, whether there is a formal or informal line of succession in which the treasurer or some other officer automatically becomes the president.

In larger clubs, the basic political campaigning techniques described in earlier chapters are often appropriate, but they should be used with great care and selectivity.

An example of how so-called slick campaign techniques can backfire was described by Nat Sorkin, a leading New York printer of political brochures. Some years ago, he ran for vice president of his synagogue. Having learned in a generation of political work how brochures are used, he developed and mailed several brochures that included everything he had seen in political brochures he had printed for other candidates: pictures of his family, his dog, and his home, and explanations of his reasons for running. His opponent simply sent out one postcard that said, "I don't own a printing plant and can't afford to send you so many fancy brochures. I believe I've earned this position, and you all know how I feel about the things that concern us. Please vote for me." The opponent won a clear victory.

Sorkin's congregation probably had never experienced a professional-style election campaign, and many members may have resented the approach without regard to the possible real merits of his candidacy. Although precedent should not control your campaign, it should provide the basis for your deliberations on tactics and strategy.

Sometimes a simple, direct piece is much more effective than a number of professionally designed brochures, particularly in a community organization election. You must always keep in mind the voters to whom you wish to appeal. You can't do something completely out of context without taking risks.

In a recent hotly contested parent-teacher association campaign, for example, the candidate was not sure the membership would recognize from his name that he espoused the religion of most of the members. He wanted to have the secretary of his church call the congregants to remind them that he was running and to ask them and their friends to vote for him. He was counseled not to do this because of the probability of adverse reactions. Such a decision cannot be made on the basis of objective data; experience and judgment should should control, supplementing any original research you can do on sensitive issues.

In larger organizations, you should consider having friends sponsor or host kaffeeklatches or teas for small groups of members, where you can explain your views on the future of the organization. These groups ideally should number 15 to 20; a larger number is an imposition on your hostess and also makes effective discussion almost impossible.

Professional research is generally unnecessary in these campaigns. However, you should make a practice of using discussion meetings and kaffeeklatches not only to get your ideas across to the members, but to listen to them and find out what they are thinking. Use these meetings to develop a program. You must give people a reason to vote for you besides geniality and access.

If your organization has 500 to 1,000 members or more, and attendance at meetings is light, you probably should prepare one simple mailing piece for those who have not attended, since the organization's hard core probably will make up their minds on other considerations. Any mailing that you do should be simply stated; avoid elaboration at all costs. Envelopes should be hand addressed: keep it constantly in mind that these are very personal campaigns. Computer letters should be ruled out completely, as they are more likely to offend than convince in non-political elections. "Nothing fancy" is probably the best strategy of all. Your letter should be signed by hand; the paper should be of good quality, but not extravagant. As in any social situation, always try to be tasteful and gracious. The return address for larger mailings should be printed, preferably in small type. These are in large measure social campaigns, and you must avoid the appearance of a high-powered political contest. This type of mailing can be supplemented, or substituted for, by a telephone call briefly asking people to vote for you and giving them a sensible reason for doing so.* These procedures require checking and transcribing membership lists against attendance lists. If attendance lists are not maintained, you may have to record attendance yourself. In developing ideas for your group, keep in mind that people tend to be uncomfortable with completely innovative concepts unless you prepare the ground very carefully.

In the early phase of campaigning, your appearance and a friendly manner will probably influence voters more than anything else. Try to listen to what's on their minds and react responsively and honestly to their sense of problems and priorities. If you criticize, do so constructively; don't relate criticism to the deficiencies, either real or imagined, of personalities. By midway through the campaign, you will have to supplement your charm with substance, being prepared to take intelligent stands on issues of interest to the membership. On election day, you can gently remind your friends and supporters how important the election is and ask them to vote.

* Sometimes you may be able to get the members' telephone numbers from the organization's secretary. But more often than not, you'll have to look the numbers up yourself.

8 Conclusion

*If this system—this towering monument to man's capacity
to live together in harmony, with tolerance, with justice,
with freedom of though, spirit and deed—is to survive,
those of us who have had the good fortune to suffer, if
you please, in the exposed position of public advocacy
have a great and abiding responsibility to talk sense, to tell
the people what the facts are, to give them the real alternatives and pose the real choices.*

—ADLAI E. STEVENSON

Dubrovnik, on the Yugoslav coast, was a powerful, independent
city-state that survived and prospered despite repeated onslaughts
over the centuries by Romans, Turks, and pirates. Visitors to the
city may see a motto engraved in stone over the entrance to the old
city hall proclaiming: "All those who enter here must place their
private passions in suspense, for public needs shall be their only
concern." In the same building are exhibited dice that were used
by the nobles of Dubrovnik in casting lots to determine who would
be governor each month.

Apparently the ruling class, for centuries, was composed of men
of such uniform distinction, ability, and integrity that the fate of the
state could be placed reliably in the hands of any one of them by a
roll of the dice, with absolute assurance that the interests of the
state would not suffer. I know of no parallel in history. I certainly
know of no American state or city legislature where a significant
degree of risk would not follow the determination of leadership and
power focus in this manner, although there may be many who believe
that in certain situations, not only would the quality of our government not be threatened by crap-shooting for power, but possibly
improvements in quality of leadership might result.

233

The point is simple: We need the best leadership we can get, yet the methods and procedures attendant to our campaigning practices provide no assurance either for the provision of able and responsible leadership or for its continuity. This book was written partially in the hope of enabling potential candidates, who may have much to contribute to society but who presently avoid campaigning out of distaste and repugnance for a "dirty business," to re-evaluate the techniques and requirements of campaigning and perhaps see that no law of God or man dictates that it must be a dirty business or that only the wealthy, dishonest, or unscrupulous can win or can hold union cards.

Seeking public office can in fact be the most productive, meaningful role a citizen can take in our society, without necessarily compromising his honor, integrity, or family values. Working within our system—one of the best in the world, since it allows change to occur peacefully—so that deficiencies are corrected and the quality of life and living is improved is not a bad way to spend a career and a life.

Since Dubrovnik's method of deciding power is not likely to be widely embraced, the preceding chapters have concentrated on the skills you'll need to campaign effectively and economically and on some of the problems you'll probably come up against. The treatment of these matters was necessarily general, since each case has its own peculiarities and no amount of preparation can prevent some feelings of terror, panic, frustration, and futility; these are normal in campaigns, even for experienced politicians. But the first time is the hardest; the terrors and emotional exhaustion are usually somewhat muted in subsequent campaigns.

The book is intended primarily to be helpful to inexperienced campaigners, whatever their political persuasion. Taken together, these chapters are an attempt at an intellectual, economical, and emotional rationalization of the campaigning process. Implicit in all the book's recommendations is the assumption that all candidates will work within the system, whatever their personal values, whatever their party. Many books in the last decade have taken the view that the system isn't working and can't work, that society's priorities have become perverted, that the government doesn't reflect the popular will, and that the seniority committee system in our legislatures allows a handful of men, often from rural areas, to dominate public policy against the popular will.

This feeling is not unique to our generation. The great political commentator Walter Lippmann noted in 1925:

> The private citizen today has come to feel rather like a deaf spectator in the back row, who ought to keep his mind on the mystery up there, but cannot quite manage to keep awake. He knows he is somehow affected by what is going on. Yet these public affairs are in no convincing way his affairs. They are for the most part invisible. They are managed, if they are managed at all, at distant centers, from behind the scenes by unnamed powers. As a private person he does not know for certain what is going on, or who is doing it, or where he is being carried. No newspaper reports his environment so that he can grasp it; no school has taught him how to imagine it; his ideals, often, do not fit with it; listening to speeches, altering opinions, and voting do not, he finds, enable him to govern it. He lives in a world which he cannot see, does not understand, and is unable to direct.*

I have lived in New York City all my life and have seen fear, hatred, and loathing take over in the last decade. Many describe the problem as emanating from racial passions that no authority or institution can successfully deal with, since the base is emotional rather than rational. I take the view that the fear of pain and death is eminently reasonable and is, in fact, human, not racial. I teach in a college located in a black ghetto, where my students describe vividly the reign of terror brought about by drug addiction and the cost of supporting the habit. Many can identify the pushers, yet the police do little and the conviction rate of dealers is quite low. The feeling of alienation that results from these and related experiences is not racial. Middle-income families of all races experience similar feelings, with the added irritation of paying additional taxes while the quality of public services deteriorates and merely getting to work becomes a traumatic, dangerous experience. It is known that heroin addiction in New York alone is a business involving hundreds of

---

* "The Phantom Public," quoted in Clinton Rossiter and James Lare (eds.), *The Essential Lippmann* (New York: Random House, 1963), p. 35.

millions of dollars, thousands of private individuals and people in government, as well as foreign governments whose permissiveness can hardly be accidental. The federal and state governments spend millions to combat this disease, which results in burglaries, muggings, murders. Yet the spreading addiction provides a fulfillment that can only be transient and results in activities that are terminal not only for the addicts. Public authorities cannot even deal with the transit graffiti problem which has become a public disgrace, let alone the drug problem which is a national terror. In rural counties that I visit in the course of my profession, I hear reports of drugs being sold in schools and of burglaries and other crimes in areas where, until recently, the crime rate was so low that there was no fulltime policeman. An obvious answer is to provide free drugs under super-vised conditions, yet many regard this course as dangerous and a possible infringement of civil rights. Vast migrations, with attendant huge public costs because of wasted investments in public facilities, take place in the nation's major cities as people try to obtain some measure of neighborhood safety, decent schools, and a minimally agreeable ambience. Policemen see corrupt administrators every day, including overly amiable judges; attorneys and businessmen participate in payoffs; and after a while, many accept this pervasive corruption as a way of doing business that makes life more convenient. After all, the consumer or the government will pick up the tab, anyway. Shoplifting is estimated to account for 3 percent of the average annual gross of the nation's department stores. The stores naturally pass on to their paying customers this 3 percent, plus the costs of increased security. (Pinkerton and similar security firms have been major growth stocks in recent years.)

In view of this widespread erosion of respect for the law, the average citizen, not surprisingly, seems to think that all politicians are in business for themselves, maximizing their private law practices and private investments while nominally being paid to protect and serve the public interest.

In a decade of political work and twenty years in government service, I have seldom heard the public interest discussed by people in power as if it were a real, tangible thing. The political interest can be served only if our leadership discusses our needs and options openly and honestly. The credibility gap is real; politicians have not been held in lower repute in our modern history, according to recent Gallup polls. The Vietnam war occurred in part because the small, well-financed China Lobby managed an effective campaign making the Chinese Communists our enemies at a time when decent, if not cordial, relations might have been possible. This took place despite the warnings of General Stilwell and other extremely able career soldiers and diplomats. Many citizens feel that, as a result of these tragic occurrences in postwar America, we as a nation are increasingly in the hands of lunatics, fools, and greedy incompetents—the whores and hustlers, the scandals of the Bobby Bakers and Sherman Adamses of each administration linger on in the public mind.

On the other hand, some hope is provided by the "New Politics," as exemplified by the 1972 McGovern primary campaign, resulting in "fresh" faces at the national Democratic convention—although this was achieved by using a quota system, an undemocratic device. But distaste and distrust resulting from that convention caused groups that are normally Democratic, such as some labor unions and some Jewish voters, to question continuing their support for the Democratic ticket. The use of blue and yellow cards by McGovern floor leaders to dictate votes was not a good example of democratic principles in action. The new hope may have been a false hope. The New Politics may emerge as a new organizational compulsion, with new people using the old techniques under a false façade of populism. The real question is whether we will be better governed as a result of these trends. Many voters—judging by the "blank" votes on many ballots and the fact that about 45 percent of the eligible voters did not vote in the 1972 presidential election—share a widespread belief that it doesn't make much difference who's in office, that no one is going to listen to the people and try to do the right thing, anyway.

Some believe that the public are getting what they deserve; they cheat, steal, compromise, lie on their taxes, concern themselves exclusively with the minutiae of making a living, don't vote, and don't participate. As Alexis de Tocqueville wrote of the United States in the nineteenth century:

> The first thing that strikes observation is an unaccountable number of men, all equal and alike, incessantly endeavor-

ing to produce the paltry and petty pleasures with which they glut their lives. Each of them, living apart, is a stranger to the fate of all the rest—his children and his private friends constitute to him the whole of mankind; as for the rest of his fellow citizens, he is close to them, but he sees them not; he touches them, but he feels them not; he exists but in himself and for himself alone; and if his kindred still remain to him, he may be said at any rate to have lost his country.

Others, whose view I share, hold that the public expect their leaders to be a little better than they themselves are and to provide a source of respected authority that can guide, consult, and lead (without looking back to see if something is gaining on them, in Satchel Paige's expression). However, too few politicians command continued respect because of their demonstrated integrity, intelligence, courage, and honesty. Even United States senators have legal practices and business interests that must in some manner compromise their ability to serve the public interest. Men like Senator Estes Kefauver, who challenged major industrial forces to serve the public good, got chewed up in the process. Men like Ralph Nader have helped change the administrative concerns of government somewhat, but only by dedicating their entire lives to consumer advocacy and the pursuit of what I regard as a public equity. Men and institutions have devoted their energies to solving the nation's housing problems, but the nation still lacks 10 million units of decent housing. Some rare public officials do try to do what needs to be done on major sensitive issues but often they are unappreciated by the very public they serve and face bitter election challenges.

Nonetheless, the current sense of futility over the major frustrations in our society and the attendant warnings of doom may not be completely justified. We may not be on our way to a paradisiacal fulfillment, but we still have the capacity as a nation, if we have the will, to provide minimal income and environmental quality guarantees, to provide sufficient housing, parks, and mass transit to allow people to live in decent environments. The people, the various interest groups in this country do largely believe in fair play and the triumph of justice, but they don't think it happens more than once in a while right now.

What has this to do with first-time campaigners? In my judgment, a very great deal. In your first campaign, even for relatively minor office, you will be shocked at the demands for favors friends and political allies will make. You'll be shocked at the number of accommodations on matters of public policy discretion you'll be asked to make as a matter of course before you serve one day in office.

If you go along with this, your political career will be set in very large measure; you will have been conditioned to accept all this garbage—for garbage it is, however frequently you'll encounter it, however often you're told, "That's the way it has to be." If you are a candidate who wants no more for yourself than to devote your life to the public service, you will find it truly tough going. And in many ways, your first campaign will control just what type of career you'll have and just what you will be able to accomplish. It is for this reason that I emphasize the necessity of being extremely cautious in your fund-raising activities.

Many good people walk away from the political life. It destroys families; thievery is common; betrayal by friends and allies is a monotonous fact; cut-throat corruption for favors and money is usual; and loyalty is sufficiently rare that campaign staffs of important legislators are hardly ever the same from election to election. People find political life callous, vicious, ungracious, shabby, and shoddy, and filled with greedy men. Those trying to do a decent job are in the minority in many localities and are often heartily detested by other politicians.

A number of things can be done to improve not only the procedures of campaigning but also those of governing—for the behavior of elected officials is necessarily influenced by the accommodations that campaigns seem always to require. I would offer the following proposals:

1. Campaign financing problems must be solved. The 1972 law allowing individual income tax deductions (up to $100 a couple) encourages more people to contribute and is a step in the right direction, as was earlier legislation requiring publication of the names of large contributors. Certainly a bill should be passed guaranteeing the major presidential candidates adequate means to reach the public; such a bill was vetoed by President Nixon. Puerto Rico already has such a practice: there, major gubernatorial candidates

are given $375,000 each from government funds for campaigning. In a similar vein, a few American radio and television stations now give free time to bona-fide candidates. The basic principle, even for local elections, should be that candidates bringing in a specified number of petition signatures should be granted some minimal funds out of public revenues so that each may be assured of the ability to communicate his program to the public.

2. Campaign fair practices acts, as they now stand, are largely words—no real muscle or penalties exist to back them up. Unscrupulous candidates send out outrageously false information and have their knuckles tapped lightly after having done considerable damage. Penalties under fair practices statutes should be imposed promptly and publicly.

3. Endorsements should be registered, as Congressman Mario Biaggi of New York proposed in 1972, since the practice of using phony endorsements of powerful political figures is widespread and, unfortunately, very effective with many voters.

4. Campaigns every two years are bound to detract from the public interest, since as much as six months of each term of office may be devoted to the campaign for reelection. A six-year term for major offices has been proposed frequently and has much merit. No term of office of city, state, or federal elective positions should be less than four years.

5. Campaign polls should be checked for professionalism before publication of results is permitted in the press and other media. In New York State a bill was introduced in 1972 to register all pollsters to insure professionalism. In Canada, publication of poll results is not permitted although, of course, candidates are permitted to commission polls for their private use. In this way, polls of uncertain quality are prevented from influencing voters.

6. Candidates' credentials—their background and their explicit views on programs, taxes, and priorities—should be published by independent groups. This is now done in some localities but the check is too often pro forma only, and so general as to be valueless. Legislation should require every candidate to make his financial situation, including his list of contributors, his personal and family assets, and seating lists at his political dinners, available to the public.

7. An elective office, except in small localities, should be a full-time job. Too many private business interests, so common in American political life, interfere with concern for the common good. Such a rule may have the effect of removing many attorneys from public office, but the system can survive the trauma, and may even be healthier for it, as a number of commentators have observed. According to Jimmy Breslin, "Our politics is rotten because it is almost exclusively made up of lawyers." * Mike Royko writes that "the undertaker-politicians and the saloon-keeper-politicians have given way to lawyer-politicians, who are no better, but they don't even buy you a drink or offer a prayer." †

8. Each candidate should be required to publish specific answers on what he would do on specific controversial capital items in his locality's budget, whom he would appoint to his staff if elected, and how he intended to solve the problems the public was concerned about. General answers should not be permitted.

9. Each board of elections should have an operating task force with power to bring legal charges for fraud, unfair campaign practices, etc. Civil suits should follow immediately. If crimes of violence —for example, children beaten for stuffing brochures in mailboxes— take place, prompt investigations should follow and criminal charges should be brought. Most states do not now have a court apparatus that can handle this problem effectively and expeditiously.

10. Ballot design should be standardized by an independent committee so that the party in power does not exert influence, thus biasing the design.

11. Gerrymandering districts makes a sham of our democratic process. The rule for congressional districts now provides that the population size be similar in each district throughout the country. This allows the party in power to draw the lines any way they wish, without regard to neighborhoods, population characteristics, or other important variables that would assure equitable representation. If computers and technicians can't agree on what is a reasonable district, it should certainly be possible for the courts to do so.

* Quoted by Michael Gartner in his review of Joseph C. Goulden, *The Superlawyers* (New York: Weybright & Talley, 1972), in the *Wall Street Journal* (New York edition), August 9, 1972.
† *Ibid.*

12. Campaign challenges and other lawsuits should not be brought to lower courts (whose judges often are involved in local politics or who owe their jobs to leaders of one party or another) but should go directly to the state appellate division. Appellate courts tend to be less political but they judge matters of procedure, while the lower courts hear arguments on facts. What is needed is a specific hearing on facts. Current procedures should be changed to reflect political realities and to guarantee objectivity.

13. On patronage requests, a victorious candidate with discretion to fill jobs should have two options: (a) He can simply say, "I'll take all referrals and pick the best," regardless of quotas or endorsements; or (b) he can take the county leader's referrals but with the proviso that if an appointee is incompetent, he'll be replaced and that sponsor's future referrals will no longer be considered.

14. Political bank accounts of individual candidates and incumbents containing funds gained from fund-raising efforts should be public knowledge. Often these funds, ostensibly raised to support party activities, are kept for individual candidates.

You will need luck and good health to be a good candidate and a good politician. A strong stomach and a thick skin wouldn't hurt. Your primary obligation conceptually is to serve the public as well as you are able, rather than to be reelected. You must choose; the first campaign will force the choice, possibly without your being aware of it.

If you have any technical questions, or any comments on the book, I would be happy to hear from you.

Appendix
Outline Timetable
for a June Primary

This book has described and analyzed the functional requirements of a campaign. This appendix puts these requirements in outline form in a time frame—that is to say, in a logical continuity. Although dates of state primary elections vary, this model traces the steps in a typical period from the decision to run to primary day, assuming a June primary. (If you win the primary, you would, of course, repeat the cycle in the general election.)

In thinking about costs, you ought to assign an amount to each function in the outline, depending on whether you intend to use amateurs or professionals, and then add up all the items. After you recover from the shock, go through the list again and subtract from those you think are less effective. Keep examining each cost against possible combinations of strategy with the advice of experienced people, until you get your basic budget total. Remember that the "first cut" tends to decide the other expenditures—if you favor direct mail, for example, there will be less for radio and television. If you can raise the amount of money that you have projected as a total, then go ahead. If not, that's a good reason not to run. Also, you may win the primary, so you ought to calculate the campaign costs of the general election as well, and judge whether you'll be able to meet these costs, making the reasonable assumption that your fund-raising capability in that case will be increased appreciably.

Time	Decision or Process Requirement	Things that Have to be Done	Cost Range
Jan. or Feb. or earlier	Precampaign phase: Decide on whether or not to run; examine financial requirements.	Check for party and political club potential support: family, friends, business associates' reaction; recognition survey (usually shows you are less well known than incumbent but also gives idea of opponents' weakness); check with party on potential funds from other candidates, etc. If you run, can you develop a personal staff? What will happen to your business and family?	Cost for recognition survey—$1,000 (not absolutely required); time taken from work in this phase —may forego normal income. Survey results may help in getting contributions.
Jan.-Feb.	Pull together background data.	Talk to politicians in your party and to political reporters on local newspapers; buy enrollment books and election maps of district from board of elections; examine census data and past voting patterns of area carefully.	Income foregone; entertainment and book expenses— approx. $75; election maps— $20 to $50.
March	Decide whether or not to make race—if no, you're still a free man. If yes, you'll have your hands full from now on. Find campaign manager and secretary and set up skeleton headquarters with their assistance.	Find small headquarters, for perhaps 5 or 6 people, with some expandability. Need 50–60 sq. ft./person; usually space has to be designed —cubbyholes or bull pens, etc. Locational factors include prestige, costs, convenience, safety, accessibility. Campaign manager should talk to real estate people—hotels, motels, offices, storefronts, and homes have all been used successfully. Keep in mind the use of headquarters and make your choice early.	Overhead: rent staff salaries, furniture rental, etc.

Time	Decision or Process Requirement	Things that Have to be Done	Cost Range
March-April	Full campaign staff (people in charge of volunteers; media; research; logistics; political liaison).		Continuing overhead costs.
	Start petitioning and canvassing.	Get experienced person to train canvassers. (Note: To make certain that petitions are legally correct, get legal advice on format, filing form, etc. Also you must usually have a committee in case you become ill, apart from normal political wear.) Determine area assignments and who is in charge of volunteers. Determine how many "good" signatures are desired and where to get them.	Care and feeding of volunteers.
	Get full campaign activities underway.	Pick printer after reviewing samples from each one considered; check out reliability—does he meet deadlines? Prepare literature to be distributed by canvassers. (This is often overlooked.)	Designing and printing.

All these March-April activites go on simultaneously. Unfortunately, usually there is not enough time for sequencing, no matter how well you plan.

Time	Decision or Process Requirement	Things that Have to be Done	Cost Range
March-April	Do sample survey to ascertain priority requirements on issues, relative standing, areas, and client groups.	Hire research consultant or start training volunteers rapidly; arrange for sample design, interviews, coding, editing, and analysis. Results should be due 15 days after first survey (March 20). This research is absolutely critical. It will be the basis for your major time and expenditure decisions and will provide the context for the issues you want to emphasize.	Varies greatly—see pp. 107–12.
	Development of campaign theme.	Hire advertising agency or media consultant, or appoint one staff member to act exclusively in this area. This phase has to be completed before the others, since for canvassing and literature distribution copy must be written and billboards, mailings, etc., coordinated. Publicity should be designed to dramatize issues and points of view and to attack opponent in carefully chosen areas where he is potentially weak.	Media costs are high.

Time	Decision or Process Requirement	Things that Have to be Done	Cost Range
March-April	Full headquarters complement should be at work.	Hire additional staff or recruit volunteers. Candidate and campaign manager should interview for key support staff spots—e.g., liaison to client groups as need is indicated by research.	Continuing overhead; maybe additional salaries.
	Publicity campaign is active.	Retain direct-mail consultant if direct mail will be used; retain telephone consultant if telephone campaign is planned (actual telephoning begins in May). Based on research, settle on client groups to be emphasized. Decide on giveaways (if any); pick supplier. If doing own mailings, make sure to have bulk rate postage data and necessary Post Office permit. Arrange for any necessary rentals of cars, trucks, or loudspeakers; buy bullhorns.	Depends on options chosen and volume desired—calls, direct mail, brochures, etc. See pp. 45, 100, 203–8. Count on more, not less, than you expect.
		Media emphases must be decided by end of March. Television and radio time must be purchased *early*.	Expensive. What can you afford? What will help?

Time	Decision or Process Requirement	Things that Have to be Done	Cost Range
March–April	Publicity (cont.)	Do your scheduling. Make it consistent with research findings; forget your intuition! Prepare key speech but try to vary it; try to speak extemporaneously as much as possible. Professional speechwriters are expensive but worth it in large-scale races.	Continuing overhead; possibly fees for writers.
		Check press and research reactions to your issues. By the end of March, you should pick the basic issue you want to hit; stay with it.	
		Fact sheet should be made for each area in your district including names of local politicians and civic leaders. (Best to include these, but if you miss one name, miss them all: the one will hate you eternally; all will forgive.)	Continuing overhead; printing or duplicating.
		Direct mail: Decide how many pieces, exactly where and what, and which day of the week. First mailing announcing your candidacy should go out in mid-April. (Brochure should be suitable for street distribution as well.)	Varies. See pp. 45, 203–8.
		Telephones: See pre-test results, approve message; prepare questions and answers on issues; settle on location; etc.	See pp. 213–18.
		Endorsements: Check research to see whose endorsement will help, and pursue it.	

Time	Decision or Process Requirement	Things that Have to be Done	Cost Range
March-April (cont.)	Publicity (cont.)	Prepare for opponent's attacks, using staff rough questioning routine, especially before press conference or tough appearance. Plan special strategies for debates and joint appearances with opponents.	Continuing overhead.
	By end of April, total budget should be set.	Analyze commitments of funds, other anticipated expenses, and resources. Once budget is settled, stay within it, despite panic.	
May	Second opinion poll to check media impact; develop issues and priority of issues; walking tour areas; area emphasis for direct mail. client-group emphasis.	Second poll results should be due early in May. Spend ½ day with research person or consultant analyzing results; then decide how you want to hit opponent(s).	More than you thought, but by this time exhaustion deadens the shock.
	Review relationship with the press.	Try to get some "action" with each campaign publication or proposal. Tie community deficiencies to opponent if some reasonable relation exists. Press is more likely to pick up short, action-oriented issue papers than longer conceptual ones.	
	Publicity.	Send out second mailing—why they should vote for you rather than opponent.	
		Design and print street literature, including palm cards and piece attackng opponent.	
		Telephone set-ups begin early in May; calling begins at end of May.	

Time	Decision or Process Requirement	Things that Have to be Done	Cost Range
May (cont.)	Review coordination of scheduling and research.	Make certain that telephone campaign is co-ordinated with speaking engagements in areas being telephoned, etc.	Continuing overhead.
June	By this time, the key issue should be staring you in the face.	Identify the key issue on the basis of your research and your sense of the way the campaign is going, and meet it straight on—but, for God's sake, pick the right one.	
Election day	The time for decisions is past!	Maintain contact with poll watchers, and have canvassers get out the vote in "favorable" areas.	
		Prepare something for radio and television for either outcome. Say what you really want to; you've been holding it in, and now you're entitled—within reason.	
		Try to relax; you've done all anyone could.	

The election day tabulations that some candidates pay for are a waste of money: In an important election, the press will do them anyway, and in any case, you'll learn the results soon enough.

Renting ballrooms is a stupendous waste of money. Have a quiet victory party a week later—and if you lose, why spend more money?

Bibliography

If you're going to campaign for the first time, you may not realize that campaign memos and the daily newspapers are the only reading you will have time for in the course of the campaign. The time to do background reading is at least one year before you start officially or unofficially to campaign.

There are hundreds of books that you might look at, but most are academic discussions of the influence of campaigning on the voter or anecdotal discussions of what a certain candidate said to his campaign manager (and author of the subsequent book). I have tried here to sort out the books that might be directly helpful to you for the specific requirements of a campaign.

Since the dynamics and the money available vary from one campaign to another, and since campaigning is an art and not a science (despite the mass of magazine and newspaper discussions of computers, political technology, etc.), I believe that, although the books listed and discussed here may help you, more often they will show you that a specific emergency response can't be made from any book. You can only try to prepare yourself as thoroughly as possible. In reading these books, bear this in mind, for in the final analysis it is *you* who must provide the unique style, the synthesis of emotion, intellect, energy, and response to issues that every campaign is and in the last analysis must be.

If you're a first-time candidate, some of these books may give you the sense of what your options are. If you're a student in a political science course, some will convey the essence and significance of campaigning and its place in the political system. Books that I would especially recommend for both groups are starred.

GENERAL BACKGROUND

Alexander, Herbert E. *Financing the 1960 Elections*. Lexington, Mass.: Heath, 1962.
——. *Financing the 1964 Elections*. Lexington, Mass.: Heath, 1966.
——. *Financing the 1968 Elections*. Lexington, Mass.: Heath, 1971. A leading authority on the financing of election campaigns explains why campaign costs have gone up so rapidly, who the contributors are, and how funds are used.

Alinsky, Saul D. *Rules for Radicals: A Radical Primer for Realistic Radicals*. New York: Random House, 1971. Alinsky was a successful organizer of groups for political action. The book points out that much effort is required to accomplish what often should be regarded as minimal public performance standards.

Beyle, Thad L. (ed.). *Planning and Politics*. New York: Odyssey, 1970. Public housing locations and other planning issues are by now almost completely political. Candidates should familiarize themselves with the issues and the options that are open to elected and appointed officials. This book can be a start in that direction.

Boorstin, Daniel. *The Image, or What Happened to the American Dream*. New York: Atheneum, 1962. An interesting discussion of politics and "pseudo-events."

*Bullitt, Stimson. *To Be a Politician*. Garden City, N.Y.: Doubleday, 1959. A strikingly thoughtful, well written account of what it's like to campaign for public office, by a man who ran twice, unsuccessfully, for Congress.

Cantril, Albert H., and Roll, Charles W., Jr. *Hopes and Fears of the American People*. New York: Universe, 1971 (also available in paperback). A statistical analysis, broken down by demographic details and based on surveys of what concerns Americans, provides a context for congressional, city, and state campaigns but is of limited utility for local campaigns.

Committee for Economic Development. *Financing a Better Election System*. New York: Committee for Economic Development, 1968. Proposals to diminish the inequities that give the edge to monied candidates.

Congressional Quarterly *Weekly Report*. Available by subscription from Congressional Quarterly, 1925 K Street, N.W., Washington, D.C. 20006. A useful source for background on issues that are important in local as well as congressional races.

Curtis, Michael (ed.). *The Nature of Politics*. New York: Avon (paperback), 1963. A wide-ranging selection of essays on politics.

Facts on File. A well-indexed summary of political events, available by subscription from Facts on File, Inc., 119 West 57th Street, New York, N.Y. 10022.

Factual Campaign Information. Washington, D.C.: U.S. Government Printing Office, 1972. A basic reference work containing tables of past election data and federal statutes that control election procedures.

Farley, James A. *Behind the Ballots: The Personal History of a Politician*. New York: Harcourt, Brace, 1938.

Flynn, Edward J. *You're the Boss*. New York: Viking, 1947. Candid picture of how the "regular organization" operated in Bronx County, N.Y. Although the once-pervasive role of the organization in big-city politics is diminishing, Flynn's description is still largely accurate.

Heard, Alexander. *The Costs of Democracy*. Chapel Hill, N.C.: University of North Carolina Press, 1960 (also available in abridged form as a Doubleday-Anchor paperback). Thorough analysis of the impacts of campaign costs on the democratic process, based on data from the 1952 and 1956 elections and still the best work on the subject. By the board chairman of the Ford Foundation.

Heckscher, August. *The Public Happiness*. New York: Atheneum, 1962. A discussion of the large public issues by a man who became one of Mayor Lindsay's commissioners.

Hofstadter, Richard. *The Paranoid Style in American Politics and Other Essays*. New York: Knopf, 1965. A lucid, balanced analysis of right-wing American politics.

Kelley, Stanley. *Political Campaigning: Problems in Creating an Informed Electorate*. Washington, D.C.: Brookings Institution, 1960. An intelligent discussion by one of the first academics to write realistically about modern American politics.

Lane, Robert E. *Political Life: Why People Get Involved in Politics*. Glencoe, Ill.: Free Press, 1959. A summary of American political behavior.

Lasswell, Harold D. *Politics: Who Gets What, When, How (With Postscript—1958)*. New York: Meridian, 1958 (paperback). An excellent discussion of what politics is all about, originally published in 1936 but still worth reading.

———. *Psychopathology and Politics*. Chciago: University of Chicago Press, 1930. A work of originality, developing the theory of neurosis and political behavior.

Lippmann, Walter. *Essays in the Public Philosophy*. Boston: Little, Brown, 1955. Brilliant insights by a man who has always tried to see what was there, not what was supposed to be there.

———. *Public Opinion*. New York: Macmillan, 1922. A discussion of the larger issues.

Lubell, Samuel. *The Future of American Politics*. New York: Harper & Row, 1965. Worth reading for general background, even if you don't agree with all his theses.

*MacNeil, Robert. *The People Machine: The Influence of Television on American Politics.* New York: Harper & Row, 1968. A comprehensive discussion of television in politics by an able newspaperman. The chapter entitled "Campaigning by Commercial" will be particularly useful to new campaigners.

Mazlish, Bruce. *In Search of Nixon: A Psychohistorical Inquiry.* New York: Basic Books, 1972. One of a number of interesting recent books that examine the psychological bases of politicians' activities. (Don't start asking yourself if you're neurotic because you want to run for office. Your motivation isn't as important as your political performance.)

McCarthy, Richard D. *Elections for Sale.* Boston: Houghton Mifflin, 1972. The high costs of campaigning and the constraints lack of money places on a candidate.

Mendelsohn, Harold, and Crespi, Irving. *Polls, Television, and the New Politics.* Scranton, Pa.: Chandler, 1970. The impact of television and political surveys on political campaigning. Useful descriptions of the importance of sampling accuracy and the interpretation of research data.

Moos, Malcolm. *Politics, Presidents, and Coattails.* Baltimore, Md.: Johns Hopkins Press, 1952. An amusing controversial story of national voting patterns in the first half of the twentieth century.

New York State College of Agriculture. *Your Road to Better Meetings.* Ithaca, N.Y.: New York State College of Agriculture, 1964. (Cornell Extension Bulletin 1134.) An excellent brief guide to organizing meetings properly and with maximum impact.

The New York Times Guide to Federal Aid for Cities and Towns. New York: Quadrangle, 1972. A helpful list of what funds are available and for what. (A federal manual, available from the Office of the President, Washington, D.C., describes the types of monetary assistance available.)

O.M. Collective. *The Organizer's Manual.* New York: Bantam, 1971. Details on the structuring of social change. Not intended primarily for political campaigns, but useful for ideas on fund-raising, organizing meetings, etc. Shows why some youth movements have been so successful: they're intelligent and they work hard.

Politeia: The Quarterly of the American Association of Political Consultants. Available from the Association, 1028 Connecticut Ave., N.W., Washington, D.C. 20036. A journal aimed primarily at political professionals rather than candidates. Interesting although not particularly helpful in planning campaign details.

Polsby, Nelson W.; Dentler, Robert A.; and Smith, Paul A. *Politics and Social Life: An Introduction to Political Behavior.* Boston: Houghton Mifflin, 1963. An excellent academic presentation.

Rosi, Richard. *Influencing Voters: A Study of Campaign Rationality.* New York: St. Martin's Press, 1967.

Royko, Mike. *Boss: Richard J. Daley of Chicago.* New York: Dutton, 1971 (also available as a Signet paperback). The Chicago Democratic machine and how it works.

Ruchelman, Leonard I. (ed.). *Big City Mayors: The Crisis in Urban Politics.* Bloomington, Ind.: Indiana University Press, 1970. Selected articles for reading by undergraduate students in political science.

Safire, William. *The New Language of Politics: An Anecdotal Dictionary of Catchwords, Slogans, and Political Usage.* New York: Random House. An amusing, instructive review, by a former member of the Nixon staff now with *The New York Times.*

Schlesinger, Arthur M., Jr. *The Crisis of Confidence: Ideas, Power, and Violence in America.* Boston: Houghton Mifflin, 1969. Contains an essay on the New Politics.

Scott, Andrew M. *Competition in American Politics: An Economic Model.* New York: Holt, Rinehart & Winston, 1970.

Scott, Hugh D., Jr. *How to Go into Politics.* New York: John Day, 1949. Revised as *How to Run for Public Office and Win.* Washington, D.C.: National Press, 1968. A rather general introduction by a U.S. senator from Pennsylvania.

Sharkowsky, Ira. *The Routines of Politics.* New York: Van Nostrand, 1970. A description of political conditioning processes, by a University of Wisconsin professor. Not an exposition of the mechanics or details of campaigning, but rather a discussion of what is customary in a larger, governmental sense.

Tolchin, Martin, and Tolchin, Susan. *To the Victor: Political Patronage from the Clubhouse to the White House.* New York: Random House, 1971. The former City Hall bureau chief of the *New York Times* and his wife, a professor of political science, describe how political patronage motivates individuals and can affect even the most major public policies.

Ujifusa, Grant; Matthews, Douglas; and Barone, Michael. *The Almanac of American Politics.* Boston: Gambit, 1972. A reference book providing brief political profiles of all 50 states and 435 congressional districts, with social and economic background and incisive commentary on each.

Voters Time: Report of the Twentieth Century Fund Commission on Campaign Costs in the Electronic Era. New York: Twentieth Century Fund, 1969. The impact of television on campaigning in general rather than in terms of the needs of individual campaigns.

Voting Rights and Residency: The Young Voter's Guide. Washington, D.C.: Youth Citizenship Fund, 1971. An examination of state laws.

Watts, William, and Free, Lloyd A. (eds.). *State of the Nation.* New York: Universe Books, 1973 (also available in paperback). A detailed survey and analysis of the public mood that provided a remarkably accurate guide as to the way voters intended to vote in November 1972.

Whale, John. *The Half-shut Eye: Television and Politics in Britain and America.* London: Macmillan; New York: St. Martin's Press, 1969. Not quite as good as MacNeil, but humorous and easy to read.

Wilson, James Q. *The Amateur Democrat: Club Politics in Three Cities.* Chicago: University of Chicago Press, 1962. A discussion of reform politics that may help those new to political clubs.

Wycoff, Gene. *The Image Candidates: American Politics in the Age of Television.* New York: Macmillan, 1968. The impacts of mass media.

GENERAL CAMPAIGN METHODS

Allyn, Paul, and Green, Joseph. *See How They Run.* Philadelphia: Chilton, 1964. A practical but somewhat simplistic manual on campaign organization.

Banati, Robert (ed.). *Winning Campaigns in the New Politics.* New York: Popular Library, 1972.

Baus, Herbert M., and Ross, William B. *Politics Battle Plan.* New York: Macmillan, 1968. More a historical study than a handbook of practical advice.

*Cannon, James M. (ed.). *Politics U.S.A.: A Practical Guide to the Winning of Public Office.* Garden City, N.Y.: Doubleday, 1960. Essays by John F. Kennedy, Adlai E. Stevenson, Richard M. Nixon, Louis Harris, and others, describing fund-raising techniques, polling, and campaign strategy. Although the details are sketchy, this useful book is interesting for the views of important political figures, including "Boss" Crump on fund-raising, Murray Chotiner's prescriptions for the campaigns of California candidates (including Richard M. Nixon in a senatorial race), and California Governor Edmund "Pat" Brown's views on the limits of research.

Cass, Don. *How to Win Votes and Influence Elections.* Chicago: Public Administration Press, 1962.

COPE (Committee on Political Education), AFL-CIO. *How to Win.* Washington, D.C.: COPE (815 16th St., N.W.), 1972. A practical booklet on campaigning, written especially for unions but useful for candidates as well.

Costikyan, Edward N. *Behind Closed Doors: Politics in the Public Interest.* New York: Harcourt Brace & World, 1966. Sketchy descriptions, by the former Democratic county leader (i.e., Tammany Hall chief) of Manhattan, of the use of political brochures, fund-raising, and canvassing. Helpful background about the role of district and county leaders and political party administrative problems.

Cutter, Cornelius. *Practical Politics in the U.S.* Boston: Allyn & Bacon, 1969.

Democratic National Committee, Office of Campaigns and Party Organization. *Campaign '72: Voter Registration Manual.* Washington, D.C.: Democratic National Committee, 1972. Good practical suggestions for registering voters.

Edwards, Lee, and Edwards, Anne. *You Can Make the Difference.* New Rochelle, N.Y.: Arlington House, 1968. A practical book for concerned conservative Republican activists.

Emmet, Grenville T. III, and Emmet, Patricia B. *What the Pros Know: The Anatomy of Winning Politics.* New York: Information, Inc., 1968 (paperback). Amateurish and incomplete but nevertheless contains useful reminders.

Ertel, James. *How to Run for Office.* New York: Sterling, 1960. Useful, though dated.

Evry, Hal. *The Selling of a Candidate, 1971.* Los Angeles: Western Opinion Research Center, 1971. A sketchy book prepared by the president of a California firm that manages candidates. Very little detail, but useful for the presentation of a point of view in campaigning.

Felknor, Bruce L. *Dirty Politics.* New York: Norton, 1966. An analysis of several particularly dirty campaigns going back to the nineteenth century. In my experience, every campaign has some "dirty" aspects, but those described here are dramatically so.

Hiebert, Ray E., et al. (eds.). *The Political Image Merchants: Strategies in the New Politics.* Washington, D.C.: Acropolis, 1971. Interesting brief papers, but of limited help for campaign specifics.

Howe, Quincy, and Schlesinger, Arthur M., Jr. *Guide to Politics, 1954.* New York: Dial, 1954. Essays on campaigning prepared for the Americans for Democratic Action. Dated but interesting reading.

*Huckshorn, Robert J., and Spencer, Robert C. *The Politics of Defeat: Campaigning for Congress.* Amherst, Mass.: University of Massachusetts Press, 1971. Careful analysis of congressional races and why certain condidates lost. The chapter on campaign organization and management is particularly useful, as is "Auxiliary Candidate Services," describing research, polling, and other campaign activities.

Johnson, Jerry. *How to Be Successful in Politics Without Really Being Competent.* New York: Vantage, 1968.

Kelley, Stanley. *Professional Public Relations and Political Power.* Baltimore, Md.: Johns Hopkins Press, 1956. A fine discussion of the first important professional campaign management firm, Whitaker-Baxter, which started the trend in California almost two decades ago. Examines the "selling of a candidate"—the use of public relations men and marketing techniques in campaigns. Now useful mostly for background.

Kirwan, Michael J. (as told to Jack Redding). *How to Succeed in Politics.* New York: McFadden-Bartell, 1964. A former congressman's reminiscences of Chicago politics and Democratic organization procedures, not intended as a focused guide to strategy and tactics.

*Levin, Murray B. *The Alienated Voter: Politics in Boston.* New York: Holt, Rinehart & Winston, 1960. A good discussion of the undecided voter and campaign techniques.

Lyford, Joseph P. *Candidate.* New York: Holt, 1959. What it's like to campaign for Congress.

*Nimmo, Dan. *The Political Persuaders: The Techniques of Modern Election Campaigns*. Englewood Cliffs, N.J.: Prentice-Hall, 1970. An excellent summary of campaign techniques, written by an academic.

Parkinson, Hank. *Winning Your Campaign: A Nuts and Bolts Guide to Political Victory*. Englewood Cliffs, N.J.: Prentice-Hall, 1970. Written by an advertising man, this book touches all the bases but is very sketchy.

*Perry, James M. *The New Politics: The Expanding Technology of Political Manipulation*. New York: Potter, 1968. A newspaperman's analyses of Milton Shapp's Pennsylvania gubernatorial campaign in 1966 (directed by Joseph Napolitan) and the campaigning methods of Governors Nelson Rockefeller of New York, Winthrop Rockefeller of Arkansas, and George Romney of Michigan. Accurate descriptions of the new technology and the detailed "routines" of political campaigning. If you read only one book for background, this is the one to read.

Pohl, Frederik. *Practical Politics*. New York: Ballantine, 1971 (paperback). The author, a well-known science-fiction writer, entered politics as a volunteer in the McCarthy presidential campaign of 1968. His book contains many useful suggestions.

Polsby, Nelson W., and Wildavsky, Aaron B. *Presidential Elections: Strategies of American Electoral Politics*. New York: Scribner, 1964. An excellent analysis of national elections by two academics. Not particularly appropriate for local candidates, but succinctly written and among the best in the field—the section on research and surveys is worthwhile. Wildavsky's books on public administration and program budgeting are well worth reading if you attain public office.

Ribicoff, Abraham, and Newman, Jon O. *Politics: The American Way*. Boston: Allyn & Bacon, 1967. A good, quick review of campaigning intended primarily for high school and college readers.

Rosenbloom, David L. (ed.). *The Political Market-Place*. New York: Quadrangle, 1972. Lists of elected and party officials and of campaign professionals and consultants whose services are available to candidates, with a bibliography and advertisements from professionals that might prove useful to some campaigners.

Shadegg, Stephen. *How to Win an Election: The Art of Political Victory*. New York: Taplinger, 1964. Revised as *The New How to Win an Election*, 1972. Probably won't be very helpful to new campaigners who need specific advice, but it is easy, interesting reading. Shadegg, the former state chairman of the Arizona Republican Party, was an adviser to Senator Barry M. Goldwater.

Simpson, Dick. *Winning Elections: A Handbook in Participatory Politics*. Chicago: Swallow, 1972 (also available in paperback). Excellent for the mechanics of petitioning, kaffeeklatches, and other such details, but not designed to help with overall campaign strategy. Simpson is an academic who ran for public office.

Swing, Meyer D. *The Winning Candidate: How to Defeat Your Political Opponent.* New York: Heinman, 1966. One of the better books, with focus on preparing press releases, managing meetings, etc.

Tufts University, The Lincoln Filene Center for Citizenship and Public Affairs. *Practical Political Action: A Guide for Citizens.* Boston: Houghton Mifflin, 1970 (paperback). An introductory book for high school students; possibly useful for new candidates.

Van Riper, Paul P. *Handbook of Practical Politics.* 3d ed. New York: Harper & Row, 1967. Somewhat dated, but nevertheless useful.

SPECIFIC CAMPAIGNS

Bruno, Jerry and Greenfield, Jeff. *The Advance Man.* New York: Morrow, 1971. Interesting description of the work of Jerry Bruno, who was active in the Robert F. Kennedy, Goldberg, and Lindsay campaigns. Greenfield is a political speech writer who has worked for Lindsay and David Garth.

Buckley, William F., Jr. *The Unmaking of a Mayor.* New York: Viking, 1966. A chronicle of the 1965 New York mayoralty campaign, which gained John V. Lindsay his first term, written with humor and considerable style by Lindsay's Conservative opponet.

Chester, Lewis; Hodgson, Godfrey; and Page, Bruce. *An American Melodrama: The Presidential Campaign of 1968.* New York: Viking, 1969. A fine description by British journalists. The section "See How They Run" is excellent for campaign dynamics and for showing how research was used in developing and handling issues.

Flaherty, Joe. *Managing Mailer.* New York: Coward McCann, 1970 (also available as a Berkeley Medallion paperback). Norman Mailer and Jimmy Breslin ran for mayor and comptroller in the New York City Democratic primary of 1969, on the theme "Make New York City the 51st State." This book, by their campaign manager, describes the not-so-uncommon anarchy of even experienced campaigners and the constant squabbling that is typical of many campaigns.

Lebedoff, David. *The Sixth Ward.* New York: Scribner, 1972. A description of the activities of a local political club.

Leuthold, David A. *Electioneering in a Democracy: Campaigns for Congress.* New York: Wiley, 1968. An analysis, by an academic, of congressional elections in the San Francisco Bay Area in 1962. A useful analysis of campaign methodology based on the author's detailed survey.

*Levin, Murray B. *Kennedy Campaigning: The System and the Style as Practiced by Senator Edward Kennedy.* Boston: Beacon, 1966. A well-documented book on Edward M. Kennedy's first senatorial campaign, 1964, describing the formulation of strategy and the dynamics of campaigning as seen by campaign participants. Very explicit about the impact of big money properly used in a sophisticated "New Politics" campaign and how an effective TV campaign was directed.

*Levin, Murray B. and Blackwood, George. *The Compleat Politician: Political Strategy in Massachusetts.* Indianapolis, Ind.: Bobbs-Merrill, 1962. One of the best books on an individual campaign, describing the dynamics of Endicott ("Chub") Peabody's race for governor of Massachusetts, and how decisions get made and unmade in the course of a campaign. See especially pp. 179-225 on polling and pp. 271-309 on the decision-making process.

McGinniss, Joe. *The Selling of the President, 1968.* New York: Trident, 1969 (also available as a Pocket Books paperback). The use of television in Richard M. Nixon's 1968 presidential campaign.

Napolitan, Joseph. *The Political Game (and How to Win It).* New York: Doubleday, 1972. Anecdotes, reflections, and reminiscences, as well as campaign memoranda from the 1968 presidential contest, by a former newspaperman who was associated with the original Kennedy group and is now a well-known campaign professional.

Shadegg, Stephen. *What Happened to Goldwater: The Inside Story of the 1964 Republican Campaign.* New York: Holt, Rinehart & Winston, 1965. A criticism of Goldwater's campaign staff and speech writers and of the press.

Sorenson, Theodore. *Kennedy.* New York: Harper & Row, 1965. Useful discussion of primaries, convention strategies, and campaign dynamics.

————. *The Kennedy Legacy.* New York: Macmillan, 1969. More intellectual than practical, but helpful in describing how John F. Kennedy responded to issues and how he developed what came to be known as "the Kennedy style."

White, Theodore H. *The Making of the President, 1960.* New York: Atheneum, 1961 (also available as a New American Library paperback).

————. *The Making of the President, 1964.* New York: Atheneum, 1965 (also available as a New American Library paperback).

————. *The Making of the President, 1968.* New York: Atheneum, 1969. The best overall accounts of the politicians and issues involved in these three presidential campaigns, but not particularly oriented toward the specific details of winning elections that might be useful in local campaigns.

RESEARCH AND SURVEYS

Abrams, Charles. *The Language of Cities: A Glossary of Terms.* New York: Viking, 1971. An excellent survey of nomenclature and the bureaucratic processes involved in housing and other urban programs.

American Society of Planning Officials. *Advisory Reports,* issued by the Society, 1313 East 60th Street, Chicago, Ill. 60637. Periodic reports on zoning and housing legislation, matters that often involve local controversies and thus may be important in campaigning.

*Backstrom, Charles H., and Hursh, Gerald D. *Survey Research.* Evanston, Ill.: Northwestern University Press, 1972 (paperback). A brilliant book that avoids mathematical statistics but describes the mechanics very well. The authors "will attribute any errors to each other." There aren't many.

Bean, Louis. *How to Predict Elections.* New York: Knopf, 1948. Bean, a well-regarded statistician, correctly predicted the Truman victory in 1948, and his book still has utility.

————. *How to Predict the 1972 Election.* New York: Quadrangle, 1972. Historical and statistical background for sorting out available data to predict the outcome of the 1972 presidential election.

Cantril, Albert H., and Roll, Charles W. *Polls: Their Use and Misuse in Politics.* New York: Basic Books, 1972. An informative book well worth reading for background before you decide what type of poll to commission.

Fenton, John M. *In Your Opinion: The Managing Editor of the Gallup Poll Looks at Polls, Politics, and the People from 1945 to 1960.* Boston: Little, Brown, 1960. A description of how Americans felt and thought about political questions.

Fitch, Lyle C., and Walsh, Annamarie Hauck (eds.). *Agenda for a City: Issues Confronting New York.* Beverly Hills, Calif.: Sage, 1970. Essays by specialists in housing, transportation, economic development, and other fields containing useful ideas and background for any campaign staff preparing position papers in larger cities.

Frankel, Martin R. *Inference from Survey Samples: An Empirical Investigation.* Ann Arbor, Mich.: University of Michigan Institute for Social Research, 1971. A technical discussion of problems in statistical sampling, useful for someone with professional statistical experience.

Hansen, Morris H.; Hurewitz, William N.; and Madow, William G. *Sample Survey Methods and Theory.* 2 vols. New York: Wiley, 1953. One of the best texts in the field. Vol. 1, *Methods and Applications,* will be most useful to campaign staffs.

Holleb, Dorothy. *Social and Economic Information in Urban Planning.* 2 vols. Chicago: University of Chicago Press, 1970. Particularly useful discussion of survey techniques; lists detailed sources for published data valuable to candidates for issue and demographic analysis.

Journal of the American Institute of Planners, 917 15th Street, N.W., Washington, D.C. 20005. A quarterly technical publication that may be valuable in local campaigns in researching local housing, taxation, transportation, and zoning issues.

Kaplan, Abraham. *The Conduct of Inquiry: Methodology for Behavioral Science.* Scranton, Pa.: Chandler, 1964. A fine text; not easy to read, but worth the effort for any serious student.

Konrad, Evelyn, and Erickson, Rod. *Marketing Research: A Management Overview.* New York: American Management Association, 1966. Articles by professionals in market research include "Television Audience Research Basics," "Measuring Advertising's Sales Effectiveness: The Problem and the Prognosis," "Advertising Readership Studies," "Pre-testing Television Commercials," "Motivational Research," and "The Art of Using Marketing Research."

*Lansing, John B., and Morgan, James N. *Economic Survey Methods.* Ann Arbor, Mich.: University of Michigan Institute for Social Research, 1971. A lucid, thorough discussion of sampling, survey design, and procedures. Useful for candidates intending to do their own polling.

Lansing, John B.; Withey, Stephen B.; and Wolfe, Arthur C. *Working Papers on Survey Research in Poverty Areas.* Ann Arbor, Mich.: University of Michigan Institute for Social Research, 1971. Methods of doing sample survey research in inner-city poverty areas.

Municipal Yearbook, issued by the International City Managers Association, 1313 East 60th Street, Chicago, Ill. 60637. An excellent source book of statistics, with particular emphasis on trends in legislation.

*National Municipal League. *The Citizen Association: How to Win Civic Campaigns.* New York: National Municipal League (47 East 58th Street, 10021), 1963 (paperback). Especially interesting for civic groups. The League issues the *National Civic Review* and many other publications of interest to local and state-wide candidates.

*Payne, Stanley L. *The Art of Asking Questions.* Princeton, N.J.: Princeton University Press, 1951. The importance of questionnaire design in research; not intended particularly for political surveys but worthwhile for its insights on the components of a quality survey.

Public Opinion Quarterly, Room 510, Journalism Building, Columbia University, New York, N.Y. 10027. Contains many interesting items on polling techniques and sample design.

The RAND Corporation, 1700 Main Street, Santa Monica, Calif. 90401, a well-known research organization, issues technical reports of value for issue and background papers in larger campaigns. A complete listing of hundreds of available reports is obtainable free of charge from the corporation.

Robinson, John P.; Rusk, Jerrold G.; and Head, Kendra B. *Measures of Political Attitudes.* Ann Arbor, Mich.: University of Michigan Institute of Social Research, 1968. A historical study of ways of measuring political attitudes, with many practical applications useful to campaigners.

Selected Scientific and Technical Reports. Springfield, Va.: Clearinghouse for Federal Scientific and Technical Information. This U.S. Government service provides scientific papers at reasonable costs on housing, taxation, pollution, urban transportation, economic analysis, and other subjects, which may be useful in preparting position papers.

Shryock, Henry S., and Siegel, Jacob S. *The Methods and Materials of Demography.* 2 vols. Washington, D.C.: U.S. Bureau of the Census, 1972. A comprehensive, painstaking work intended for technicians but of value to the research staff of any professional campaign.

Stephan, Frederick J., and McCarthy, Philip. *Sampling Opinions.* New

York: Wiley, 1960. A competent book for use as background in doing attitudinal surveys.

Survey Research Center, Field Office, Institute of Social Research, University of Michigan. *Interviewer's Manual.* Ann Arbor, Mich.: Survey Research Center, 1969. A training manual explaining how to record and edit and other sampling procedures; brief and to the point. Valuable for setting up your own research.

Tallmer, Jerry. Six articles in the *New York Post,* October 30, 1972-November 4, 1972. This is the best newspaper analysis of polling processes and problems I have seen.

U.S. Department of Commerce. *County City Data Book.* Washington, D.C.: U.S. Government Printing Office. Published several times a decade, this standard reference work provides data on all counties and cities. Topics include land areas, budgets, employment, farm production, race, and income. The best single overall summary available.

U.S. Department of Commerce, Bureau of the Census. *Atlantida: A Case Study in Household Sample Surveys,* prepared for the Alliance for Progress. 14 vols. Washington, D.C., U.S. Government Printing Office, 1966. This work, the most thorough one I know of, covers all aspects of planning a household sample survey program.

————. *Congressional District Computer Profiles for the . . . Congress.* Washington, D.C.: U.S. Government Printing Office. Statistical tabulations, issued every two years, for the congressional districts as districted for the November election, including data on population, employment, and housing as well as scale maps showing the boundaries of each district.

————. *Congressional District Data.* Washington, D.C.: U.S. Government Printing Office. Biennial summaries of census data conveniently arranged in one booklet per state, providing district maps, population, housing, and voting data for each congressional district.

————. *Current Population Survey.* Washington, D.C.: U.S. Government Printing Office. This periodic survey of 50,000 American families provides information throughout the year on the demographic characteristics of the population, including age, labor force, income, and other characteristics such as school enrollment trends and the number of 18-to-20-year-old voters. A serious candidate should familiarize himself with these data and with the methods used.

————. *Decennial Census.* Washington, D.C.: U.S. Government Printing Office. These data, the most complete set available, unfortunately become dated rapidly, so that by 1974, for example, the 1970 figures will have lost their value for local analysis, while by 1978 they will be almost entirely worthless. Campaign staff will have to use local sources —even rough estimates from local health departments and planning boards—and/or other Bureau of the Census publication to update.

————. *Directory of Federal Statistics for Local Areas.* Washington, D.C.: U.S. Government Printing Office, 1966.

————. *Directory of Federal Statistics for States.* Washington, D.C.: U.S. Government Printing Office, 1967.

————. *Directory of Non-Federal Statistics for States and Local Areas.* Washington, D.C.: U.S. Government Printing Office, 1969. These three inexpensive, thorough publications can be invaluable in helping campaign staffs wade through the abundance of government data. Data for small communities is extremely difficult to track down without these guides.

————. *Introduction to Small-Area Geographic Subdivisions for Which the U.S. Bureau of the Census Collects and Tabulates Data.* An excellent brief description of the various types of local areas for which U.S. Census data are available. Obtainable without charge from the Data Access and Use Laboratory, Social and Economic Statistics Administration, Bureau of the Census, U.S. Department of Commerce, Washington, D.C. 20233.

————. *Metropolitan Area Statistics.* Washington, D.C.: U.S. Government Printing Office. A convenient reprint (costing only 35¢) of a section of the annual *Statistical Abstract* offering a survey of data for 155 metropolitan areas, including population change, employment, voting patterns, business patterns, and housing.

————. *The 1970 Census—and You: A General Introduction to Census Data.* Washington, D.C.: U.S. Government Printing Office, 1971. A basic ten-page guide to census data and their practical applications, for the layman.

————. *Sampling Lectures.* 2 vols. Washington, D.C.: U.S. Government Printing Office, 1968. A fine exposition of basic sampling theory; quite brief compared to the monumental, extremely detailed *Atlantida* study cited above. Worth studying if you intend to do your own sample surveys of political opinion.

————. *Statistical Abstract of the United States.* Washington, D.C.: U.S. Government Printing Office. All the important statistics in one annual volume, but not down to the level of small communities.

————. *Supplemental Courses for Case Studies in Surveys and Censuses.* (Demography Lectures, ISP Supplemental Course Series, No. 25.) Washington, D.C.: U.S. Government Printing Office, 1969. Very useful if you're doing your own surveys.

————. Social and Economic Statistics Administration. *County Business Patterns.* Washington, D.C.: U.S. Government Printing Office. These annual reports providing employment trends by industry and by county are excellent for use in economic issue development. They are appropriate for use by laymen as well as by the economists for whom they are designed.

*U.S. Executive Office of the President, Bureau of the Budget. *Household Survey Manual.* Washington, D.C.: U.S. Government Printing Office, 1969. The best single publication describing the methodology of professional surveys, very useful for the candidate doing his own opinion surveys.

U.S. Executive Office of the President, Office of Management and Budget. *Catalog of Federal Domestic Assistance Programs.* Washington, D.C.: U.S. Government Printing Office. An annual listing of the federal financial aid programs available to states, cities, and communities.

In addition to the foregoing, regional offices of the U.S. Bureau of Labor Statistics provide current analyses of trends in wages, unemployment, prices, and manpower.

VOTING PATTERNS

Bailey, Harry A., Jr., and Katz, Ellis (eds.). *Ethnic Group Politics.* Columbus, Ohio: Merrill, 1969. A general reader.

Burdick, Eugene, and Brodbeck, Arthur J. (eds.). *American Voting Behavior.* Glencoe, Ill.: Free Press, 1959. Excellent essays, especially Brodbeck's comparison of electioneering with the techniques of psychotherapy. Somewhat dry reading overall, but interesting for the serious student.

Campbell, Angus, et al. *The American Voter.* New York: Wiley, 1960. Probably the definitive statistical analysis.

DeVries, Walter, and Tarrance, Lance. *The Ticket Splitter: A New Force in American Politics.* Grand Rapids, Mich.: Eerdmans, 1971. A study of the independent voter in Michigan, which has increasing application throughout the United States.

Friedheim, Jerry. *Where Are the Voters?* Washington, D.C.: National Press, 1968. Interesting for breakdowns by client groups.

Fuchs, Laurence H. (ed.). *American Ethnic Politics.* New York: Harper & Row, 1968. Good essays by Daniel Patrick Moynihan on the Irish voter, James Q. Wilson on the Negro voter, and others.

Hawkins, Brett W., and Lorinskas, Robert A. (eds.). *The Ethnic Factor in American Politics.* Columbus, Ohio: Merrill, 1970. An academic presentation of ethnication as a critical factor in American political life.

Kent, Frank R. *The Great Game of Politics: An Effort to Present the Elementary Human Facts about Politics, Politicians, and Political Machines, Candidates and Their Ways, for the Benefit of the Average Citizen.* Garden City, N.Y.: Doubleday, 1923. The subtitle says it all. Still worth reading for background and for pleasure, even though it won't change any campaign decisions.

———. *Political Behavior: The Heretofore Unwritten Laws, Customs, and Principles of Politics as Practiced in the United States.* New York: Morrow, 1928. Like its predecessor, one of the first books that tried to tell it straight. Out of date, but good for comparing how politicians viewed the voters then and how they do now. Charmingly written, with a high level of candor.

Key, V. O., Jr. *Politics, Parties and Pressure Groups*. 5th ed. New York: Crowell, 1964. A widely used text that contains useful information on the national campaigning process.

———. *Public Opinion and American Democracy*. New York: Knopf, 1961.

Lazarsfeld, Paul F.; Berelson, Bernard; and Gaudet, Hazel. *The People's Choice: How the Voter Makes up his Mind in a Presidential Campaign*. 3d ed. New York: Columbia University Press, 1968 (paperback). A standard work.

McPhee, William N., and Glaser, William A. (eds.). *Public Opinion and Congressional Elections*. Glencoe, Ill.: Free Press, 1962. Thirteen essays on voting behavior.

Murphy, Reg, and Gulliver, Hal. *The Southern Strategy*. New York: Scribner, 1971. An interesting analysis, by two journalists, of Southern voting strategy.

Novak, Michael. *The Rise of the Unmeltable Ethnics: Politics and Culture in the Seventies*. New York: Macmillan, 1972. A provocative description of American Greeks, Italians, Slavs, and other ethnic groups in American life.

Phillips, Kevin P. *The Emerging Republic Majority*. New Rochelle, N.Y.: Arlington, 1969 (also available as an Anchor paperback). How the Republicans can unite client groups to develop a continuing dominance in national politics. Widely quoted and allegedly used in the Nixon presidential reelection strategy.

Pool, Ithiel de Sola; Abelson, Robert; and Popkin, Samuel. *Candidates, Issues and Strategies: A Computer Simulation of the 1960 and 1964 Presidential Elections*. Cambridge, Mass.: M.I.T. Press, 1964. Academically oriented, but useful in providing a context for evaluating campaigns.

Scammon, Richard M. (ed.). *America at the Polls: A Handbook of American Presidential Election Statistics, 1920-1964*. Pittsburgh: University of Pittsburgh Press, 1965. Statistical analysis of presidential elections by the former director of the U.S. Bureau of the Census.

———. *America Votes*. 8 vols. Originally published (1956) by Macmillan, New York; more recently by Congressional Quarterly, Washington, D.C. A handbook of contemporary election statistics.

Scammon, Richard M., and Wattenberg, Ben J. *The Real Majority: How the Silent Center of the American Electorate Chooses its President*. New York: Coward McCann, 1970. A widely read and discussed book, worth looking at even if you don't agree with the authors' thesis.

POLITICAL ADVERTISING

American Association of Advertising Agencies. *Political Campaign Advertising and Advertising Agencies*. Available on request from the association, 200 Park Avenue, New York, N.Y. 10017.

American Newspaper Publishers Association, Bureau of Advertising.

23 Winning Ideas for Political Advertisers. Available from the association, 750 Third Avenue, New York, N.Y. 10017.

Broadcasting Yearbook, 1735 De Sales Street, N.W., Washington, D.C. 20036. A compendium listing basic data and personnel of television and AM and FM radio stations throughout the nation as well as marketing information and other data for interest to political advertisers.

Direct Mail Advertising Association. *How to Win Your Election with Direct Mail.* Available from the association, 230 Park Avenue, New York, N.Y. 10017. Brief, simple information about the use of direct mail in politics; can help candidates by telling them where to find direct-mail agencies and how to pick the right one.

McCaffrey, Maurice. *Advertising Wins Elections.* Minneapolis: Dillon, 1962.

Seehafer, Gene F., and Laemmar, Jack W. *Successful Television and Radio Advertising.* New York: McGraw-Hill, 1959. A useful text despite its age, with helpful chapters on writing TV and radio commercials, testing programs and commercials, measuring sales effectiveness, time buying, spot TV and radio advertising, and a glossary, which may facilitate communication between candidates and media representatives.

Votes Unlimited. *Campaign Specialties.* Retail catalog available on request from Votes Unlimited, Ferndale, N.Y. 12734. A priced commercial shopping list for buttons, shopping bags, and other giveaway items.

Index